Tools for Schools

Applications Software for the Classroom

SECOND EDITION

Michael Land
Midwestern State University

Sandra Turner
Ohio University

Wadsworth Publishing Company

I(T)P® An International Thomson Publishing Company

Belmont, CA • Albany, NY • Bonn • Boston • Cincinnati • Detroit • Johannesburg
London • Madrid • Melbourne • Mexico City • New York • Paris • Singapore
Tokyo • Toronto • Washington

Education Editor: Sabra Horne

Assistant Editor: Claire Masson

Editorial Assistant: Kate Barrett

Marketing Manager: Jay Hu

Project Editor: Jennie Redwitz

Print Buyer: Karen Hunt

Permissions Editor: Jeanne Bosschart

Designer: Cuttriss and Hambleton

Art Editor: Bobbie Broyer

Copy Editor: Donald Pharr

Cover: Cuttriss and Hambleton

Cover Images: © 1996 PhotoDisc Inc.

Compositor: Joan Olson

Printer: Courier/Kendallville

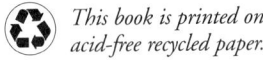 *This book is printed on acid-free recycled paper.*

Printed in the United States of America
2 3 4 5 6 7 8 9 10

For more information, contact Wadsworth Publishing Company, 10 Davis Drive, Belmont, CA 94002,
or electronically at http://www.thomson.com/wadsworth.html

International Thomson Publishing Europe
Berkshire House 168-173
High Holborn
London, WC1V 7AA, England

Thomas Nelson Australia
102 Dodds Street
South Melbourne 3205
Victoria, Australia

Nelson Canada
1120 Birchmount Road
Scarborough, Ontario
Canada M1K 5G4

International Thomson Publishing GmbH
Königswinterer Strasse 418
53227 Bonn, Germany

International Thomson Editores
Campos Eliseos 385, Piso 7
Col. Polanco
11560 México D.F. México

International Thomson Publishing Asia
221 Henderson Road
#05-10 Henderson Building
Singapore 0315

International Thomson Publishing Japan
Hirakawacho Kyowa Building, 3F
2-2-1 Hirakawacho
Chiyoda-ku, Tokyo 102, Japan

International Thomson Publishing
Southern Africa
Building 18, Constantia Park
240 Old Pretoria Road
Halfway House, 1685 South Africa

Library of Congress Cataloging-in-Publication Data

Land, Michael.
    Tools for schools: applications software for the classroom/Michael Land, Sandra Turner.—2nd ed.
    p.   cm.
    Turner's name appears first on the earlier edition.
    Includes bibliographical references and index.
    ISBN 0-534-21492-4 (pbk.)
    1. Computers—Study and teaching—United States. 2. Computer-assisted instruction—
United States. 3. AppleWorks. I. Turner, Sandra V. II. Title.
LB1028.43.L365 1997   96-36362
371.334—dc20

Contents

Chapter 2: Communicating with Graphics 29

Chapter 3: Preparing and Using Slide Shows 69

Chapter 6: Problem Solving with Spreadsheets — 167

Chapter 7: Hypermedia: Working with HyperStudio — 211

Chapter 8:
Telecommunications: The World Wide Web and E-Mail 241

Chapter 9:
Integrating Technology into the Curriculum 275

Appendixes 297

Glossary 327

Index 331

Preface

The goal of this book is to help educators use applications or tool software to teach topics in the K–12 curriculum. In ever-increasing numbers of classrooms, students are writing with a word processor, using databases in social studies and science, publishing their work with desktop publishing software, using spreadsheets to analyze data in mathematics and social studies and displaying the results in graphic formats, creating their own learning environments with hypermedia, communicating with others worldwide, and searching data banks on the Internet.

During the last ten years, the emphasis in computer education has gradually shifted from an emphasis on programming and the study of the computer itself to the use of applications or tool software. We have observed that not many teachers and students have opportunities to apply programming skills to solve real-world problems. However, applications software is easier to learn than programming, and almost everyone who learns to use it sees an immediate application in her or his own work. Consequently, the computer becomes a practical tool that teachers and students can use in all areas of education.

About the Book

As with the original book, we revised the text for a one-semester course in computer applications for teachers and prospective teachers. The book provides specific ways to use word processing, graphics, slide shows, page layout, databases, spreadsheets, charting, hypermedia, and telecommunications software to teach subject-area objectives in the K–12 curriculum.

The book is written at a beginning level for teachers who have had little or no prior experience with computers. However, even those teachers who have had some experience with technology will benefit from the sample activities and teaching ideas in each chapter. The approach is practical and applied rather than theoretical. Because we believe that people learn by doing, a hands-on approach is used to introduce each type of application. This approach gives teachers experience that they can use to prepare lessons and activities appropriate for the subject area and grade level that they teach.

Changes to This Edition

Changes to the edition have been so extensive that this is practically a new beginning for the book:

- ❏ The word processing, database, and spreadsheet chapters have been rewritten for use with ClarisWorks.
- ❏ The graphics chapter has been completely rewritten.
- ❏ There is a new chapter on page layout and desktop publishing.

In addition, there are three new chapters on areas that have generated a great deal of excitement since the first edition of this book was published:

- ❏ A new chapter on slide shows or presentations,
- ❏ a new chapter on hypermedia, and
- ❏ the telecommunications chapter has been replaced with a chapter on e-mail and the World Wide Web

For the chapters on word processing, graphics, slide shows, page layout, databases, and spreadsheets, we have selected ClarisWorks; for hypermedia, we have selected HyperStudio; and for a web browser, we have selected Netscape, although the user can use a different web browser without difficulty in this chapter. All three of these applications are popular, run on both Macintosh and Windows, are relatively easy to learn, and are appropriate for use by both students and teachers.

We had almost completed the initial revision of the book for the Macintosh when it was suggested that we attempt to accommodate both Windows and Macintosh with one book. We agreed that we would attempt such a task but that we would first finish the Macintosh version. When we began to determine what might need to be changed for Windows, to our surprise there were very few changes. Many universities and public schools use both Windows and Macintosh, so we have structured the book so that users of either type of operating system can use the book and even move back and forth with the same document or file; this is also an accommodation for users who have one type of computer at home and a different one at school. The following is a list of accommodations or guidelines we have used:

❏ Almost all the screen figures are Macintosh (because we at first thought this was going to be a Macintosh-only book). However, almost all the features we refer to in the figures are usually very similar, if not identical, for both operating systems.

❏ The disks that come with the book are DOS-formatted disks so that users of Windows and Macintosh can use the same disks.

❏ We have used names with eight or fewer letters for file names. Although you can use long file names with both Macintosh and Windows, neither platform recognizes long file names from the other. In addition, we have appended three-letter extensions to file names for the benefit of Windows users. Ironically, you won't see the extensions when opening a file in Windows, but you will see the suffix when displaying the contents of a disk or folder on the Macintosh. If you are using a Macintosh, just disregard the extensions.

❏ When giving step-by-step instructions in cases where there is a difference between the operating systems, we have used symbols to note the difference: **M** for Macintosh and **W** for Windows 95.

The Tools Disks

Tools for Schools comes with two disks containing files associated with the book. A special disk icon will appear in the margin 🖫 to indicate that you are to open a file from this collection. The files are organized into folders corresponding to each chapter. Most of the ClarisWorks files, except libraries, have been saved as stationery files so that the user does not accidentally save over the original file.

Special Features of the Book

In addition to the Tools disks, several other special features have been incorporated into the book:

❏ Numerous examples and teaching ideas that are appropriate for teachers at both the elementary and secondary levels

❏ Question-and-answer sections

❏ Screen displays to help you in verifying that you are proceeding as expected

❏ Important terms highlighted in boldface in the text and defined in the glossary in nontechnical terminology

❑ A bibliography at the end of each chapter listing articles and books for further reading

❑ End-of-chapter exercises that give you an opportunity to check and extend your understanding

❑ A World Wide Web site maintained by Wadsworth in support of the book

❑ A separate instructor's guide

Using ClarisWorks, HyperStudio, and Netscape with the Book

You will need ClarisWorks 4, HyperStudio 3, and Netscape (or some other web browser) for the type of computer you are using. You should have either a PC with Windows 95 and at least 8 megabytes of RAM or a Macintosh with System 7.1 or higher and at least 8 megabytes of RAM. Depending upon the computer and operating system you are using and the size of the computer monitor, your screen will vary somewhat from the screen figures in the book.

Acknowledgments

We especially want to thank our spouses for their understanding both during the writing of the original book and the revised edition. We also want to thank the following reviewers for their thoughtful comments: Nancy Evans, Lincoln University; James Gaffney, Xavier University; William Gibbs, Eastern Illinois University; Donn Ritchie, San Diego State University; and Neal Strudler, University of Nevada.

To the staff at Wadsworth, we owe our sincere gratitude for their confidence in us and our ideas and for their gentle nudges to complete the revision: Sabra Horne, Claire Masson, Kate Barrett, and Jennie Redwitz.

Introduction

There are millions of computers now being used in the public schools. The availability and decreasing prices of hardware and the availability of better software have had a major impact on schools' approach to computer use.

Tutor-Tutee-Tool Framework

In 1980, Robert Taylor proposed a framework for understanding the diverse uses of computers in education: the computer as tutor, as tutee, and as tool. As a tutor, the computer presents some subject material, the student responds, the computer evaluates the response, and then the computer determines what to present next. The computer tutor can tailor its presentation to accommodate a wide range of student differences and can keep complete records on each student's progress. This mode of using the computer is also called computer-assisted instruction (CAI) and has been broadened to include simulations and problem-solving software.

In order to use the computer as a tutee, the student programs the computer, communicating with the computer in a language it understands. Because you can't teach what you don't understand, the student learns what he or she is trying to teach the computer. Students also gain insight into how the computer works and, ideally, into their own thinking processes. Students who program the computer have a sense of being the master of the computer rather than being its subject.

To function as a tool, the classroom computer needs useful software—software that will make a student's work easier and more efficient. For example, students could use the computer for writing, for drawing, for analyzing and graphing data, for composing music, for accessing information in large databases, for collecting data for a science experiment, for constructing hyperlinks among common threads of data, and for communicating and sharing information with other people. In the tool mode, as in the tutee mode, the student is in control. However, in the tool mode the computer is not the subject of instruction. A tool is not an end in itself, but a means to an end.

Although all three modes—tutor, tutee, and tool—are important, the use of the computer and technology as a tool is currently viewed by many computer education specialists as the most valuable way to use computers in classrooms.

What Is Applications Software?

Software that enables the computer to be used as a tool is called applications or productivity software. In business and industry, computers and technology are viewed primarily as aids to productivity. In businesses, database-management software is used to store employee records, large mailing lists, and inventories; word-processing software is used for producing form letters and to avoid retyping edited documents; spreadsheet software is used for preparing budgets and making financial projections; desktop publishing and graphics software is used for preparing professional-quality documents; slide show or presentation software is used for training and for making professional presentations; hypermedia software is used for training and for making presentations; and the Internet is used for an increasing range of tasks, including getting up-to-date information, providing up-to-date information, and communicating with field sites and branch offices.

Applications or productivity software originally made its way into the elementary and secondary schools when school administrators realized that it could be a useful tool for managing school administrative tasks. Once the software was in the schools, teachers recognized that it could be used by both teachers and students as an instructional tool.

In this book, we focus on eight categories of applications or productivity software: word processing, graphics, page layout or desktop publishing, slide show or presentation, database, spreadsheet and charting, hypermedia, and telecommunications. We will show you how to use the software yourself and how to use it with the students in your classroom. We believe that the best way to learn is by doing. In keeping with this philosophy, our approach is to encourage you to use the computer as a personal tool first, and then to think about how to use it in your classroom.

Integrating the Computer into the Curriculum

Tools themselves do not teach; neither are they the object of instruction. A tool is a means to an end, so it makes sense that the computer as a tool should be integrated throughout the school's curriculum. In a computer-integrated curriculum, there is no need to add new computer-related objectives to a school's curriculum. Rather, schools examine the traditional curriculum and determine when it may be appropriate to develop computer-related learning activities for existing curricular objectives. For example, if your English curriculum includes a research paper, the students could use the Internet to find relevant references and then use a word processor to write and revise the paper. If you are teaching rocks and minerals in science, you could develop a database to help students identify unknown rocks. If you study bar, line, and pie graphs in mathematics, bring in newspaper articles containing various statistics and have the students use a graphing application to illustrate the data. If your social studies curriculum includes a unit on South American countries, use a database to make comparisons among the countries.

Why Teach with Applications Software?

Of course, each of the activities mentioned above can be taught without using a computer. What, then, are the advantages of using technology as a tool?

First, students can produce professional-looking work in less time. For example, using a graphing application saves time that would otherwise by spent in laboriously drawing bar graphs, and the results look better.

Second, the computer offers teachers a different method for attaining curricular objectives that are currently not well met. For example, although language arts teachers agree that revision is an important step in the writing process, it is not practical to expect students to rewrite a paper several times by hand.

Third, technology tools can provide students with activities that develop higher-level thinking skills—skills that involve creating, analyzing, synthesizing, and evaluating. Working with a database of the United States presidents, for example, students can sort the data to confirm or reject the hypothesis that a president is more likely to be elected to a second term if the nation is at war. With spreadsheets, variables can be systematically changed to analyze the effects of different assumptions.

An additional benefit of using technology is that students learn to use tools that are commonplace in the work force. Students learn these computer skills in a relevant and useful context.

We are in the midst of the Information and Communications Age. Our total collected body of knowledge is expanding so rapidly that most of us have difficulty staying up-to-date, even in our own fields of specialization. In this era, knowledge of facts is not as important as the ability to find information when it is needed, to analyze and synthesize it, and to apply the conclusions to new situations. With the computer as a tool, students can focus more on thinking.

1

Word Processing and Writing

OBJECTIVES

Use the word processor to write and edit documents, save them on disk, and print them.

Plan instructional activities that use word processing to enhance the K–12 curriculum.

WRITING IS AN INTEGRAL part of the school curriculum. The ability to write clearly and concisely is important in all content areas, from language arts and social studies to mathematics and science.

Word processing is a tool for writing. With a word processor, students can easily correct and revise whatever they have written. Usually, students do not like to revise and edit their work. They are reluctant to clutter up their compositions with changes and insertions. With word processing, though, students begin to view their work as part of a process of revision. When students do not have to worry so much about mistakes, they can focus on the content of their writing. They are freer to express themselves and to experiment. Word processing also gives students pride in their writing because the copy is neatly printed and looks professional.

Word processing is also a useful tool for teachers. Teachers can use word processing to prepare student handouts, lesson plans, tests, parent letters, and reports. With a word-processed document, it is easy to make changes in handouts and to prepare alternate forms of a test for different classes.

In this chapter you will learn how word processing can be used to enhance students' writing across the curriculum. First, however, we will assist you in learning to use a specific word processor, ClarisWorks, that is powerful enough for your personal use yet can be successfully used by elementary students.

Getting Started with ClarisWorks

The best way to learn about word processing is to try it. We will assume that you have a computer with ClarisWorks 4.0 (or later) installed on your hard drive. In addition, you should prepare a folder on your hard drive named `Tools` in which you copy the files from the `Tools` disks that accompany this book. You will also need a blank disk for storing your own files, or if you are using your personal computer, you may save your files directly to your hard drive.

Opening an Existing File

The `Tools` folder on your hard drive contains a variety of files that you will use throughout this book. When you want to work with one of these files, or with a file that you have created or saved, you must open it. Opening a file loads it into the memory of the computer. The simplest way to do that is to double-click the icon of the file you want to open.

Consider the analogy of a desktop to refer to the computer's memory. Imagine yourself sitting at your desk. The documents you have written are in different folders in a filing cabinet. The filing cabinet is analogous to a disk, either the hard disk or a floppy disk. When you want to work with one of the documents, you open the drawer, take out the file folder you want, and put it on your desktop. Thus, loading a file from a disk into the computer's memory is similar to pulling a file folder out of the drawer and putting it on your desktop. (In the case of opening a file from disk, however, you are placing a *copy* of the file into memory; the original is still on the disk.)

Double-clicking on a ClarisWorks file loads both the file and the ClarisWorks application into memory.

The files in this chapter are located in the `01wp` folder of the `Tools` folder unless noted otherwise.

The file *Starting* was saved as a stationery file. When you open a stationery file, the document is given the name *Untitled* so that you don't accidentally save over the original file.

Let's open the file Starting. To open the file, double-click the Starting file icon. Your screen should look like Figure 1.1. Notice that the title or name of the file in the title bar is at the top of the **document** window. The menu bar runs across the top of the screen above the document **window.**

Figure 1.1
Document window showing some of the contents of the file Starting

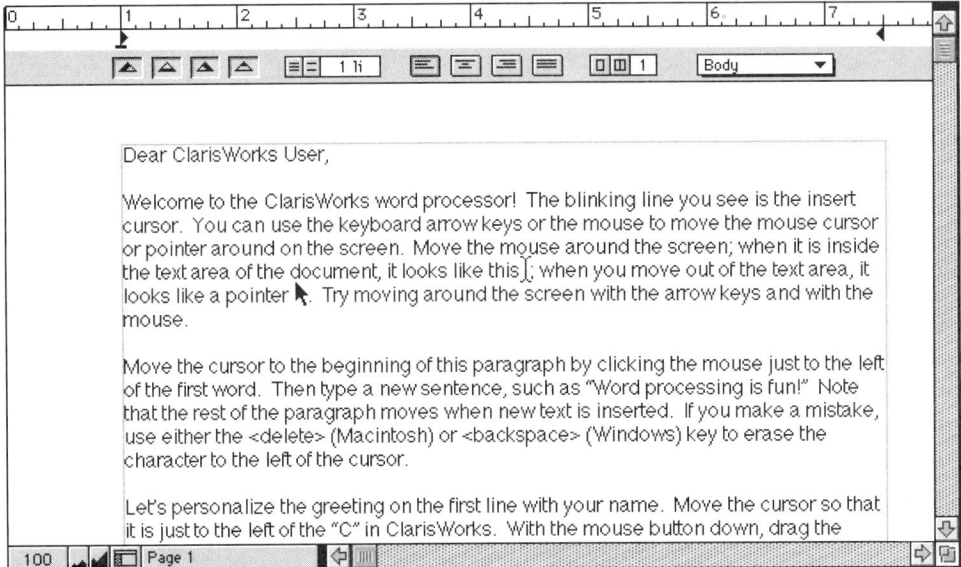

Dear ClarisWorks User,

Welcome to the ClarisWorks word processor! The blinking line you see is the insert cursor. You can use the keyboard arrow keys or the mouse to move the mouse cursor or pointer around on the screen. Move the mouse around the screen; when it is inside the text area of the document, it looks like this; when you move out of the text area, it looks like a pointer. Try moving around the screen with the arrow keys and with the mouse.

Move the cursor to the beginning of this paragraph by clicking the mouse just to the left of the first word. Then type a new sentence, such as "Word processing is fun!" Note that the rest of the paragraph moves when new text is inserted. If you make a mistake, use either the <delete> (Macintosh) or <backspace> (Windows) key to erase the character to the left of the cursor.

Let's personalize the greeting on the first line with your name. Move the cursor so that it is just to the left of the "C" in ClarisWorks. With the mouse button down, drag the

Inserting and Deleting Text

Read the letter on the screen to learn how to move the cursor, insert text, and delete text. The full text of the document appears in Figure 1.2.

Another way to delete text is to select it, then choose *Edit/Cut* or *Clear*.

Figure 1.2
Text of the `Starting` file

Dear ClarisWorks User,

Welcome to the ClarisWorks word processor! The blinking line you see is the insert cursor. You can use the keyboard arrow keys or the mouse to move the mouse cursor or pointer around on the screen. Move the mouse around the screen; when it is inside

the text area of the document, it looks like this $\mathcal{I}$; when you move out of the text arrow,

it looks like a pointer $\blacktriangleright$. Try moving around the screen with the arrow keys and with the mouse.

Move the cursor to the beginning of this paragraph by clicking the mouse just to the left of the first word Move. Then type a new sentence, such as "Word processing is fun!" Note that the rest of the paragraph moves when new text is inserted. If you make a mistake, use the delete key to erase the character to the left of the cursor.

Let's personalize the greeting on the first line with your name. Move the cursor so that is is just to the left of the "C" in ClarisWorks. With the mouse button down, drag the mouse to the right to highlight the words ClarisWorks User but don't include the comma. With the two words selected, begin typing your name. Easy, isn't it?

This letter is longer than one screenful, so move your cursor down to continue reading. One way to move down the document is to click in the scroll area at the right of this document window. When you do, the letter will scroll up the screen. You can either drag the scroll box, click below (or above) the scroll box, or click the down (or up) arrow at the bottom (or top) of the scroll area. To go to the beginning of the

document quickly, hold either the <option> key $\boxed{\text{M}}$ or the <alt> key $\boxed{\text{W}}$ down while clicking the scroll area above the scroll box. Use the same basic technique to move to the end of this letter and add your own postscript stating what happens when you click in the scroll area below the scroll box.

One more thing. The paragraph above looks too long. Let's make a separate paragraph out of the first two sentences. Move the insert cursor to the end of the

second sentence, just past the period, and press the <return> $\boxed{\text{M}}$ or <backspace>

$\boxed{\text{W}}$ key twice. Now the other part of the paragraph has a couple of spaces at the beginning of the first line. See if you can remove those two spaces.

Mike

P. S. By the way, if you choose `Edit/Preferences.../Show Invisibles`, you can see the symbol that is placed there when you press the <return> key ↵. To "turn off" this feature, choose `Edit/Preferences.../Hide Invisibles`.

Writing a Letter

Suppose you want to use ClarisWorks to write a letter to your family or a friend. To start a new word processing document, choose `File/New.../Word Processing/OK`. An empty word processing document will appear on the screen. The current name of the document is `Untitled`, as indicated in the title bar. Start your letter by typing the current date and pressing the **M** <return> or **W** <enter> key twice. Begin writing your letter. As you type the first line of your letter, notice that the text "wraps around" when it gets to the right margin. The **word wrap** feature means that you don't need to press **M** <return> or **W** <enter> at the end of each line. In fact, you should *not* press it again until you are ready to start a new paragraph. If you press it at the end of each line, the word processor will not be able to adjust the margins properly each time you make insertions and deletions in your text.

Complete your letter by typing at least two paragraphs and proofreading on the screen, making changes and corrections as necessary.

Changing the Style of Text

In your letter, find a word that you would like to underline.

You can use a triple-click to select a line of text and a quadruple-click to select an entire paragraph.

❏ With your mouse, double-click the word to select it.

❏ Now choose Underline from the `Style` menu.

You can also choose items such as underline from the Shortcuts palette available under `File/Shortcuts/Show Shortcuts`.

Now use the same technique to select a word or phrase, and boldface the word or phrase. You may also want to try out some of the other styles listed under `Style`. Normally, you would not want to clutter a document with a wide variety of styles, but since you are exploring, feel free to try all of the styles listed under the menu item `Style`.

Changing the Alignment of Text

Suppose you would like to center your name and return address at the top of your letter.

Some people use the term justification rather than alignment to refer to the same process. You can also change the alignment after the text has been typed.

❏ Move to the top of the document window, click the mouse button, and press **M** <return> or **W** <enter> twice to move the date down.

❏ Move the insert cursor to the top line and then click the center alignment symbol 🔲 on the ruler at the top of your document window.

❏ Now type your name and address.

If you want your name and address to appear in boldface, select your name and address and choose Style/**Bold.**

Changing Font and Size

At this point, you may want to explore the items under Font and Size on the menu bar. To get an idea of what different **fonts** and sizes look like, simply select the text that you want to change and then choose a different font under Font and a different size under Size. Even though it's okay to explore with different fonts right now, in your own work you should use only one or two different fonts per page and be consistent in a document with the font and size that you use. The size that is most frequently used in word processing is usually 10 or 12 **points.**

Saving a File to a Disk

Your letter is currently stored in the computer's memory but not on disk. If you were to turn your computer off without saving, you would lose your letter. Consequently, you need to save it on a disk. Saving a file to a disk is like putting a copy of the letter in a file folder and storing it in your filing cabinet for future reference.

To save a copy of your letter to a disk, you need to insert a formatted floppy disk now.

❏ Choose File/Save.
❏ When the dialog box appears on the screen, type in the name you want to give the file.
❏ Then point and click to find the disk you want to save the **file** on.
❏ When you have located the disk, click the Save button.

You should develop the habit of saving your work regularly, perhaps every twenty minutes if you are working on a long document. A simple pressing of **M** ⌘-S or **W** <ctrl>-S is all that is needed. Then, if there is a power failure or something happens to your computer, you have lost only what you wrote since the last time you saved. Each time you save a ClarisWorks document, the previous version of the file is replaced by the updated version.

A document refers to the contents of a file displayed in a window on your computer. A file refers to a copy of that document saved on a disk.

Printing a Word Processing Document

If you have a printer connected to your computer, be sure the printer is turned on at this time. With your document showing on the screen,

❏ Choose `File/Print…`.

❏ When the print dialog box appears on the screen, click the `Print` or `OK` button.

The printed version of your document is called a **hard copy.** Now close the document that appears on the screen by choosing `File/Close`.

If you get a message when you attempt to close the document about whether to Save, Don't Save, or Cancel, click the `Save` button if you want to save it.

Other Word Processing Features

Although you can do a lot of word processing with the fundamentals you have learned so far, most word processors have several powerful features that simplify the task of editing your text: finding and replacing words or phrases, deleting a block of text, and moving a block of text to a different location in the document. We have designed a hands-on activity that lets you learn about these features as you actually try them at the computer:

❏ Open the file `MoreFtrs` with `File/Open…`.

Follow the directions on the screen. You will be making a lot of changes to the document, but the original is still intact on disk. So, if you become confused and want to start over,

❏ Close the document with `File/Close`.

❏ Choose `Don't Save` when prompted. Then open another copy of the file with `File/Open…`.

The text of the `MoreFtrs` document is shown in Figure 1.3.

If you accidentally save the file, don't worry. Remember, we saved the original document as a stationery file, so when you open it, the name of the document appears as `Untitled`. There is little chance you would accidentally save over the original file.

Figure 1.3
Text of the `MoreFtrs` file

Using Additional Word-Processing Features

<u>Finding text and replacing text</u>

Several paragraphs down we have consistently misspelled the word "cursor"!
With a word processor it is simple to replace every occurrence of "curser" with "cursor."
- Choose `Edit/Find Change/Find Change...` and the `Find/Change` dialog box will appear on the screen. You can reposition the real `Find/Change` dialog box on the screen by pointing to its title bar, holding the mouse button down, and dragging.
- Type `curser` into the `Find` box and `cursor` into the `Change` box.
- You now have two choices. You can either click the `Change All` button and all of the items will be changed or you can choose the `Find Next` button and make an individual decision on each item found. The latter choice is the safest, so click the `Find Next` option. Keep in mind you do not want to change the word in the paragraph above this one!

You may want to go back and replace the misspelled words and try the `Change All` option to see how it differs from the `Find Next` option.

Finding text is similar to replacing text; when you do not want to replace text, however, you leave the Change box empty.

<u>By the way...</u>

You have been making a lot of changes to this document, but the original is still safely on disk. If you make a confusing mess of this document, you can go to `File/Open...` to place a new copy of the document on the Desktop.

<u>Deleting a block of text</u>

You have already learned to delete with the <delete> or <backspace> key, which erases the character to the left of the curser when pressed. If you have lots of patience, you can use this technique to delete large blocks of text, but there is an easier way. Suppose you wanted to delete the entire paragraph just preceeding this one.
- Select the entire paragraph by pointing and dragging or quadruple-clicking within the paragraph.
- Choose one of the following options-
    - Choose `Edit/Cut`, or
    - Choose `Edit/Clear`

Now suppose you want to delete the first sentence of the paragraph above. Highlight the sentence so that you have selected the sentence itself and the two spaces after the period. If you make a mistake in highlighting, just click the mouse once and begin selecting text again. Perhaps the easiest way to select this text is to begin at the end of the sentence (Just to the left of the word "If"!), hold the mouse button down, push up (away from you) to the next line of text and drag all the way to the left until the word You is selected, and release the mouse button. Then choose one of the options offered in the previous paragraph.

Continued

<u>Moving a block of text</u>

Sometimes you decide after you have written something that a paragraph and its heading or an entire section should be in a different order. Let's move this section and its heading to the beginning of the document. Select this heading and this section by pointing, clicking, and dragging. They are two techniques you can use.

<u>Technique 1</u>
- Choose `Edit/Cut`
- Move to the top of the document
- Click the mouse on the line just above the header <u>"Finding text</u> ..."

- Press the <return> **M** or <enter> **W** key twice to make room for the new paragraph and to place a line after the new paragraph
- Use the keyboard up arrow to move the curser up one line

- Choose Edit/Paste to paste the new paragraph. You may need to press the <return> **M** or <enter> **W** key to place a blank line between paragraphs. That's it!

<u>Technique 2</u>
- For this technique, you can either close this document and open a new copy or move this section back to its original position.
- Select this entire section with the technique you used in Technique 1 above.
- Then pause momentarily, hold the mouse button down on the selected text, drag and drop the text into its new location.
- You make have to make a few minor editing changes once you have dropped the text.

<u>Copying a block of text</u>

The difference between copying text and moving (or cutting) text is that when something is copied, it is not deleted from where it was, and you end up with a duplicate copy of the text. The procedure for selecting text is identical to that you used for moving text. Once it is selected, however, you choose `Edit/Copy`, rather than `Edit/Cut`. Then you place the curser where you want to paste the text and choose `Edit/Paste`. Try this technique to place a copy of this section at the end of this document.

<u>ClarisWorks Help</u>

To access Help–

If **M**, then choose

? /Index from the upper right corner of the screen. Then follow the instructions on the screen.

If **W** , then choose

<u>H</u>elp/<u>I</u>ndex...

The ClarisWorks **application** has many features. Some of the features of the word processor include the ability to change margins, set tab marks for columns, change vertical spacing, change fonts, and set headers and footers. These features and others are discussed in the document, in the questions and answers section that follows, and in the activities at the end of this chapter.

You have been introduced to the fundamentals of using the ClarisWorks word processor. Later in this chapter, we will discuss some of the other features of ClarisWorks.

Word Processing and the Writing Process

Writing can be thought of as a three-stage process: prewriting, composing, and revising. The **prewriting stage** includes planning what you are going to say, gathering information from other sources, and outlining and organizing your ideas. In the **composing stage** you actually write a rough draft without worrying about details such as spelling, grammar, or the best choice of words. During the **revision stage** you reread what you have written to see how you can express your ideas more clearly and concisely. You also correct spelling and grammar and try to find the precise word for the meaning you intend.

Using the Computer for Prewriting

Although word processing is usually thought of as a tool for the composing and revising stages of writing, the computer can be an effective tool for prewriting as well. Prewriting activities that involve the use of the computer include **freewriting, invisible writing, prompted writing,** using **templates,** and **outlining.**

FREEWRITING Writing teachers often recommend freewriting as the first step in the writing process. In freewriting, you write quickly and without reflection whatever thoughts come to mind. Word processing programs are useful tools for freewriting because they make it easier to write quickly. Also, the computer seems like an audience to some people, so freewriting can feel as natural as speaking. Ten minutes of freewriting can help students get in a good frame of mind for writing. After freewriting, students realize that they do have ideas and information to express.

INVISIBLE WRITING Invisible writing is a variation of freewriting in which the computer screen is turned off. When you cannot see what you are typing, you are forced to focus on the flow of ideas rather than on editing. Your thinking is not distracted by trying to read the text on the screen. When the screen is turned on again, you can analyze what you have written and begin to organize your ideas.

Freewriting and invisible writing are most successful when students are comfortable with the keyboard. If the student cannot type well and needs to hunt for individual letters on the keyboard, freewriting will be difficult because he or she will be concentrating on typing rather than on the ideas. Also, the physical surroundings need to be quiet and without distractions.

⊟ PROMPTED WRITING Another way that teachers can use the computer to stimulate and guide students' writing is with on-screen questions and prompts. Teachers can create prompted writing documents for their students by using any word processing application. To see an example of prompted writing, open the file `Special` and write a sentence or two in response to each prompt. When you have finished, follow the instructions on the screen to remove the prompts, save your document, and print it. Prompted writing files are available both commercially and in the public domain for many word processing applications.

TEMPLATES Whereas prompted writing files are designed to stimulate thoughts, word processing templates are designed to organize thoughts. A template sets up the form of a document. For example, a template for a book report might include these categories:

Title:

Author:

Setting:

Sketch of the main character:

Other important characters:

Summary of the plot:

Your opinion of the book:

A template for a science lab report might include the following headings:

Purpose of the experiment:

Hypothesis:

Apparatus:

Procedure:

Results:

Conclusions:

Discussion:

In addition to helping organize a report, a template saves time because it can include formatting information such as centering the title, underlining the cate-

gory headings, and setting tabs for columns. Many people create their own templates for whatever word processing they do repeatedly. For example, a teacher may have a template for lesson plans or one for form letters that are sent home to parents.

In some ways a word processing template resembles a written form to be filled in. A template, though, is more flexible than a printed form. You can add, delete, and change the given information as appropriate. Also, you are not limited to a blank line of a specific length, as on a printed form.

OUTLINING   With templates, the format of a document is given to you, but outlines allow you to plan and structure your own writing. After a writer has brainstormed ideas and gathered information, outlining helps to organize and evaluate the information.

Most word processing programs have outlining features. To see an example of a ClarisWorks outline, open the file `Outline1`.

Computer Activities for the Composing Stage

Word processing works well for the composing stage of writing. One advantage of word processing is that you can write in a nonlinear fashion: you can write later paragraphs before earlier ones. You can merge into one document parts that were written separately. You can insert text between parts of an outline. You can also load from a disk a letter you wrote to one person and modify it slightly to make it appropriate for another person. Teachers can develop activities for their students that take advantage of the inherent flexibility of the word processor.

SKELETON STORIES   Skeleton stories require a minimum of original writing because students simply fill in the blanks to complete a story. As an example, open the file `Skeleton` and insert your own words in place of each set of parentheses. For students who find composing to be a painful and difficult process, skeleton stories allow them to quickly and easily create a first draft that looks good and is complete.

ADD-ON STORIES   Writing need not be an individual endeavor. Indeed, for many adults, writing is collaborative. One way to encourage collaborative writing in the classroom is by using add-on stories. The teacher suggests a topic, and the first student in the group types a sentence or short paragraph to start the story. Each student in a group of five or six takes a turn typing another sentence or paragraph into the computer. If there are several computers available, students can rotate around the room, adding to each story in turn. One teacher gave the following assignment: "Write a story about a bird that lived in a special place." If you open the file AddOn, you can see how a seven-year-old started the story (Daiute, 1985) and get your class (or your friends) to help finish it.

LANGUAGE EXPERIENCE WRITING   In language experience writing, primary-age children dictate their stories to the teacher or to a teacher's aide. The teacher or aide types the story into the word processor using the child's exact words, with correct spelling and punctuation. The child can see his or her words on the screen and then receive a printout. The rationale for the language experience approach is that young children are able to tell more sophisticated stories than they can write, and their lack of keyboarding and handwriting skills should not limit their creative expression. As an added benefit, students are highly motivated to read what they have written, even if the words are beyond the normal primary vocabulary.

Computer Tools for Revising

Once students have written a first draft, they can use spelling checkers and thesauruses and text-analysis programs to evaluate their writing.

SPELLING CHECKER   A **spelling checker** compares each word in your document with the words in its dictionary and identifies those not in the dictionary as "suspect." For each word that is suspect, ClarisWorks gives you a choice of Replace, Check, Skip, Learn, or Cancel.

Using a spelling checker helps you identify and correct many misspelled words and typographical errors. For example, the application can recognize that *recieve* is misspelled and alert you that you typed *hte* when you meant *the*. But misspelled words in one context might be correct in another. For example, it would not notice if you use *to* when you mean *too* or if you type *form* instead of *from*. Another limitation is that many correctly spelled words, such as proper names and technical terms, are not in your dictionary. However, ClarisWorks will let you prepare a customized dictionary, but you need to be careful that the words you add are correctly spelled.

A spelling checker can be a useful tool for students who recognize its limitations. When a suspect word is identified, the student is forced to decide if it is misspelled and then to find out what the correct spelling is. A spelling program is also a very good proofreader, catching errors like *ot* that can easily slip past your eyes.

PRACTICE WITH A SPELLING CHECKER   If you need or want to practice with the ClarisWorks spelling checker,

❏ Open the file `SpellChk`.

❏ Choose `Edit/Writing Tools/Check Document Spelling`....

❏ When the spelling checker reaches a word with questionable spelling, the `Spelling` dialog box will appear (Figure 1.4) with these choices: `Replace`, `Check`, `Skip`, `Learn`, `Cancel`.

❏ If the correct spelling of the word appears, you can replace the original spelling by highlighting the correct spelling and clicking the `Replace` button or using the key combination at the left of the word.

Figure 1.4
Spelling dialog box

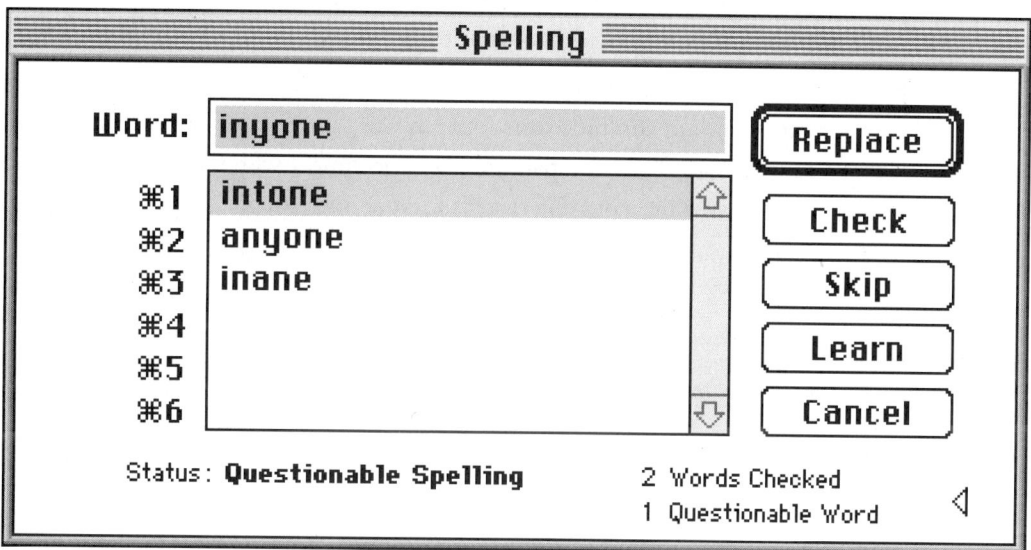

If you want to see the questionable word in context, click either **M** the arrow at the bottom right of the dialog box, or **W** the context>> button and the word will appear in context to allow you a better decision.

If you are not offered an acceptable choice, you can click in the rectangle to the right of `Word:` (where the offending term is) and edit the spelling yourself.

🖫 **THESAURUS** A thesaurus will suggest synonyms for words that you select. Students can use the first word that comes to mind when they are composing and then check the thesaurus for a better word when they are revising. If you want to try out the ClarisWorks thesaurus,

❑ Open the file Thesrus. We are going to make this story more interesting by replacing the words in all capitals with words suggested by the thesaurus.

❑ Select the word *SAD* by double-clicking it.

❑ Choose Edit/Writing Tools/Thesaurus..., and the dialog box in Figure 1.5 will appear on the screen.

❑ You will be offered five choices—Lookup, Last Word, Cancel, Replace—or you can enter another word into the Find box. If this is the first word you have looked up in this document, the Last Word choice will be ghosted and not be available as a choice.

❑ If you see a word that you want to substitute for the original word, you can either double-click the new word or click it once and then click the Replace button. If you prefer to look at more choices, click on one of the words or terms offered and then click the Lookup button.

❑ Continue this procedure for each word in your document that is in all capitals. Then compare your new document with the original text. How is the story different? Is it more interesting?

Figure 1.5
Thesaurus dialog box

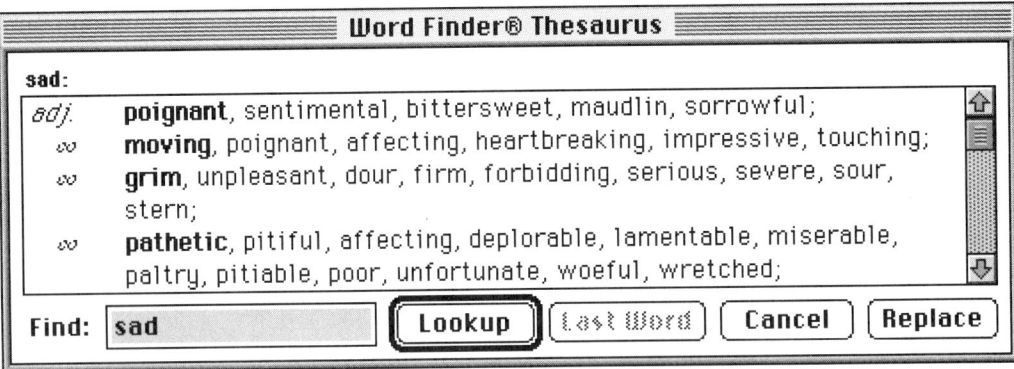

TEXT-ANALYSIS APPLICATIONS Text-analysis programs analyze a word-processed document and give the student feedback about word frequency, sentence length, readability index, passive voice, sexist language, homonyms, unmatched quotation marks, and other possible usage errors. Some of these applications also "outline" the document by printing the first and last sentence of each paragraph so you can examine the transition from the concluding sentence of one paragraph to the topic sentence of the next. Students can use this information to correct usage errors and to revise their writing so that it is clearer and more coherent.

Even without these kinds of applications, students can do some simple text analysis with a word processor. By the time most students reach high school, they are aware of their own common usage errors. For example, a student who often confuses *its* with *it's* can find every occurrence of those two words and check the usage against memorized rules. Students can also delete every sentence except the first and last in each paragraph (after first saving the original file and renaming it), and read the resulting sentences for continuity and coherence. (See Appendix E for information about the effectiveness of using word processing with students.)

Word Processing Activities in the Curriculum

Although word processing should be an integral part of any school's writing curriculum, it can also be used as a tool in a variety of content areas. The `Tools` disks that came with this book contain a collection of word processing activities for the classroom. Each of the activities is designed to teach a particular content-area objective as well as to teach or provide practice with one or more specific word processing skills. Table 1.1 lists the names of the files, the content areas, the content-area objectives, and the word processing skills in which each activity provides practice. Assume the role of a student, and open each activity and try it. We hope these activities will stimulate your ideas about how word processing can be incorporated into your own school's curriculum.

Table 1.1
Word Processing Activities for the Curriculum

File Name	Content Area	W.P. Skill	Content-Area Objective
Add-On	language arts	insert	To write collaboratively
Category	problem solving	strike through insert	To identify relationships among words To identify the nonexample of a concept in a list
Combine	language arts	insert, delete, move	To combine short, simple sentences into compound or complex sentences
Current	social studies	insert	To analyze a news story for relevant information To summarize information
Fraction	math, language arts	type numbers	To solve simple fraction problems
Homonyms	language arts	delete	To use homonyms correctly in a sentence
Identity	math	(none)	To practice with the identity properties
Jumbled	language arts	move	To sequence sentences in the correct order
MathSent	math, language arts	type text	To convert number facts to word sentences
Outline1	health, language arts	outlining	To organize information into an outline
Outline2	social science	outlining	To organize information into an outline
PartSpch	language arts	macro	To recognize parts of speech
Punctn	language arts	insert	To correct punctuation in a paragraph
Repeated	language arts	find, thesaurus	To substitute a more specific word for a general word
Replace	problem solving	replace	To use successive trial and error to solve a problem
Run_Ons	language arts	insert, delete	To identify and correct run-on sentences
Skeleton	language arts	insert, delete	To stimulate creative writing
Special	language arts	insert	To stimulate writing about personal experiences
Story	language arts	teacher or aide enters story	To stimulate and record a story in a language experience activity

If you have access to the ClarisWorks education stationery files listed below, explore them to get ideas for your own classroom:

About Stationery

Course Syllabus

Dept. Memorandum

Event Flyer

Lab Report

Olympic Project

Parent Letter

Personal Stationery

Rain Forest Project

Research Paper Presentation

To Do List

Writing an Essay

Questions and Answers

Q1: **How do I remove a paragraph return character?**

A: Move the insert cursor to the right of the paragraph return character and press the **M** <delete> or **W** <backspace> key. Use the same technique to remove a tab setting. If you don't know what these symbols look like, choose `Edit/Preferences...` and then select `Show Invisibles/OK` or click the Show Invisibles icon ⟨⟩ from the Shortcuts palette. The symbol for a paragraph return is ↵ and for a tab is ➤.

Q2: **When I am editing a paper I have written, I would like to be able to save the edited version and keep the original version. Can I do that?**

A: To save your edited version under a different name, choose `File/Save As...`. When the Save dialog box appears, enter the new name and click the `Save` button. Now you have a copy of both files.

Q3: **I know it's important to make a backup copy of any file I have. Then, if something happens to my disk, I will be able to use my backup copy. How do I do this?**

A: See Appendix A or B for making backup copies.

Q4: **Is there any way I can search for tab settings or paragraph return settings?**

A: Use `Edit/Find/Change/Find/Change...`. In the Find dialog box, enter \t or \p, depending upon which one you want. Then click `Find Next`.

Q5: **How can I set page numbers in a ClarisWorks word processing document?**

A: You need to insert a header or footer (`Format/Insert Header` or `Footer`). Then choose `Edit/Insert Page #...`.

Q6: **Can you use footnotes in ClarisWorks?**

A: To place a footnote in ClarisWorks, place the insert cursor to the immediate right of the word or phrase you want to footnote, choose `Format/Insert Footnote`, and then enter your footnote.

Q7: **How do I set tabs in a word processing document?**

A: On the ruler at the top of the document window, you will find four icons at the left end of the text ruler: left justify ▲ , center ▲ , right justify ▲ , and align on decimal ▲ . Depending upon the justification you want to set with a tab setting, drag a copy of that icon and drop it on the ruler at the location you want.

Q8: **I can't remember the keyboard equivalents for performing operations such as paste, and I don't like to keep pulling down menus. Is there another way I can perform these operations?**

A: You can use the **Shortcuts palette** to perform many operations by simply clicking the icon that is associated with an operation. You can display the palette with `File/Shortcuts/Show Shortcuts`. By placing the mouse point over an icon on the palette, it will display its function on the screen.

Q9: **What is a stationery file?**

A: A **stationery file** is a file that opens with the name `Untitled`. Typically, one saves a template this way. Since the name of the document is not the same as the file, there is little chance that you will overwrite the original file. You can save a document as a stationery file with

❑ `File/Save As`....
❑ When the dialog box appears, choose `Stationery`.
❑ Enter the name you want to use.
❑ Locate the folder or disk in which you want to save.
❑ Click the `Save` button.

Q10: **I have word processing files from other word processors that I need to open. Can I open them with ClarisWorks?**

A: You can open (or save) a variety of word processing files saved on other applications.

❏ Use `File/Open…`.

❏ When the dialog box appears, hold the mouse button down on `Document Type`, pull down to `Word Processing`, and release to show only word processing files. If you are looking for a particular type of word processing file, point to `File Type`, pull down to the one you are looking for, and release.

Q11: **Do I have to enter all my text before I can use outlining?**

A: You can outline as you enter your text. Select new topics and movement from the `Outline` menu. Select a style from either the Stylesheet (`View (Window)/Show Styles`) or the Paragraph Styles Menu `Body ▼`.

Q12: **What does Insert do?**

A: `File/Insert` allows the user to insert the contents of a file (but not a ClarisWorks word processing file) of the types indicated in the dialog box under `Show`.

Q13: **Can I divide a word processing document into columns?**

A: You can click the Column Indicator `□ Ⅲ 1` icon to divide the document page into two or more columns, or you can use text frames (see Chapter 2) for more flexibility.

Q14: **How can I change to double spacing in a word processing document?**

A: Click the Line-Spacing control icon `≡ ≡ 1 li` on the left side of the ruler with the insertion cursor in the paragraph where you want to change the spacing.

Activities

1. Open the activity files listed in Table 1.1 and try each one of them. Evaluate the appropriateness of using the computer in each case. Which activities take advantage of the capabilities of the computer, and which could be done just as easily with pencil and paper? Save your completed activities on your data disk.

2. Use the ClarisWorks word processor to compose a letter to the parents of students who will be in your classroom this year.

3. Plan a word processing activity for your students that teaches both a word processing skill (or gives practice in a skill already introduced) and a content-area objective.

4. If you have access to the ClarisWorks education stationery files, choose one you are interested in and modify it to apply to your situation.

5. Prepare a one- or two-page résumé outlining your educational and professional background.

6. For this activity, use either a piece of your own writing or that of a friend or student. For every paragraph in the document, delete all but the first and last sentence. Analyze the resulting sentences for continuity and coherence. If the writing is not yours, give feedback to that person.

7. Prepare a list of common grammar mistakes that you make. What features of a word processing application might you use to locate these kinds of mistakes?

8. Identify a word processing activity that you frequently perform. Prepare a template for this activity or task, and save the document as a stationery file.

9. If you have access to a copy of The Writing Center program and the accompanying notebook, explore several of the numerous writing activities and templates available with it.

Summary

Word processing is a tool for writing. With a word processor, you can easily correct and revise whatever you have written. As a teacher, you can create a variety of curriculum activities that teach content-area objectives as well as word processing skills. You can create templates or forms for whatever written work you do repeatedly.

Students who use word processing are more likely to think of writing as a process of revision rather than as finished copy. Freed from worrying about mistakes, they can focus on the content of their writing.

Word processing was one of the first computer applications to be widely used with desktop computers, and it is still the most widely used computer application. Its popularity is due to its usefulness—it truly makes writing easier. In the next chapter, you will be working with graphics, so you will be able to use text frames and graphics to increase the appeal of your word processing documents.

Key Terms

application 10	points 7
backup 21	prewriting stage 11
composing stage 11	prompted writing 11
document 4	revision stage 11
file 7	Shortcuts palette 22
fonts 7	spelling checker 14
freewriting 11	stationery file 22
hard copy 8	template 11
invisible writing 11	window 4
outlining 11	word wrap 6

References

Bangert-Drowns, R. (1993). The word processor as an instructional tool: A meta-analysis of word processing in writing instruction. *Review of Educational Research, 63,* 69–93.

Barton, R. (1993). *Teaching across the curriculum with the Macintosh and The Writing Center in the one computer classroom.* (ERIC Document No. ED 358839)

Bernhardt, S. (1990). Teaching college composition with computers: A time observation study. *Written Communication, 7,* 342–374.

Boone, R. (Ed.). (1991). *Teaching process writing with computers* (rev. ed.). (ERIC Document No. ED 338218)

Brady, L. (1990). Overcoming resistance: Computers in the writing classroom. *Computers and Composition, 7*(2), 21–33.

Bright, T. (1990). *Integrating computers into the language arts curriculum.* (ERIC Document No. ED 326884)

Cochran-Smith, M. (1991). Word-processing and writing in elementary classrooms: A critical review of related literature. *Review of Educational Research, 61,* 107–155.

Cochran-Smith, M., Paris, C., & Kahn, J. (1991). *Learning to write differently: Beginning writers and word processing.* Norwood, NJ: Ablex.

D'Odorico, L., & Zammuner, V. (1993). The influence of using a word processor on children's story writing. *European Journal of Psychology of Education, 8*(1), 51–64.

Doolittle, P. E. (1991). *Vygotsky and the socialization of literacy.* (ERIC Document No. ED 377473)

Duin, A., & Gorak, K. (1992). Developing texts for computers and composition: A collaborative process. *Computers and Composition, 9*(2), 17–39.

Grejda, G., & Hannifan, M. (1992). Effects of word processing on sixth graders' holistic writings and revisions. *Journal of Educational Research, 85*(3), 144–149.

Grow, G. (1995). *The do it wrong approach to writing.* (ERIC Document No. ED 381780)

Gunn, C. (1990). Computers in a whole language classroom. *Writing Notebook, 7*(3), 6–8.

Hunter, W. (1991). A brief report on three recent summaries (Technography Place). *Writing Notebook: Creative Word Processing in the Classroom, 8*(4), 34–35.

Kantrov, I. (1991). Keeping promises and avoiding pitfalls: Where teaching needs to augment word processing. *Computers and Composition, 8*(2), 63–77.

Miller, L. (1994). Putting the computer in its place: A study of teaching with technology. *Journal of Curriculum Studies, 26*(2), 121–141.

Moeller, B. (1993). *Literacy and technology. News from the Center for Children and Technology and the Center for Technology in Education.* (ERIC Document No. ED 362245)

Montague, M. (1990). Computers and writing process instruction. *Computers in the Schools, 7*(3), 5–20.

Nydahl, J. (1991). Ambiguity and confusion in word-processing research. *Computers and Composition, 8*(3), 21–37.

Owston, R., Murphy, S., & Wideman, H. (1992). The effects of word processing on students' writing quality and revision strategies. *Research in the Teaching of English, 26,* 249–276.

Platt, C. (1993). Mystery pen pals. *Learning, 22*(2), 74.

Reissman, R. (1992). Using computers. The plot thickens. *Learning, 21*(4), 43.

Schramm, R. (1991). The effects of using word processing equipment in writing instruction. *Business Education Forum, 45*(5), 7–11.

Simic, M. (1994). *Computer assisted writing instruction.* (ERIC Document No. ED 376474)

Snyder, I. (1993). Writing with word processors: A research overview. *Educational Research, 35*(1), 49–68.

Snyder, I. (1994). Writing and word processors: The computer's influence on the classroom context. *Journal of Curriculum Studies, 26*(2), 143–162.

Stratton, B., & Grindler, M. (1991). *SMILE: Using photography to enhance reading/writing instruction.* (ERIC Document No. ED 333341)

Valeri-Gold, M., & Deming, M. (1991). Computers and basic writers: A research update. *Journal of Developmental Education, 14*(3), 10–12, 14.

Waite, J. (1995). Typographic principles for word processing students. *Business Education Forum, 50,* 28–32.

Warschauer, M. (1995). *E-mail for English teaching: Bringing the Internet and computer learning networks into the language classroom.* (ERIC Document No. ED 389211)

Williamson, B. (1993). *Writing with a byte. Computers: An effective teaching methodology to improve freshman writing skills.* (ERIC Document No. ED 376474)

Wresch, W. (Ed.). (1991). *The English classroom in the computer age: Thirty lesson plans.* (ERIC Document No. ED 331087)

Communicating with Graphics

OBJECTIVES

Create and edit draw and paint graphics.

Create instructional materials and lessons with graphics.

Unless otherwise noted, the files referred to in this chapter are located in the `02gr` folder of the `Tools` folder.

THE VISUAL IMPACT of the world around us is something that most of us take for granted. Think for a moment about a favorite book or story from your childhood. What do you recall? Chances are that you visualize images involving vivid graphics or pictures that once again give you great pleasure. Images or graphics are a significant means of enhancing communication. Try to imagine a newspaper, a magazine, or a textbook without graphics; it would be significantly different. In this chapter you will be working with graphics so that you can supplement your own instructional activities. How can a teacher use graphics in the curriculum? You can use them to give a more pleasing appearance to handouts, to stimulate writing, to supplement lessons on shape and texture, to illustrate concrete concepts in a range of teaching areas, to prepare a slide show, to illustrate an idea in a hypermedia lesson, or as a means of student creative expression. There are dozens of ways to use graphics in the classroom. The more you learn about graphics, the more ideas you will get!

There are two basic types of computer graphic images. Some graphics are composed of a series of dots (**pixels**) on the screen and are called **paint graphics;** others are mathematically described objects called **draw graphics.** Claris-Works has both draw and paint graphics.

Pixel is short for picture element, an individual point or dot on the computer screen. Paint graphics are often referred to as bitmapped graphics because each pixel on the screen corresponds (is "mapped") to a bit in video RAM. Draw graphics are often called vector graphics because the images are composed of mathematically described objects and paths.

Draw Graphics

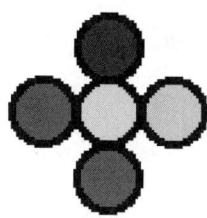

Whenever you want simple shapes such as lines, squares, or circles, you will probably elect to use draw graphics. Each shape you draw is an **object.** You can combine objects with other objects and **frames** to create a design such as a map, a logo, or a form.

. . . .

Exploring with Draw Tools

We are going to begin by giving you the opportunity to explore with the draw tools. Start ClarisWorks; when prompted for the type of document, choose `Drawing`. The **Tool panel** is located on the left side of the document window (Table 2.1). The Tool panel in a draw document is composed of three sections. The four items in the top section include the selection and frame tools, the next section contains ten draw tools, and the bottom section contains the fill sample, fill palettes, pen sample, and pen palettes.

An object *is a mathematically defined element such as a circle or a line, or it can be a paint, text, or spreadsheet frame. A frame is a type of object; every object has a border (that you can hide if you elect) and a fill (which is the area within the border).*

If you need assistance identifying the tools,

Ⓜ *Choose ?/*`Show Balloons`*, and then point at the item you want identified with the pointer.*

Ⓦ *With the pointer, point at the item you want identified and wait a couple of seconds.*

The Tool panel is composed of three sections.

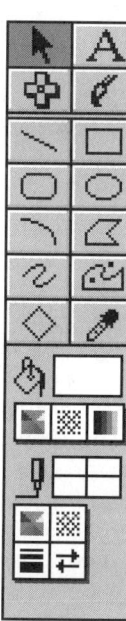

Table 2.1
Drawing and Painting Tools Located on the Tool Panel

Tool Icon	Name of Tool	Purpose
	Arrow pointer	Select objects and frames.
	Text tool	Create a text frame.
	Spreadsheet tool	Create a spreadsheet frame.
	Paint tool	Create a paint frame.
	Line tool	Draw line. With Shift key down, draws perfect horizontal or vertical line.
	Rectangle tool	Draw a rectangle. To draw a square, hold Shift key down as you drag.
	Rounded Rectangle	Draw a rounded rectangle. To set radius of corners, click tool and select RoundtoolCorners from Options menu.
	Oval tool	Draw oval. To draw a circle, hold Shift key down as you drag.
	Arc tool	Draw arc.
	Polygon tool	Draw irregular polygon; click, drag, click; to end, double-click.
	Freehand tool	Draw curving or irregular lines.
	Bezigon tool	Draw a Bezier curve; click, drag, click; to end, double-click.
	Regular Polygon tool	Draw a regular polygon. To set the number of sides, choose Polygon Sides from Options menu. In Paint, double-click the tool.
	Eyedropper	Pick up an object's fill and pen attributes; in Paint, picks up the color.
	Selection Rectangle tool	Selects all or part of a paint graphic. To leave white space surrounding a graphic, hold the Shift key down as you drag the Selection tool over an image.
	Lasso	Selects an irregularly shaped paint graphic; drag around area with the Lasso.
	Magic Wand	Selects adjacent pixels of the same color and patterns; can fine-tune a small part of a paint image.
	Brush	Paint brushstrokes in the selected color and pattern; double-click Brush to change shape.
	Pencil	Paint fine lines in current fill (not pen) color; hold Shift key down to draw perfect horizontal or vertical lines. Double-click to alternate between 100% and 800% zoom levels.
	Paint bucket	Fill area with current fill attributes. To fill an area containing many colors, select the area and choose Fill from the transform menu.
	Spray can	Paint a flow of dots in current fill color; double-click to edit spray size.
	Eraser	Erase what you drag over; double-click erases the entire paint document/frame.

LINE TOOL

❏ Choose the **Line tool** by clicking the icon on the Tool panel.

❏ Drag the mouse for a short distance on the screen with the mouse button down.

You should see a straight line that will look something like this . (If the line is not selected, use the **Arrow pointer** to select the line by clicking it. You will know the object is selected when you observe the "handles" on the object.) Now that you have the line selected, we are going to explore some of the characteristics of the border and the fill that you can change, such as the color, pattern, and width of the line.

Look near the bottom of the Tool panel to locate the section that contains the pen samples and pen palettes, marked by the **pen sample icon** (see Figure 2.1). Experiment with Pen Color, Pen Pattern, Width, and Arrows by using the following instructions:

❏ From the palette below the pen sample icon , choose a pen color by placing the mouse pointer over the Pen Color icon, then depress the mouse button, pull over to the color you want, and release the mouse button.

❏ Choose a pen pattern by placing the mouse pointer over the Pen Pattern icon. Then depress the mouse button, pull over to the color you want, and release the mouse button.

❏ Choose a 6-point line width by placing the mouse pointer over the Width icon. Depress the mouse button on the icon, pull down to the 6 pt. line, and release the mouse button.

❏ Choose the line tool again, then hold the mouse button down, drag across the screen, and release the mouse button. Now let's modify the characteristics of this line.

❏ With the line still selected, change the color, the pattern, and the width of the line with the technique above. Try different variations of arrows by selecting an item from the arrow icon while your line is still selected.

❏ Now try drawing a new line while you hold the <shift> key down. You will be able to make a perfect vertical or horizontal line or a line at a 45° angle, depending on the initial movement you make with the mouse.

If ClarisWorks has already been started, then point to `File/New.../Drawing/OK.`

The second or middle section of the Tool panel contains ten draw tools.

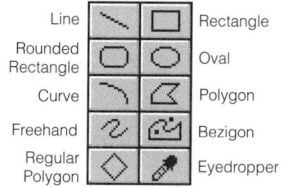

You can "tear off" a copy of the color palettes by pointing to the palette, holding the mouse button down, dragging across the screen, and then releasing the mouse button.

Figure 2.1
Section of the Tool panel showing the pen palettes

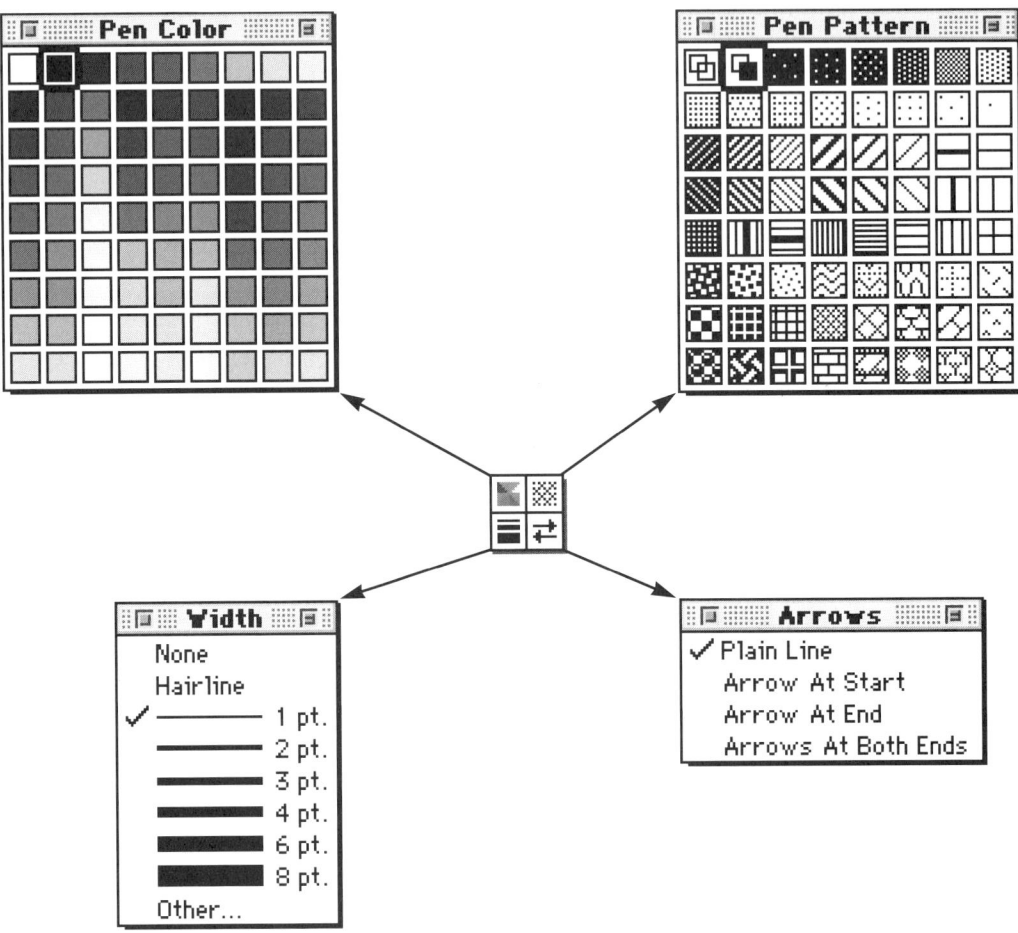

If you are going to use the same tool to draw several objects, you can double-click the tool you want to use and then draw as many objects with that tool as you need without reselecting the tool each time you draw an object.

Now we are going to explore with each of the other draw tools. For each of the remaining draw tools, you can set either pen characteristics (Figure 2.1) or fill characteristics ✋▢ (Figure 2.2) before or after you draw your objects. Try various combinations of color, patterns, and line characteristics with each tool.

Figure 2.2
Section of the Tool panel showing the fill sample and the fill palettes

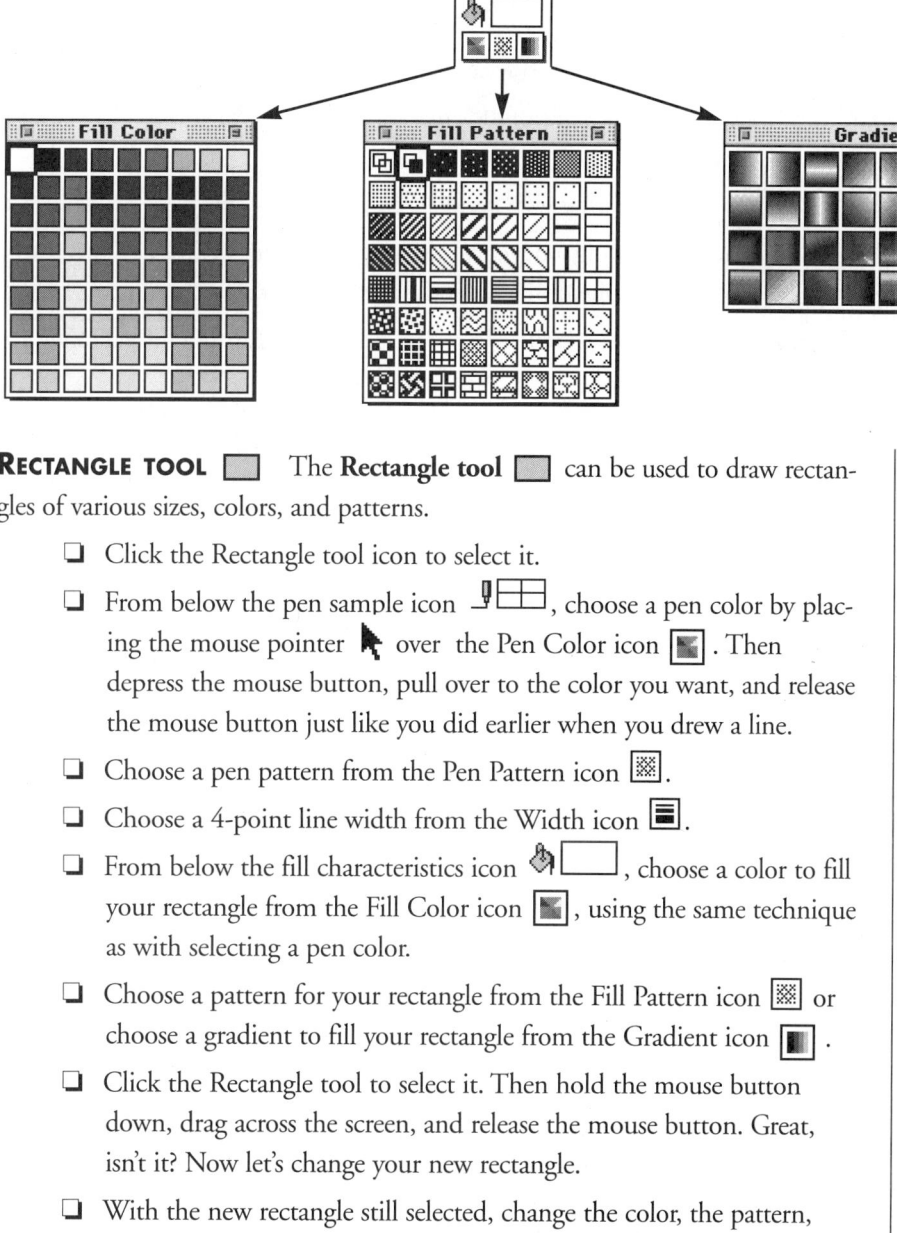

RECTANGLE TOOL ▯   The **Rectangle tool** ▯ can be used to draw rectangles of various sizes, colors, and patterns.

❏ Click the Rectangle tool icon to select it.

❏ From below the pen sample icon ▯, choose a pen color by placing the mouse pointer ▮ over the Pen Color icon ▮ . Then depress the mouse button, pull over to the color you want, and release the mouse button just like you did earlier when you drew a line.

❏ Choose a pen pattern from the Pen Pattern icon ▦ .

❏ Choose a 4-point line width from the Width icon ▤ .

❏ From below the fill characteristics icon ▯, choose a color to fill your rectangle from the Fill Color icon ▮ , using the same technique as with selecting a pen color.

❏ Choose a pattern for your rectangle from the Fill Pattern icon ▦ or choose a gradient to fill your rectangle from the Gradient icon ▮ .

❏ Click the Rectangle tool to select it. Then hold the mouse button down, drag across the screen, and release the mouse button. Great, isn't it? Now let's change your new rectangle.

❏ With the new rectangle still selected, change the color, the pattern, and the width of the line and the fill pattern and fill color, or try choosing or changing the Fill Gradient ▮ .

❏ Now try drawing a new rectangle while you hold the <shift> key down. You will be able to make a perfect square with this technique.

OVAL TOOL ⬭ You can use the **Oval tool** ⬭ to draw various kinds of ovals with various colors, patterns, and gradients.

- ❏ Select the color, the pattern, and the width of the line and the fill pattern and fill color or the Fill Gradient ▣ you want to try first.

- ❏ Click the Oval tool to select it.

- ❏ Hold the mouse button down, drag across the screen, and release the mouse button.

- ❏ Try experimenting with various colors, patterns, and sizes of ovals.

- ❏ Now try drawing a new oval while you hold the <shift> key down. You will be able to make a perfect circle with this technique.

ROUNDED RECTANGLE TOOL ▢ You can use the **Rounded Rectangle tool** ▢ to draw rectangles with rounded corners.

- ❏ Choose the Rounded Rectangle tool by clicking its icon.

- ❏ Set the radius of the corners by first selecting `Round Corners…` from the `Options` menu. Make the choice you want to try and click OK.

- ❏ Draw your rounded rectangle by dragging diagonally across the screen with the mouse button down.

- ❏ With the new rounded rectangle selected, change the color, the pattern, and the width of the line and the fill pattern and fill color, or try choosing or changing the Fill Gradient ▣.

- ❏ Draw a rounded rectangle while you hold the <shift> key down. What happens?

ARC TOOL ⤵ You use the **Arc tool** ⤵ to draw arcs of various sizes, shapes, and patterns.

- ❏ Choose the Arc tool and draw a series of arcs.

- ❏ Explore various colors, patterns, line widths, fill patterns, fill colors, or fill gradients with your arcs. Among your choices, select a solid color (▣ from among the choices as you hold the mouse button down on the Fill Pattern icon ▦) or a pattern, and with another one, no fill pattern (⊞ from among the choices as you hold the mouse button down on the Fill Pattern icon ▦).

POLYGON TOOL ◿ The **Polygon tool** ◿ is used to draw irregular polygons.

- ❏ Click the Polygon tool icon to select it.

❑ With the mouse button down, click somewhere on the screen where you want the drawing to begin. Then drag the mouse (mouse button up) a short distance across the screen and click again; continue dragging and clicking.

❑ When you have the shape that you want, double-click to end if the ending point is not the same place as the starting point.

❑ Explore various colors, patterns, line widths, fill patterns, fill colors, or fill gradients with the Polygon tool.

FREEHAND TOOL ∿   You can use the **Freehand tool** ∿ to draw curving or irregular lines.

❑ Choose the Freehand tool.

❑ With the mouse button down, draw a pattern on the screen and release the mouse button.

❑ Explore various colors, patterns, line widths, fill patterns, fill colors, or fill gradients with this tool.

BEZIGON TOOL 🔲   You use the **Bezigon tool** 🔲 to draw a **Bezier curve,** which is a curve drawn through points that you specify.

❑ Choose the Bezigon tool by clicking its icon on the Tool panel.

❑ You use the same technique to draw with this tool as you used with the Polygon tool. With the mouse button down, click somewhere on the screen where you want the drawing to begin. Then drag the mouse (mouse button up) a short distance across the screen and click again; continue dragging and clicking. When you have the shape that you want, double-click to end if the ending point is not the same place as the starting point.

REGULAR POLYGON TOOL ◈   Use the **Regular Polygon tool** ◈ to draw a variety of regular polygons.

❑ Select the tool by clicking its icon on the Tool panel.

❑ Set the number of sides by choosing `Polygon Sides` from the `Options` menu; enter the number of sides (3 to 40), and click OK.

❑ Draw your polygon by holding the mouse button down, dragging the mouse across the screen, and then releasing the mouse button.

🖫 **EYEDROPPER** 🖊   You use the **Eyedropper** 🖊 to pick up the color and pattern of an object and then use that color and pattern to fill an object or to draw another object.

*To open a graphic library,
choose File/Library/Open...
When you locate the library,
click the Open button.*

*You don't have to use drag and
drop; you could use copy and
paste, or you could click the
object you want and then click
Use on the library palette.*

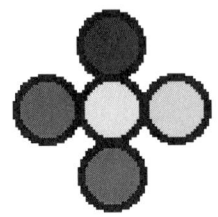

*Your new logo will look
like this one.*

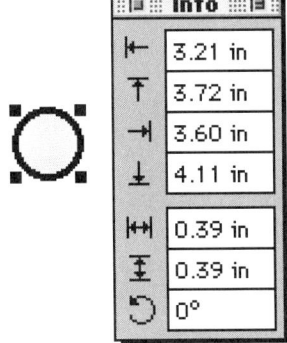

*This is your circle and the
Info palette; the dimensions
of your original circle will
probably be different from ours
in the graphic above.*

- ❏ Open `Lbry_ch2` (located in the `02gr` folder) inside a draw document.
- ❏ When the library appears on the screen, **drag and drop** a copy of graphic Object 1.
- ❏ Select the Eyedropper.
- ❏ Then click the object you just pasted into your draw document. The color and pattern of the object are now shown in the fill sample icon 🎨▭ .
- ❏ Select a draw tool and draw a new object; it should have the same color and pattern as the original object.
- ❏ You can change the color of an existing object by clicking the Eyedropper on the object while holding the **M** <command> (⌘) or the **W** <ctrl> key down after you have clicked on the item whose characteristics you want to copy.

That's the last of the draw tools; now let's practice constructing a graphic that we could use as a logo for a newsletter. The logo will consist of five circles with the edges touching.

- ❏ Start a new drawing document.
- ❏ Select the Oval tool ⬭ .
- ❏ With the <shift> key down, drag to draw a small circle.
- ❏ Choose the appropriate color, patterns, and line width that you want.

We want circles of exactly 0.33 inch in diameter. To accomplish this,

- ❏ Choose `Object Info...` from the `Options` menu.
- ❏ If your circle isn't selected, click it with the pointer to select it and observe the dimensions of your circle in the `Info` palette, particularly in the boxes just to the right of the width ↔ and the height ↕ icons. If the value in these locations is not 0.33, then
- ❏ Type .33 in the ↔ and the ↕ boxes; then click anywhere outside the `Info` palette. Your circle is now exactly .33 inch in diameter!

You're ready now to make duplicates of your circle. We need a total of five circles, so, with your circle selected,

- ❏ Point to `Edit/Duplicate` four times to make four duplicates of your circle.

❏ Make the color or pattern in each of your circles different by selecting one circle at a time and then selecting appropriate colors and patterns.

Now we need to orient our circles to begin forming our logo. We need three of the circles to be arranged vertically. To accomplish this,

❏ With the pointer, select and drag individually three of the circles until they are arranged vertically.

❏ We need to align the three circles perfectly, so select all three of the circles by holding the <shift> key down as you select them (or by drawing an imaginary box around them with the pointer tool).

❏ Choose Align Objects... from the Arrange menu (Figure 2.3).

❏ Then select Left to Right/Align centers/OK. (Top to bottom should be None.)

Figure 2.3
Align Objects dialog box

Here are three circles arranged vertically. Don't worry that they are not perfectly aligned yet; we will take care of that momentarily.

Align Objects

Top to Bottom
- ◉ None
- ○ Align top edges
- ○ Align centers
- ○ Align bottom edges
- ○ Distribute space

Left to Right
- ○ None
- ○ Align left edges
- ◉ Align centers
- ○ Align right edges
- ○ Distribute space

Sample

[Cancel] [OK]

Vertically, your three circles should be aligned perfectly. However, they are probably not in the appropriate position in relation to their borders; we want the borders to overlap. Use the up and down keyboard arrows to move the circles in relation to each other. Because we need the selected object to move only one

To go to 200% magnification, point to the Zoom Percentage box `100` in the lower left of the document window and choose 200.

pixel at a time when we tap an up or down arrow key, we need to turn the `Autogrid` setting off. To do this,

❏ Point to `Turn Autogrid Off` on the `Options` menu.

❏ Select the circle you want to move and use the keyboard up or down arrow key to position the borders so they overlap; you may want to go to 200% magnification. Keep doing this until you have the three circles aligned the way you desire.

To keep these three objects aligned, we are going to group them so they act like a single object. To do this, select all three objects and point to `Arrange/Group`.

Next we are going to align the two remaining objects on either side of our group of three objects. When you have placed the last two circles on either side,

❏ Select all of the objects by pointing to `Edit/Select All` (if there are no other objects in your document) or by drawing an imaginary line, with the pointer, around the objects you want to select.

❏ With all of the circles selected, point to `Arrange/Align Objects…`.

❏ Choose `Align centers` from the `Top to Bottom` choices. (The `Left to Right` choice should be `None`.) Then choose `OK`.

Now use the same technique with the keyboard arrow keys as you did with the first three circles, except this time use the right and left arrow keys to align the objects. When you have the objects aligned as you want them, select all the objects that make up your logo and group them with `Arrange/Group`. If you want to keep your logo, you need to save the document.

Paint Graphics

You can paint a graphic or picture by turning individual pixels on and off with the painting tools. The real-world analogy to a paint graphic is a painting or a portrait. Unlike draw objects, a paint graphic is composed of one or more pixels. In a paint document, all the tools that you used as draw tools in a draw document are now painting tools. In addition, a paint document has eight additional tools that your draw document did not have when you were working with a draw object.

Shown here is a square of 25 pixels; 13 of the pixels have been turned off.

Exploring with Painting Tools

Start a new painting document. First, explore the use of the ten tools that you previously explored in the draw environment. As in the draw environment, combine the use of these ten tools with the fill palettes and the pen palettes (Table 2.1 and Figure 2.1).

BRUSH TOOL 🖌 The following eight tools are unique to the paint environment. You use the **Brush tool** 🖌 to paint brush strokes in a variety of shapes, sizes, colors, and patterns.

- ❏ Double-click the Brush tool icon and choose the brushstroke you want.

- ❏ Select the color and pattern from the fill palettes that you want.

- ❏ Use the mouse as a brush; when you want to leave a stroke on the screen, depress the mouse button and drag.

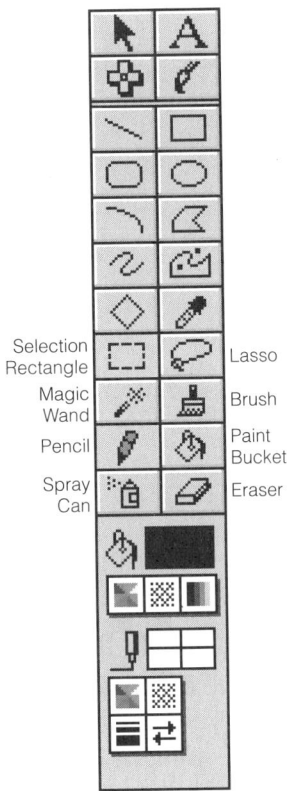

Selection Rectangle · Lasso
Magic Wand · Brush
Pencil · Paint Bucket
Spray Can · Eraser

Here is the Tool panel in a Paint document with the eight new tools in the Tool panel labeled.

If the paint tip of the Paint Bucket is not inside a closed area, you will fill the entire document with the color or pattern you have selected. If this occurs, you can undo by choosing Edit/Undo. If you are filling a small area, you may want to go to 200%, 400%, or even 800% magnification so that you have more control over what you are doing.

PENCIL TOOL You use the **Pencil tool** to paint fine lines with the current fill attributes (not the pen attributes).

❑ Click the pencil tool icon to select it.

❑ Drag the pencil (mouse button down) to paint a fine line in the current fill color.

❑ To draw a perfectly straight horizontal or vertical line, hold the <shift> key down as you draw. If you want to alternate between 100% and 800% view, double-click the Pencil tool icon.

PAINT BUCKET You use the **Paint Bucket** to fill an enclosed area with the current fill attributes.

❑ You need an unfilled, closed figure on the screen, so use a tool such as the Rectangle tool to draw a closed figure that is not filled (click from among the choices you get when you hold the mouse button down on the Fill Pattern icon).

❑ Choose the color and pattern from the fill palettes that you want to use as a fill.

❑ Click the Paint Bucket icon (the icon above the Eraser , *not* the one associated with the fill characteristics icon).

❑ With the paint tip of the Paint Bucket positioned inside the closed figure you want to fill, click the mouse button. Your figure should be filled with the color and pattern that you selected.

For more practice with the Paint Bucket, drag and drop a copy of the graphic Girl from the Lbry_ch2 file and place it in a paint document.

❑ Select a fill color and a fill pattern that might be appropriate for the hair color of the girl in the graphic that you just placed into your document.

❑ Select the Paint Bucket.

❑ Place the tip of the Paint Bucket on some area of the girl's hair, and click. If part of the hair was not colored, then use the same procedure on that part of the picture.

❑ Use this same technique to color the bow in her hair. Keep this graphic to use with another painting tool momentarily.

SPRAY CAN The **Spray Can** is used to paint a flow of dots with the current fill attributes.

❑ Choose the Spray Can by clicking its icon.

❏ Drag the mouse across the screen (mouse button down) to paint a mist of dots in the current fill color.

❏ To change the spray size, double-click the Spray Can icon and enter dot size (1–72) and flow rate (1–100). Then click OK and drag the mouse across the screen again with the mouse button down.

The next four tools that we describe are paint editing tools.

ERASER 🖌 The **Eraser** 🖌 is used to erase what you drag over an area with the mouse button down. To practice with the Eraser, you need to have several items on the screen that you don't care if they are erased! If you don't have something on your screen, you need to sketch a couple of things first.

❏ Choose the Eraser by clicking its icon once.

❏ With the mouse button down, drag the Eraser across a painted area on the screen. You should leave an erased trail.

❏ Now double-click the Eraser on the Tool panel. What happens? The entire contents of the paint document should have been erased.

SELECTION RECTANGLE TOOL ⬚ The **Selection Rectangle tool** ⬚ is used to select all or part of a paint graphic. You need to have a paint graphic showing on the screen to practice with this tool.

❏ When you are ready to try out the Selection Rectangle, choose it by clicking its icon.

❏ First, try selecting an entire graphic by holding the mouse button down at a point slightly above and just to the left of the graphic you want to select.

❏ Then drag (mouse button down) diagonally across the graphic to a point just to the right of and just below the graphic.

❏ Release the mouse button and you will see a marquee (which looks a lot like the Selection Rectangle) around the graphic you selected. There are a variety of things you can do when you have a graphic selected. To move the selected graphic, move the mouse until you see the pointer. Then hold the mouse button down and drag the graphic to another position on the screen.

❏ To select just a part of a paint graphic, use the same basic technique just described but select only a part of the graphic.

LASSO 🪢 The **Lasso** 🪢 is used to select an irregularly shaped graphic or a graphic in a crowded area. You will need some paint graphics on the screen to practice with this tool.

You don't really have to begin at the upper left of a paint graphic. You can begin at any of the other three corners of the graphic. The idea is that you must cover the entire part of the graphic that you want to select.

❑ When you are ready to practice, select the Lasso.

❑ With the mouse button down, drag the mouse in a circular movement to surround the area you want to select, whether it be the entire graphic or just a part of it.

❑ To move the selected graphic, point to it until you get the pointer, and then hold the mouse button down and drag the graphic to a new position.

MAGIC WAND ✦ The **Magic Wand** ✦ is used to select shapes that are difficult to lasso and is the last paint editing tool we will describe. By clicking a paint area with the Magic Wand, all the adjacent pixels of the same color are selected. Then you can delete or change the color and pattern of the selected area.

❑ You need from `Lbry_ch2` the graphic `Girl` whose hair color you changed earlier.

❑ When you have the graphic on the screen, choose an appropriate lip color from the fill colors.

❑ Select the Magic Wand by clicking its icon.

❑ With the tip of the Wand, click the lips of the girl; when you click, you will be able to observe that the lips have been selected.

❑ Choose `Transform/Fill`. You just changed the lip color of the graphic.

Graphic File Formats

We have been working with two types of graphics, paint (bitmapped) and draw (object-oriented or vector). Paint or bitmap formats work well for images such as paintings, photographs, and digitized video. One of the disadvantages of paint graphics is that they require a tremendous amount of memory when working with them and a tremendous amount of disk storage space. Conversely, draw or vector formats work well with charts, graphs, line art, CAD graphics, and images with simple shapes. Although paint graphics can be used to represent more things than draw graphics, draw graphics do not require as much memory or storage space.

It may be confusing when you read or hear about PICT, EPS, PCS, TIFF, TGA, and a whole range of other graphics formats (Appendix D). All these formats refer to the file format or structure of the data used to place or record an image on a disk, as contrasted with the two basic types of graphics, paint and

draw. In some cases, the same file format can be used to store more than one type of graphic. Why, then, are there so many different graphics file formats? Because each combination of graphic type and file format has both advantages and disadvantages.

In ClarisWorks, you can save in only one graphics file format, PICT, on the Macintosh but in two file formats with Windows: the Macintosh picture format, PCT, and Microsoft Windows Metafile format, WMF. However, you can open or insert from among a variety of graphics file formats (Appendix D).

Sources of Graphics

There are various sources of graphics you can use with ClarisWorks. You and your friends can paint and draw your own graphics in ClarisWorks or other paint and draw applications. A good way to store them is in ClarisWorks libraries that you have organized by topic or by lessons. In addition, ClarisWorks comes with a collection of graphics organized by topic into libraries. To access these libraries, point to `File/Library/Open...`.

CLIP ART COLLECTIONS You can also use commercial or public domain clip art collections in floppy disk and CD-ROM formats. Just make sure that the graphics files are in one of the formats indicated in Appendix D.

GRAPHICS SCANNERS Scanners are especially useful in giving your work a professional look. Graphics scanners are almost as easy to use as a photocopy machine.

DIGITAL CAMERAS Cameras such as the Apple QuickTake and the Kodak DC 50 are great for you and your students for capturing your own color digital pictures indoors and out.

VIDEO DIGITIZERS Digitizers or frame grabbers such as VideoLabs FlexCam video camera and ComputerEyes are great for grabbing video frames.

THE INTERNET There are literally thousands of graphics and pictures on the Internet. Many of them are in GIF format, but you should be able to open them with ClarisWorks (Appendix D). If you are using the Netscape Navigator browser, you can gain access to any graphic appearing on the screen by simply holding the mouse button down over the picture and following the directions on the screen.

Sample

Sample i

Sample ii

You can also save graphics as a ClarisWorks file, but that is not a standard graphic file format. You can tell by observing the file icon the difference between a ClarisWorks file (Sample), a PICT file *(Sample i), and a PCT file* W *(Sample ii).*

M *You can also take a snapshot of what appears on the screen by holding down the shift-⌘-3 keys. This procedure will place a PICT file on the hard drive with the name* Picture *followed by a numeral.*

W *To capture the screen, press the <print screen> key, then paste the resulting graphic into a paint or draw document.*

Legal Issues Concerning Graphics

Graphics are very easy to alter; this characteristic of electronic images has created a misunderstanding of what is legal and what is not legal regarding the use of images. You can create an original graphic from your own ideas, and you can alter your own original work. However, there may be a problem if your graphic too closely resembles an image produced by someone else and you plan to use it in a commercial product. This idea can become particularly complicated if you scan images; changing a few pixels does not make the graphic yours (Turner & Land, 1994).

If a picture is protected by **copyright,** then the owner has the exclusive right to reproduce, sell, or publish the picture. A work that is protected by copyright will usually have a copyright notice such as this:

Copyright © 1997 by Sarah Marie Land

Even though a graphic is copyrighted, you may still be able to use it. The copyright owner can give you permission, or you may be entitled to fair use of the graphic without permission. Fair use allows limited use for limited purposes such as for nonprofit educational purposes. The critical point is that the use not adversely affect the commercial value of the original work. If you are using graphics created by someone else, your best protection is to secure the permission from the holder of the copyright (Turner & Land, 1994).

Frames, Objects, Documents

You may be at the point where you are confused about frames, objects, and documents. A document saved on disk or other storage medium is called a file. Frames and objects are items that can be selected with the pointer tool and are located within a document. One way to identify an object or frame, then, is to click it with the pointer. If it has handles, then it is either a frame or an object. A frame is a special type of object; think of a frame as a container for text, paint graphics, or numerals. An object is not a container, although you can change the appearance of the color and pattern of its interior.

Table 2.2 shows what objects you can place into what document types. Note that you cannot have databases in any other document type, although you can paste data from a database into word processing, paint, and spreadsheet documents and frames, along with draw documents. In addition to the combinations shown in this table, you can have text and spreadsheet frames in or on other text and spreadsheet frames.

Table 2.2

Types of Objects that Can Be Placed in Documents

Objects	Word Processing	Database	Draw	Paint	Spreadsheet
Text frames	✓	✓	✓	1	✓
Draw objects	✓	✓	✓	1	✓
Paint frames	✓	✓	✓	2	✓
Spreadsheet frames	✓	✓	✓	1	✓
M QuickTime movies	✓	✓	✓	1	✓

1. Draw objects, text frames, and spreadsheet frames placed into paint documents become paint whenever the user clicks outside of the frame.
2. The paint frame does not work in a paint document.

The Paint tool ✒ is the tool you use to draw a paint frame in a document (other than a paint document). It is not used to paint! Consequently, we refer to the actual tools with which you paint as painting tools.

How do you get objects, frames, and data into documents and other frames? The procedure is actually straightforward. Use the following items for practice.

1. Use the text, paint, and spreadsheet tools to place those types of frames into a document. Use the various drawing tools to draw vector objects in a document.

❑ Start a new drawing document.

❑ Choose the Paint tool ✒ .

❑ To create a paint frame, drag diagonally across the screen for about an inch with the mouse button down.

❑ You can work directly inside the paint frame, or you can choose either **M** `View/Open Frame` or **W** `Window/Open Frame` (with the frame selected) to work within the paint frame. Try a couple of the painting tools.

❑ If you are in an open frame, close the frame by clicking the close window box.

❑ Now choose the Text tool **A** .

❑ To create a text frame in a draw document, drag diagonally across the screen for a couple of inches with the mouse button down; then release the mouse button and begin typing.

❑ Now choose the Spreadsheet tool ⊹ .

❑ To create a spreadsheet frame, drag diagonally across the screen for a couple of inches with the mouse button down. Then release the mouse button. You have a tiny spreadsheet frame!

Start a new word processing document. Show the Tool panel by pointing either to **M** `View/Show Tools` or **W** `Window/Show Tools`. Now create paint, spreadsheet, and text frames in your new word processing document with the appropriate tools. To create a text frame within a word processing document, you need to hold the **M** <option> or **W** <alt> key down as you drag with the Text tool; note that you must enter text into the text frames or it will disappear. Now try the draw tools.

You can also show the Tool panel by clicking the `Show/Hide Tool` icon ▥ at the bottom left of the document window.

2. Use copy/paste or drag-drop to move a copy of a frame or object from one document or location to another. When you paste an object or frame into a word processing document or text frame and the Text tool is selected, the object will be treated as **in-line** text rather than a separate object; consequently, as you edit and add text, the location of the object will be adjusted automatically. If the pointer tool is selected when you paste, the object will be treated as a separate object.

3. Use insert (File/Insert...) to place the contents of text files, graphics files, spreadsheet files, or M QuickTime movies into existing documents or frames.

In the Classroom

The following examples illustrate how you can begin to use graphics in your classroom. We present these ideas to stimulate you to develop your own ideas and encourage you to share these ideas with your colleagues.

Art

REPLICATE THE STYLE   This activity was designed for an art class after a visit to an art exhibit. Have students draw or paint a picture in the same style as their favorite piece of art from the exhibit.

EXPLORE PERSPECTIVE   In a paint document or frame, have students make a series of paintings with one of the tools. In turn, the students can select each of the paintings and explore with changes of perspective with `Transform/Perspective`, and then drag on one of the handles.

Mathematics

SHAPES WITH COMMON ATTRIBUTES   This activity was designed for K–4 mathematics to assist students in recognizing shapes that have common attributes. Ask students to draw two large intersecting circles, one representing shapes with four sides and the other representing red shapes. Have them draw two different shapes appropriate for each of the three regions. One variation is for the teacher to draw the intersecting circles and a variety of shapes outside the circles. The students would use the pointer to move the shapes to the appropriate region.

TYPES OF SYMMETRY   This activity was designed for grades 4–6 in mathematics. Use the Rectangle tool ▭ and the Regular Polygon tool ◇ to draw three designs, one with only horizontal symmetry, one with only vertical symmetry, and one with both horizontal and vertical symmetry. Print out the designs and give them to your students. Ask your students to identify the type of symmetry you used.

Which of the basic regular polygons (square, rectangle, triangle, pentagon, hexagon) can be drawn with both horizontal and vertical symmetry? Students can test their answers by drawing these shapes.

💾 **FOUR BY FOUR PUZZLE**   This activity was designed for an elementary mathematics class. This file is in the `02gr` folder and is called `4x4`. Students are to place the four different shapes on the grid so that only one of each shape appears in each column, row, and diagonal (inspired by an activity in *Claris-Works 2.0 in the Classroom,* 1993).

TANGLE WITH A TANGRAM   This activity (file `Tangram Challenge`, which is a stationery file that comes with the educational version of ClarisWorks) for elementary mathematics lets students manipulate tangram pieces electronically to combine the pieces to conform to a single shape.

Science

MENDEL'S LAWS OF GENETICS   This activity was designed for grades 7–8 to illustrate Mendel's laws of genetics. Prepare a colored graphic of flowers to show Mendel's experiment in which he crossed red flowers with white flowers; include through the F2 generation. Draw or paint one flower; duplicate it and place onto other areas of the screen; color them last. One variation is to do the same thing with pairs of characteristics.

SKETCHING A CELL   This activity was designed to allow science grades 7–10 to identify or illustrate the parts of a basic animal cell. Sketch a typical animal cell and label the following parts with the Text tool: cell membrane, nucleus, nucleolus, mitochondrion. This activity could also be used for plant cells or specialized cells.

💾 **DNA BASE TEMPLATES LIBRARY**   This simple library (`DNA_Lbry` in the `02gr` folder) was developed so a teacher or a student could have easy access to the four bases that make up a DNA molecule. The graphics can be used as a teaching or learning activity in a document, they can be used to construct a slide show on DNA, or they can be printed out so that students can manipulate them by hand.

Language Arts

WHICH SHAPE WAS FLIPPED?   This activity was designed for preschool–grade 1 language arts to improve visual discrimination. Place a picture, shape, or letter into each of four sections of a draw document. Then use `Arrange/Transform` and either `Flip Vertically` or `Flip Horizontally` to change one of the objects. The students need to identify the one that is different. This activity can help students discriminate between the letters *b* and *d* and other kinds of right–left confusion.

PREPARE A REBUS DOCUMENT   This activity can be used to stimulate writing on almost any topic in either a word processing document or a draw document. Either you or your students can supply the graphics. A **rebus** is a representation of words or syllables by pictures of objects, such as:

In ⬆ this week, we talked about living in a large 🏙 .

. . . .

Other

💾 **TIMELINE**   These templates (`Timeln1` and `Timeln2` are in the `02gr` folder) were designed so teachers and students could build timelines in a variety of subjects. `Timeln1` was designed so the timeline graphic is on the master page; you need to be in `Page View` to see the timeline. `Timeln2` was designed so the timeline is not on the master page; the graphic has been placed across six pages. As a variation, either you or your students could prepare a library of time markers, text frames, and graphics appropriate for instructional topics ranging from art through zoology. Topics might include the progression of reptiles through geological time, an illustration of your family genealogy, an illustration of changes in art styles through a particular period of time, or a sequence of historical events.

MAKE A MAP   This activity for social studies allows students to practice the skills of a cartographer. They can draw maps of rooms, parks, downtown, or other geographic areas. You may want to prepare a library of map symbols that the students can use in drawing their maps. If you have access to the book *ClarisWorks 2.0 in the Classroom* (1993), note that one of the files that comes with the book contains map symbols.

Graphics Documents for the Teacher and the Curriculum

Graphics can be an integral part of every classroom, whether in combination with word processing or by itself. Table 2.3 lists the graphics files in the folder 02gr of the Tools folder. Open each one of them, explore them, and decide which ones you can use and which ones you would change.

Table 2.3

Graphic Files for the Teacher and the Curriculum

File Name	Content Area	Computer Skills	Content Area Objective
4x4	problem solving, geometry	drag an object	to identify patterns
Crtficat	teacher tool	enter text	to recognize achievement with a certificate
DNA_Lbry	science	copy from library align shapes	to explore the structure of DNA
Geoboard	geometry	draw lines	to construct figures of a selected perimeter
Lsn_Lbry	teacher tool	copy from library	to copy items from library to prepare a lesson plan
Lsn_Plan	teacher tool	type text, copy frames	to prepare a lesson plan
Mk_Ur_On	language arts, social studies	enter text and/or graphics	to compose a brief message to someone such as a friend, a character in a story, or a historical figure (make your own card)
PickPath	problem solving, geometry	none	to analyze, describe, and offer various solutions to one problem
Snowflk	art, problem solving	duplicate, flip vertically and horizontally, align, group, rotate	to explore shapes and create a design with one's name
Timeln1 Timeln2	all	enter text and graphics	to prepare a timeline in a given content area
Web1, Web2	teacher or student tool	copy from library or prepare text frames and lines	to prepare a content analysis on a topic

If you have access to the stationery education files that come with Claris-Works, explore the following drawing files:

Annual Report	Classroom Icons
Business Cards	Fax Cover Sheet
Certificate A	For Sale Sign
Certificate.One	Function Lesson
Certificate.Two	Social Studies Project
Class Seating Chart	Tangram Challenge

Questions and Answers

Q1: **How can I quickly tell the difference between paint and draw graphics?**

A: In ClarisWorks, it's easy to tell what type of document you are in; the environment appears after the document name in parentheses (PT for paint and DR for draw). However, that does not tell you if the graphic in the document is paint or draw unless it is a paint document, in which case everything in the document is paint. When you are in a draw, word processing, spreadsheet, or database document, double-click the graphic frame or object with the pointer; if the painting tools show on the Tool panel, then it is a paint graphic. It they do not appear, then the object is either a draw object or a spreadsheet, text, or **M** QuickTime movie frame.

Q2: **Sometimes I need to make changes in a draw object that are not possible with draw. How can I convert a draw object into a paint graphic so I can make changes?**

A: With the document open that contains your draw object,
- ❑ Select the Paint tool ✎ .
- ❑ With the Paint tool, draw a paint frame slightly larger than the draw object with which you are working.
- ❑ Copy or cut your original draw object.
- ❑ Select the new paint frame and point to Open Frame under **M** View or **W** Window.
- ❑ Then paste the draw object into the frame window.
- ❑ Edit your graphic with the painting tools; then close the window of the frame. Your graphic is now a paint graphic.

Q3: **Can I convert a paint graphic to a draw object?**

A: Yes, you can. If your paint graphic is in a paint document,
- ❑ Move the graphic to the upper left of the document window.
- ❑ Decrease the size of the screen area with Document... under the Format menu by changing the number of pixels.
- ❑ Save the document as a Macintosh Picture (PICT or PCT) file.
- ❑ Either insert or open the file as a draw document.

If the paint graphic is in a spreadsheet or a text frame or document, then copy and paste the graphic into a draw document and save as a Macintosh Picture (PICT or PCT) file.

Q4: **Why would I want to change a paint graphic into a draw object?**

A: A draw graphic uses a great deal less memory than a paint graphic.

Q5: **I'm confused about the difference between a draw object and a paint frame; since they can both be selected with the pointer tool, aren't they both objects?**

A: A frame is a type of object; therefore, a paint *frame* is an object and can be selected with the object tool. However, the contents of a paint frame consist of pixels and must be selected with the Selection Rectangle tool ▢ or the Lasso ◯ .

Q6: **What is Photo CD?**

A: Photo CD is a method developed by Eastman Kodak for the storage of images on CD-ROM at a fraction of the cost of other methods. One format—Photo CD Master—is available through many film-processing outlets. With this process, each image is written to a CD-ROM disk in five resolutions ranging in size from 72k to 18MB. This particular format requires 35mm film and can store up to 100 images on a CD-ROM disk in one or more sessions.

Q7: **How can I put pictures I take with my 35mm camera on Photo CD?**

A: You need to identify a Photo CD transfer site somewhere near you. If you have access to the Internet, you can search for the nearest local transfer site.

The line on the left is the original; the line on the right is enlarged, demonstrating aliasing.

Q8: **What is aliasing?**

A: Aliasing is the effect that occurs when you enlarge a paint graphic. The effect appears as jagged edges or staircasing and occurs because a paint image has a fixed resolution.

Q9: **What are raster graphics?**

A: Raster graphics is another name for paint or bitmapped graphics.

Q10: **What is dithering?**

A: Your eye interprets a pattern of small black and white pixels as gray. Consequently, monochrome paint applications can be used to display grayscale images (by a pattern or mixture of black and white pixels) in a process called dithering or halftoning.

Q11: **What do the initials RGB and CMYK refer to?**

A: A range of colors can be created by mixing a small number of primary colors. The two main mixing paradigms in computer applications are RGB (red, green, blue), an additive color process, and CMYK (cyan, magenta, yellow, black), a subtractive color process.

Q12: **I want to make a mirror image of one of my graphics. Can I do that?**

A: Yes, we assume you are using draw, so
- ❏ Select your image (a picture of a person with her/his arms in different positions works best for comparison purposes) and make a duplicate copy with `Edit/Duplicate`.
- ❏ Drag the copy away from the original.
- ❏ Then, with the copy selected, choose `Arrange/Transform` and then select `Flip Horizontally`. Make another copy of the original and select `Flip Vertically`. Are either of these a traditional mirror image? If not, what would it take to make a mirror image?
- ❏ Make another copy or duplicate from the original object.
- ❏ This time choose `Arrange/Transform/Rotate`. Rotate 180 degrees once (paint) or 90 degrees twice (draw).

You can also flip and rotate text frames.

Q13: **Paint takes up so much room; is there anything I can do when I am using paint so that it does not take so much memory?**

A: Try the following techniques while in a paint document or in a paint frame:
1. Choose `Format/Document...` (Figure 2.4). Change the size of the paint area by entering smaller numerals in the `Pixels across` and the `Pixels down` slots. Your screen probably has 72 pixels per inch, so you can use that numeral to calculate the size of the area you will need.

2. Point to `Format/Resolution & Depth...` (Figure 2.5).
Changing the Depth value to a smaller number will require less
memory; it will also result in fewer choices for color on the
associated palettes.

Figure 2.4
Document dialog box

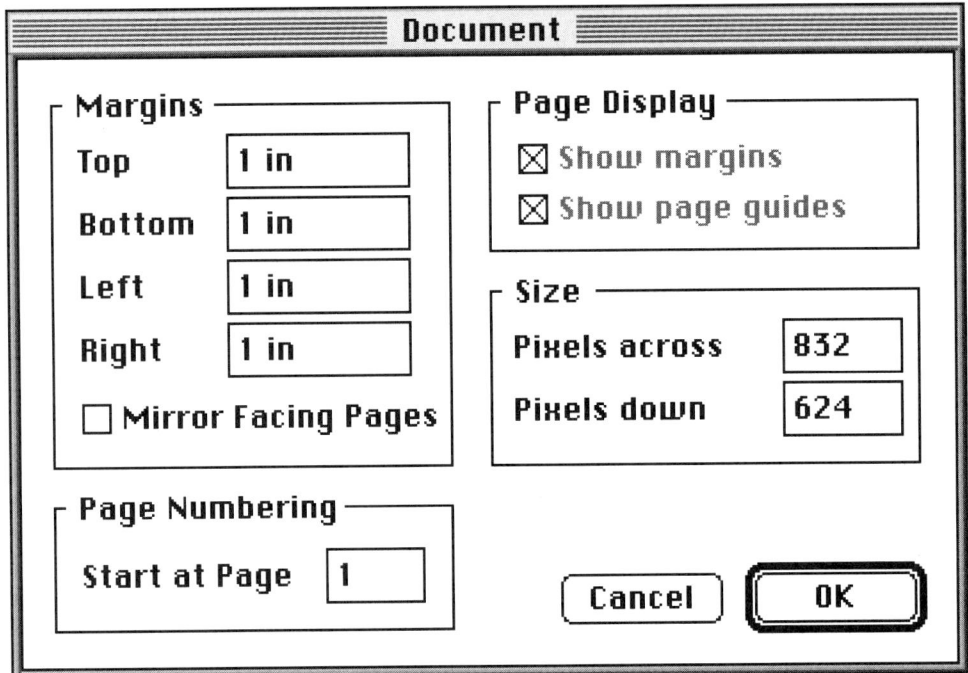

Figure 2.5
Resolution and Depth dialog box

Resolution and Depth

┌Resolution────
- ⦿ 72 DPI
- ○ 144 DPI
- ○ 288 DPI
- ○ 300 DPI
- ○ 360 DPI

┌Depth────
- ○ Black & White
- ○ 4
- ○ 16
- ⦿ 256
- ○ Thousands
- ○ Millions

Memory 117K

[Cancel]   [[OK]]

Q14: **Some of my graphics appear to have a clear wide frame around them or at least on one or two sides. Can I get rid of that area?**

A: Your graphic probably started out as a paint graphic, was saved as a Macintosh Picture (PICT or PCT) file, and then probably was opened or imported as a draw graphic. If you will either select the graphic with the Lasso and place the paint graphic in a draw document before you save or reduce the display area in the paint document, you can avoid this nuisance. If your graphic already has the clear frame, you can paste it into a paint document or frame. If you want to use the graphic as a draw graphic, then go through the procedure of changing it back to a draw graphic.

Q15: **When I try to make some of my graphics smaller by resizing with the pointer, part of the graphic disappears. What's wrong?**

A: You are probably trying to resize the boundary of a paint frame rather than the actual graphic. Try selecting the graphic with the Rectangle Selection tool or the Lasso; then you can reduce the size with `Arrange/Transform/Scale by Percent....`

Q16: **Ⓜ How do I get an idea of what a graphic file looks like without actually opening it?**

A: You can preview the contents of a file by clicking the `Preview` button (unless an image is already showing) after choosing `File/Open` or `Insert.`

Activities

1. You can create interesting designs with the following technique:

❏ Use the Freehand tool to draw a small object in either paint or draw.

❏ With the object selected, duplicate it by pointing to `Edit/Duplicate`. A duplicate copy will appear overlapping the original.

❏ You can leave the copy or move it to another position.

❏ With the duplicate selected, make several more duplicates; they will continue the pattern that you began with the first duplicate.

❏ Now select each object individually and make each one a different color and/or pattern.

2. Use the following activity to practice flipping and rotating objects:

❏ Start a new draw document.

❏ Point to `File/Insert...` (with the pointer selected) and open the file named `Natasha`.

❏ Make a duplicate of the object and drag it to the right of the original.

❏ With the copy selected, point to `Arrange/Transform/Flip Horizontally`. Is the duplicate a mirror image of the original?

❏ Make another duplicate of the original object (then drag it below the original).

❏ Point to `Arrange/Transform/Flip Vertically`. Is this duplicate a mirror image of the original?

❏ Make yet another duplicate of the original object and drag away and below from the original.

❏ Point to `Arrange/Transform/Rotate 90` twice. Is this image a mirror image of the original? Is it a mirror image of the first duplicate?

3. Select one of the teaching and learning activities in this chapter, or use your own ideas, and prepare a detailed lesson illustrating the integration of graphics into a lesson appropriate for your classroom.

M *If you need a place to store graphics, you can use the* Scrapbook *(accessed under the Apple icon at the upper left corner of the screen on a Macintosh). Simply use copy and paste or drag and drop to place graphics (or text) in or to copy graphics (or text) from the* Scrapbook.

Copy/paste will not work properly with this activity.

4. Select one of the following items and prepare appropriate graphics:

a. perspective in art

b. picture to stimulate creative writing

c. abstract versus surrealistic sketch

d. representations of the word *ate* versus *eight; tear* (from the eyes) and *tear* (to rip) or other combinations of words

5. Open the file 4x4. Change the puzzle in the following manner: make every object the same color, but give each member of a shape group (for instance, the circles) a different pattern. Repeat the same four patterns for each shape group. Change the instructions, asking students to arrange the objects so that only one of each shape and pattern appears in each column, row, and diagonal. Save as a stationery file (inspired by an activity in *ClarisWorks 2.0 in the Classroom,* 1993).

Another variation on this puzzle is to combine each different pattern with a different color but to leave the instructions the same. Does this have any effect on the solution? What effect would you expect on the students?

6. Use the template Timeln1 or Timeln2 to construct a timeline in an academic area of interest to you.

7. Design a logo or letterhead for

❑ a classroom or school newsletter

❑ a school club

❑ your classroom

❑ a special project

8. Prepare a map showing

❑ how to get to school from your house

❑ the buildings on your school campus

❑ your neighborhood

❑ downtown

❑ a favorite park

9. Prepare a graphics library for

❑ examples of various art styles

❑ a story students have read or heard

❑ a lesson on DNA

❑ a geometry lesson

❏ items found on a topographic map

❏ dinosaurs

❏ lab equipment

❏ examples of people from various ethnic groups

❏ a weather map

❏ maps of the world

❏ a lesson on common insects

10. Prepare

❏ a seating chart

❏ an organizational chart

❏ a chart showing the basic evolution of plants

❏ a floor plan for a house

❏ a floor plan for a perfect classroom

11. If you have access to the graphics application KidPix (or other paint or draw applications), explore with it and decide if it would be appropriate for use in your classroom.

For each of the following activities, you will be practicing with a tool or technique not previously covered in this chapter:

12. **Reshape Pointer** ✛ Draw an arc, bezigon, freehand shape, polygon, or regular polygon draw object and then try reshaping it by pointing to `Arrange/Reshape`. Use the **reshape pointer** ✛ to drag an anchor point to a new location.

13. **Resizing a Draw Object** Make three copies of a draw object you want to resize, and try each of the following:

❏ Place the pointer on a handle of the selected object and hold the mouse down as you drag.

❏ With a copy of the original draw object, hold the <shift> key down as you place the pointer on a handle of the selected object and hold the mouse button down as you drag.

❏ Select another copy of the object and choose `Arrange/ Transform/Scale by Percent`. Enter the values you want and click `OK`.

❏ Select the last copy of the object and choose `Options/ Object Info`. Type in different values into the `Info` palette and then click outside of the palette.

Compare the results you got with each of these techniques for resizing. What advantages and disadvantages does each one have?

14. **Smooth an Object** Draw a bezigon, freehand, or polygon draw object; then, with the object selected, choose `Arrange/Transform/Smooth` or `Unsmooth`.

15. **Connect the Starting Points of Two Objects** Use the following technique to prepare an interesting design by connecting the starting points of two objects:

❏ Draw two objects with either the Bezigon, Freehand, Polygon, or Curve tools.

❏ Select one of the objects.

❏ Choose `Arrange/Reshape...`.

❏ Copy or cut the selected object.

❏ Select the second object.

❏ Choose `Edit/Paste`.

The objects are now connected as a single object.

16. **Connect Two Objects from End to Starting Point** Try connecting the end of one object to the start of a second object with the following technique:

❏ Draw two objects with the Bezigon, Freehand, Polygon, or Curve tools.

❏ Select one of the objects.

❏ Choose `Arrange/Reshape...`.

❏ Copy or cut the selected object.

❏ Select the starting point of the second object.

❏ Choose `Edit/Paste`.

The objects are now connected end to start!

17. **Reshape with Control Handle** Draw an object with the Bezigon tool.

❏ With the object selected, choose `Arrange/Reshape`.

❏ Click an anchor point and drag either end of the control handle with the reshape pointer ⊕.

—Control handle

18. **Painting with an Image** Use the following technique to get an interesting effect in a paint frame or document:

❏ Choose a paint image or picture with the Selection Rectangle tool or the Lasso.

❏ Hold either the M `<option><command>` keys or the W `<ctrl><alt>` keys down as you drag the image with the mouse.

19. **Free Rotation** Practice free rotation of objects with the following technique:

❏ Select an object.

❏ Then choose `Arrange/Free Rotate`.

❏ Drag the object by a corner handle to rotate.

❏ Choose `Arrange/Free Rotate` again to deselect.

Try the same technique with text in a text frame. Also try a 90° rotation with `Arrange/Transform/Rotate 90°`.

20. M **Opaque, Transparent, Tint** Practice overlapping patterns and colors in paint with the following procedure:

❏ Draw a black rectangle about 3 inches wide.

❏ Choose `Options/Paint Mode.../Opaque`.

❏ Choose a white fill color, and paint a rectangle over the left third of the black rectangle.

❏ Change to `Transparent Pattern`, and paint a rectangle with a white fill on the middle third.

❏ Now change to `Tint`, and try either a white or yellow fill on the right third.

21. **Transform: Shear, Distort, Perspective, Rotate..., Scale by Percent...** Practice transforming part or all of a paint image with the following directions:

❏ Select all or part of an image.

❏ Choose `Transform` and then try each of the following: `Shear, Distort, Perspective, Free Rotate, Resize`. Now drag on one of the handles.

❏ Try `Flip Horizontally, Flip Vertically, Rotate..., Scale by Percent...` by first selecting all or part of a paint image.

Now try the same techniques with a text frame in a paint document or paint frame.

22. Fill From the file `Lbry_ch2`, place the graphic `Elisabeth` in a paint document or frame to practice the following. Place a yellow vertical or horizontal stripe on the dress by

❏ Selecting an area on the dress with the selection rectangle.

❏ Now choose a bright fill color to contrast with the existing color.

❏ Then choose `Transform/Fill`.

To reverse the colors of the entire image,

❏ Select the image.

❏ Then choose `Transform/Invert`.

23. Pick Up From file `Lbry_ch2`, use graphics `Elephant` and `Design` for this activity.

❏ Place the graphic `Design` in a paint document.

❏ Place the graphic `Elephant` in the same document.

❏ Select the elephant with the Lasso.

❏ Drag the selected graphic over the design.

❏ Choose `Transform/Pick Up`.

❏ Drag the elephant away from the design graphic to observe the effects.

24. Place several text frames, paint frames, and draw objects in a draw document. Overlap part of each frame and object. Under `Arrange`, explore the following options: `Move Forward`, `Move To Front`, `Move Backward`, `Move To Back`. An object must be selected before it can be moved.

Summary

One of the advantages of draw graphics over paint graphics is that you can enlarge, reduce, refill, reshape, and rotate them without loss of quality. One of the advantages of paint graphics is that you have much more flexibility in what you can illustrate than with draw graphics. By taking advantage of the characteristics of both types of graphics, you can prepare a wide range of graphics appropriate for use in the classroom.

Graphics and pictures aren't just something to make your word processing documents look nicer. They can add a completely new perspective to many activities in language arts, science, mathematics, and social studies. In the following chapters, you will learn more about the use of graphics for preparing slide shows and presentations, newsletters, hypermedia learning activities, and charts and graphs. If you have an outstanding ability to create your own pictures and graphics, that's great; if you don't, you can still make effective use of graphics. With practice and patience, you can locate a wide range of existing graphics that are appropriate for your needs. As much as anything else, the right graphic can help turn a good lesson or activity into a great lesson.

Key Terms

Arc tool 36

Arrow pointer 33

Bezier curve 37

Bezigon tool 37

Brush tool 41

copyright 46

drag and drop 38

draw graphics 30

Eraser 43

Eyedropper 37

frame 31

Freehand tool 37

in-line 49

Lasso 43

Line tool 33

Magic Wand 44

object 31

Oval tool 36

paint graphics 30

Paint Bucket 42

pen sample icon 33

Pencil tool 42

pixel 30

Polygon tool 36

rebus 52

Rectangle tool 35

Regular Polygon tool 37

reshape pointer 63

Rounded Rectangle tool 36

Selection Rectangle tool 43

Spray Can 42

Tool panel 31

Zoom Percentage box 40

References

Beauchamp, D. G. (Ed.). (1990). *Investigating visual literacy: Selected readings from the annual conference of the International Visual Literacy Association.* (ERIC Document No. ED 352051)

Brown, J. (1991). Images for insight: From the research lab to the classroom. *Journal of Computing in Higher Education, 3,* 104–125.

Burson, G. (1990). Using charts and graphs to teach immigration history. *OAH Magazine of History, 4*(4), 46–49.

ClarisWorks 2.0 in the Classroom. (1993). Santa Clara, CA: Claris Corporation.

Dugdale, S., *et al.* (1992). Visualizing polynomial functions: New insights from an old method in a new medium. *Journal of Computers in Mathematics and Science Teaching, 11*(2), 123–141.

Gossette, F., & Wheeler, J. (1993). Computer mapping in a regional geography course. *Journal of Geography, 92,* 28–34.

McCain, T. D. E. (1993). *Teaching graphic design in all subjects.* (ERIC Document No. ED 367298)

Mustoe, M. (1994). *The versatility of Photo CD technology in the classroom.* (ERIC Document No. ED 382270)

Poohkay, B., & Szabo, M. (1995). *Effects of animation & visuals on learning high school mathematics.* (ERIC Document No. ED 380122)

Scali, N. (1992). Using art to enrich writing and reading (a literature, writing, and art activity). *Writing Notebook: Creative Word Processing in the Classroom, 9*(4), 42–43.

Silverstein, O. (1995). *Imagery in scientific and technological literacy for all.* (ERIC Document No. ED 380090)

Turner, S., & Land, M. L. (1994). *HyperCard: A tool for learning.* Belmont, CA: Wadsworth.

Preparing and Using Slide Shows

OBJECTIVES

Design, create, and edit instructional slide shows.

Plan instructional activities using a slide show.

THIS CHAPTER TEACHES YOU to design, edit, and construct a slide show or presentation appropriate for use in the classroom with ClarisWorks. How can you and your students use a slide show to accomplish curriculum objectives?

Students can construct or use a slide show to

❏ Present a proposal for recycling in science class.

❏ Present an original advertisement for selling a product that would appeal to them.

❏ Prepare and present a book report.

❏ Present their lab investigations.

❏ Show deception in advertising.

❏ Illustrate the sequence of events in a story.

❏ Illustrate the proper sequence of dance steps with a digitized movie.

❏ Illustrate the movement of the earth and moon in relation to the sun with a digitized movie.

❏ Demonstrate basic art techniques and concepts, such as perspective.

❏ Show original artwork they have produced.

❏ Illustrate propaganda techniques.

❏ Present words or phrases in a second language.

You can use a slide show to

- ❏ Introduce students and parents to the course or classroom on the first day or week of school.
- ❏ Introduce a new unit to students.
- ❏ Give examples and nonexamples of concepts or ideas.
- ❏ List and present sequences of events in a content area.
- ❏ Present an assignment.
- ❏ Present the main points in a lecture or discussion.
- ❏ Summarize the main points in a lesson, unit, or presentation.
- ❏ Present a test or quiz.
- ❏ Prepare handouts.
- ❏ Prepare transparencies.

Getting Started

When you use ClarisWorks to prepare and present a **slide show** or presentation, the pages of the document are the slides, ClarisWorks is the projector, and the monitor is the screen. You can prepare a slide presentation with any document type except communications, but the most versatile and easiest document type to use to prepare a slide show is drawing.

Exploring a Slide Show

Start ClarisWorks and open the file Position (Source: Sylvia Broussard, West Foundation Elementary School). The draw document that appears on your screen contains six pages demonstrating the meanings of words by position.

- ❏ To view the contents of this document as a slide show, choose one of the following: **M** View/Slide Show…, while holding the <option> key down, or **W** Window/Slide Show…, while holding the <ctrl> key down.

- ❏ To go to the next slide, click the mouse. Go through each screen of the presentation.

- ❏ To quit the presentation, press the q key on the keyboard.

To get to the options that you can set on a slide show (Table 3.1 and Figure 3.1), choose either **M** Select View/Slide Show… or **W** Select Window/Slide Show….

Another way to advance to the next slide is to press the down arrow on the keyboard.

Table 3.1
Options for a Slide Show

Objective	Steps
To make a slide opaque or transparent	Click the page icon under Order until it is [■] for opaque and [□] for transparent.
To hide (not use) a slide	Click the page icon under Order until it is [⋮]
To change the order of a slide	Place the pointer on the Page (slide) number and drag up or down.
To end a slide show	Press the letter q to quit.
To fit the slide within the screen boundaries	Click Fit to screen under Slide Options.
To center the slide horizontally and vertically	Click Center under Slide Options.
To have the pointer show during a slide show	Click Show cursor under Slide Options.
To make one slide fade out and the next slide fade in	Click Fade under Slide Options.
To keep the slide show going continuously	Click Loop under Slide Options.
To make the slide show go to the next slide automatically	Click Advance every *n* seconds; enter the number of seconds.
To change the background color for the slide show	Point to Background and pull over to the color you want.
To change the color around the slides in the slide show	Point to Border and pull over to the color you want.
M To make a QuickTime movie automatically play	Click Auto play under QuickTime Options.
M To make all movies on a slide play at the same time	Click Simultaneous under QuickTime Options.
M To display a slide until a movie has finished	Click Complete play before advancing under QuickTime Options.
To return to the previous slide during a slide show	Tap the up arrow on the keyboard.
To return to the document	Click Done.

Source: *ClarisWorks 4.0 User's Guide* (1995). Claris Corporation, Santa Clara, CA.

Figure 3.1
Dialog box showing the options for a slide show. (The Fade and QuickTime options are found only on the Macintosh version.)

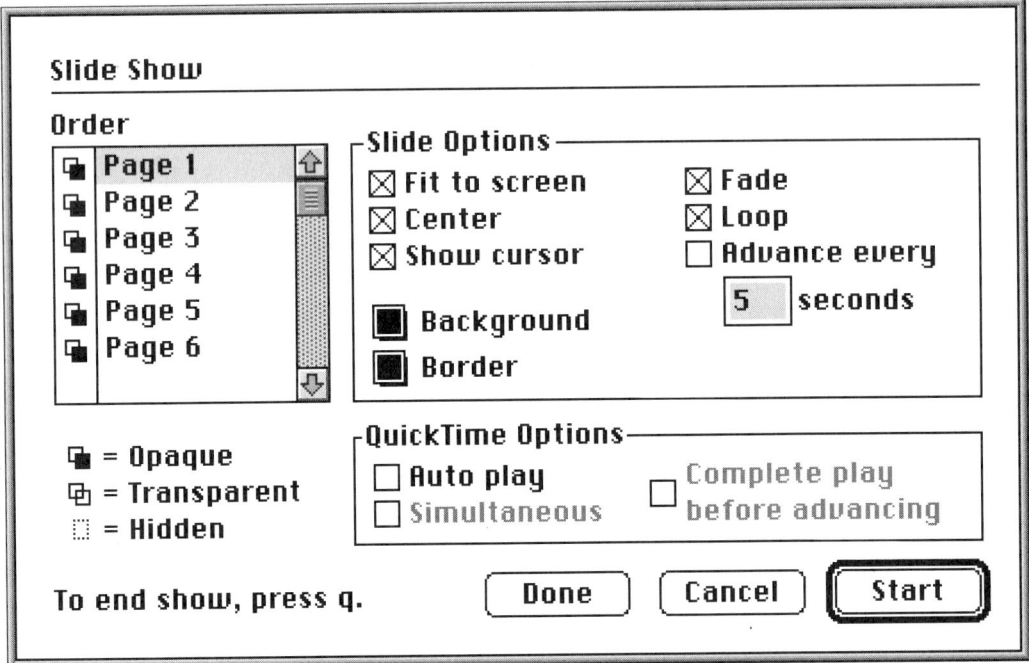

❏ Under Slide Options, the presentation comes with the following options selected (Fit to screen, Center, Show cursor, Fade [**M** only], and Loop). Explore the options in this section by selecting various combinations and then viewing the presentation by clicking the Start button.

❏ Change the Background and the Border colors by holding the mouse button down on those options, and then pulling over to the color you want to try.

❏ When you have finished exploring with the various options, click either the Done or the Cancel button to return to the document itself.

Choosing the Done button will keep the most recent options you have selected; choosing the Cancel button reverts to the options you had chosen when you originally chose View (Window)/Slide Show….

Now we are going to explore the components of the document layout. On page one of the document, there are two locked text frames. To see the borders of the text frames,

❏ Choose the pointer and then click on an area containing text; you should be able to see the handles on the selected objects. Some objects on the screen are also located on the **Master Page.**

❏ To get to the Master Page, choose the pointer tool, and then choose `Options/Edit Master Page`. Everything on the Master Page will show on every page of the document unless you hide it with another object on the page.

❏ Explore the effects of changing the color and pattern of the objects on the Master Page.

❏ To return to the document page, choose `Options/Edit Master Page`.

❏ Now view the slide show to observe the effects of the changes you have made.

❏ When you have finished experimenting, close the document.

You will need to unlock the objects on the Master Page before you can edit them. To unlock the objects,

❏ *Choose `Edit/Select All`.*

❏ *Choose `Arrange/ Unlock`.*

Constructing a Slide Show

In this section, you will learn how to start a slide show from a simple template, from scratch, and with the ClarisWorks Assistant. The Assistant is the name that ClarisWorks uses for the ability of the computer and the software to assist in performing certain tasks.

Slide shows are easiest to prepare in ClarisWorks by starting with a draw document. To make it easier for you to concentrate on putting your first slide show together, we have constructed all of the text frames and graphics that you will need for the following activities.

▪ STARTING WITH A SIMPLE TEMPLATE In this activity, you will prepare a slide show for a concept attainment lesson about triangles.

❏ Open the file `Triangle`, which is a simple template for a slide show. The document (Figure 3.2) consists of one object on the Master Page, a rounded-corner rectangle.

❏ You will also need to open the library `Tri_Lib` (`File/Library/ Open...`); all the objects you need for constructing your slide show are in this library (Figure 3.3), or you can elect to prepare your own objects.

Figure 3.2
Document showing the Master Page

Figure 3.3
Contents of library `Tri_Lib`

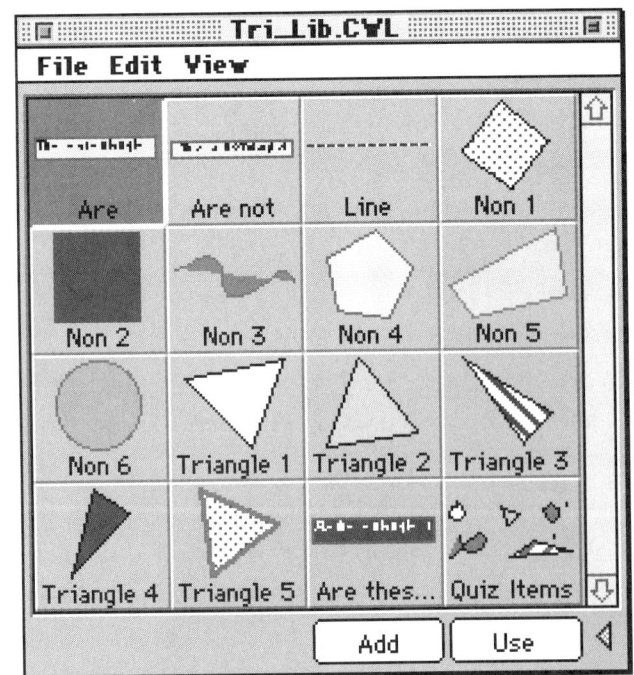

At this time you should have the document `Triangle` showing on the screen on the Master Page. One way to tell if you are on the Master Page is to glance at the page indicator at the bottom of the document window (see Figure 3.2); if you are on the Master Page, those words will appear. To get an idea of how your completed document will appear, see Figure 3.4. The final product will have six pages; right now, your document has only one page. You need to format the document so it will have six pages, three across and two down. To accomplish this, you can't be on the Master Page, so

❏ Choose `Options/Edit Master Page` and release the mouse button.

❏ Choose `Format/Document...`.

❏ Enter 3 in the `Pages Across` box and 2 in the `Pages Down` box.

❏ Click the `OK` button.

❏ Resize the document window so that you can see all six pages.

Figure 3.4
Six pages of the slide show when completed

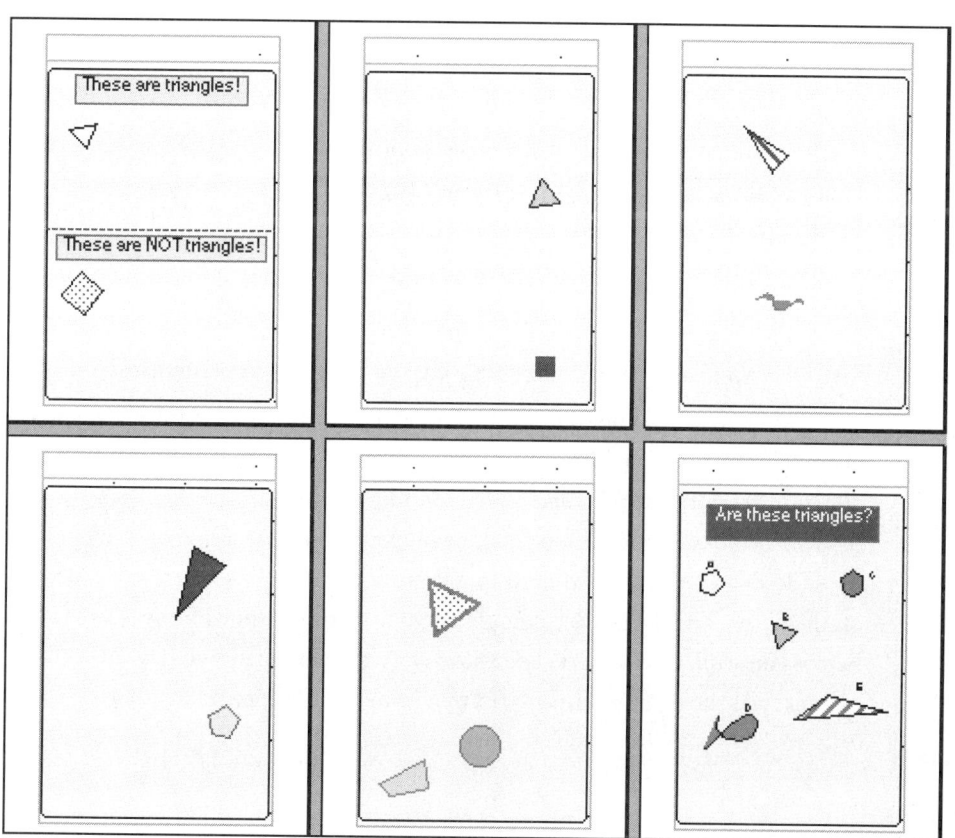

The pages or slides are counted or presented in the following sequence: all of the slides in the first row from left to right, then the second row, and so forth.

As an alternative to drag-drop, you can use the Copy and Paste technique, or you can
❏ *Click the place on the document where you want the object to be placed.*
❏ *Click the object you want to place.*
❏ *Then click the Use button on the library palette.*

Triangles and nontriangles share the number of the page they were meant to be placed on, except Nonexample 6, which can be placed on any of the first five pages.

Now you will place three objects on the first page (Figure 3.4), the two text frames naming the objects to be placed on their respective halves of the screen, and a horizontal line dividing the screen into top and bottom halves. From the library `Tri_Lib`,

❏ Drag off a copy of the text frame `Are` and drop it near the top of the upper half of the screen (Figure 3.4). Adjust the position of the frame with the keys on the keyboard and/or by dragging with the mouse.

❏ Drag off a copy of the text frame `Are not` and drop it just below the center of the screen. Adjust the position of the frame until you are satisfied with it.

❏ Drag off a copy of the item named `Line` from the library and drop it on the first page to divide it into top and bottom halves.

Next you are going to place the geometric objects on the various pages of the document. The example triangles are named `Triangle`, followed by an integer, and the nontriangles are named `Non`, followed by an integer. Each of the first five pages will have at least one new triangle and at least one new nontriangle, with one page having two new nontriangles. The easiest way to place a copy of an object on the page is to use the drag and drop technique. When you run your presentation, the graphics from each previous page will show on all successive pages (for the first five pages) because of the way we have formatted the template, so keep this in mind as you place the objects on the page.

After you have placed all of the objects on the first five pages or screens, place a copy of the following objects on the last page: `Are these?` and `Quiz items`. To accomplish this,

❏ Place the text frame `(Are these?)` near the top of the screen.

❏ Place the `Quiz items` object on the last page.

Save what you have prepared so far, giving the file an appropriate name.

Try viewing your slide show with various combinations of items on the Slide Show dialog box (see Table 3.1 and Figure 3.1). You may want to view the presentation at least once with the original settings. If you change the `Background` color to a medium or dark color, you should see a title on each page of the slide show. You may also need to adjust the location of some of the objects on the pages. That's it; you've completed your first slide show! Be sure to save it. Before you work on the next slide show, close the document window of your current slide show. If the library you were using is still open, close it also.

STARTING FROM SCRATCH   Your next slide show will be an inductive concept attainment lesson on oxymorons. If you don't know what an oxymoron is, you will by the time you complete this presentation! We will supply all the data for the lesson in a library, but you are certainly free to prepare your own objects and text. To begin your new slide show,

❑ Start a new drawing document by choosing `File/New.../Drawing/OK`.

❑ Set all four margins to .4 in case you want to print out a copy later.

❑ Choose `Format/Document...`. You will need nine pages for this slide show, so select the combination of pages across and down that you want to work with (such as three across and three down) and then click OK.

❑ Point to one of the following: **M** `View/Page View` or **W** `Window/Page View`.

❑ To get a view of at least six of the pages, choose 25% on the `Zoom Percentage` box. Adjust the size of the document window to show as many pages as possible.

🖫 To get an idea of how the first page or slide will appear, look at Figure 3.5. Pages or slides 2 through 6 will look similar to this first slide when you run the slide show. When you look at the document pages, however, slides 2 through 6 will look like Figure 3.6. After you have constructed and run the slide show, you will understand the differences in appearance. We have constructed and included all the data necessary for your slide show in the library `Oxy_Lib` (see Figure 3.7). However, you are free to construct your own or to modify the items in the library.

Figure 3.5
Page one of your oxymoron slide show

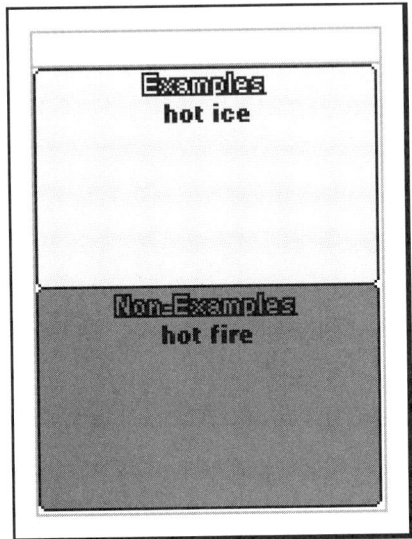

Figure 3.6
Page two of your oxymoron slide show

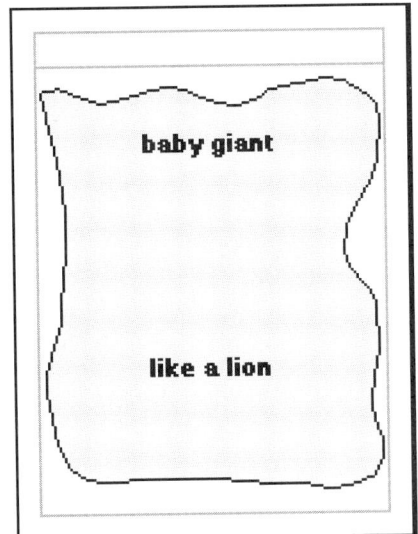

Figure 3.7
Library for your oxymoron slide show

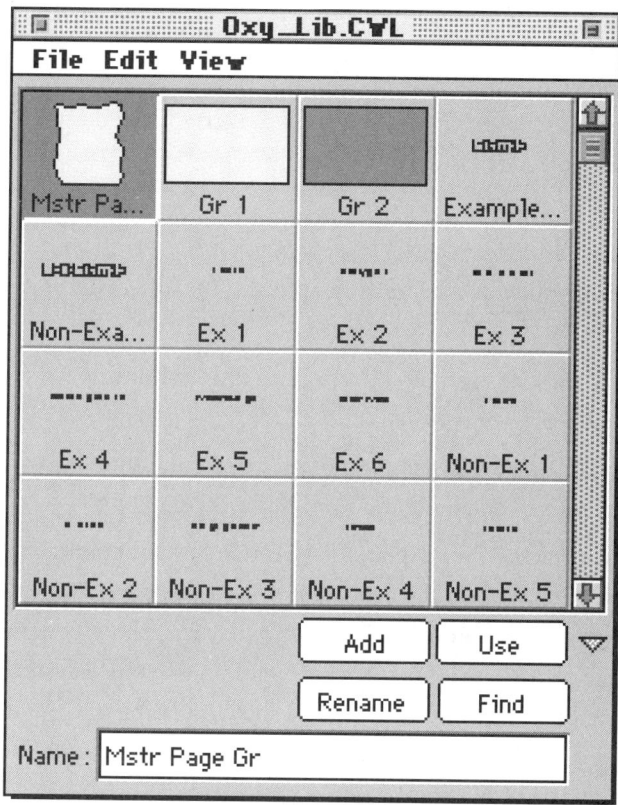

❑ Open the library with `File/Library/Open…`.

❑ Go to the Master Page by pointing to `Options/Edit Master Page`. We will place the irregularly shaped graphic (the first object in the library; it's named `Master Page Gr`) on the Master Page, so

❑ Drag off a copy of the object `Master Page Gr` and drop it on the Master Page. Adjust the placement as necessary by dragging and/or with the keyboard keys.

❑ When you are satisfied with the placement of the graphic, you can exit the Master Page with `Options/Edit Master Page`. You're now on the first page and ready to place six items on the page: two graphic objects and four text frames.

❑ Enter the header `What am I?` (`Format/Insert Header`) with the following characteristics: 48 point, bold, centered, and white text color.

If you need to make fine movements with the arrow keys, point to `Options/Turn Autogrid Off`. Then each tap on a keyboard arrow key will move a selected object one pixel on the screen.

❑ Drag off a copy of graphic `Gr 1` from the library, drop it on the upper half of the first frame (check to be sure you're on the first page!), and adjust its position.

❑ Drag off a copy of graphic `Gr 2` from the library, drop it on the lower half of the first frame, and adjust its position.

❑ Drag off a copy of the text frame `Examples Label` and drop it just below the top edge of the graphic on the upper half of the frame (Figure 3.5).

❑ Drag off a copy of the text frame `Non-Examples Label` and drop it just below the top edge of the graphic on the lower half of the frame (Figure 3.5).

❑ Drag a copy of the first example (`Ex 1`) and drop it just below the text frame containing the word `Examples`.

❑ Drag a copy of the first nonexample (`Non-Ex 1`) and drop it just below the text frame containing the word `Non-Examples`.

You've finished the first frame of your slide show! (You may want to select and lock all the objects you have placed on the first frame so that you don't accidentally move an object.) Frames two through six will be somewhat tedious because of the placement required of the text frames. Everything on frame one will show on frame two; everything on frames one and two will show on frame three, and so on through frame six. Therefore, the placement of the text frames (examples and nonexamples) on these pages is critical if you want your slide show to have a professional appearance. To assist you in the precise placement of the text frames, you may want to go to the Master Page and draw (temporary) lines to guide the placement of the text frames (Figure 3.8). When you are ready to begin placing the text frames on pages two through six, you cannot be on the Master Page. When you are out of the Master Page,

❑ Drag off a copy of the next example (`Ex 2`) and drop it on the upper half of page two in a position so that it does not block the example that will be showing through from page one when you run the presentation.

❑ Drag off a copy of the next nonexample (`Non-Ex 2`) and drop it on the lower half of page two in a position so that it does not block the nonexample that will be showing through from page one when you run the presentation.

Continue this process until you have placed all of the examples and nonexamples on pages two through six.

Figure 3.8
Guidelines drawn on the Master Page for placement of text frames

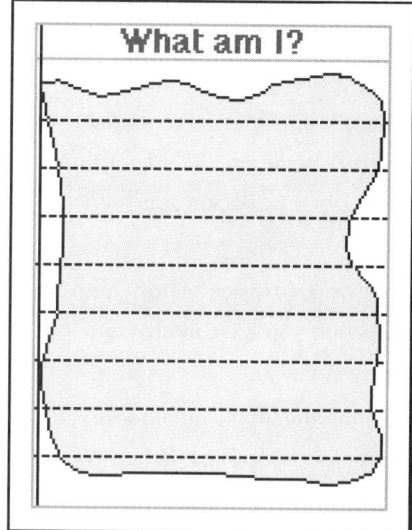

If you draw guidelines on the Master Page, you need to remove them once you are satisfied with the placement of the text frames.

You're now ready to complete the last three pages. One by one, drag off a copy of the last three objects in the library (Txt-p. 7, Txt-p. 8, Txt-p. 9), drop them on the corresponding pages, and adjust their placement. Now you need to set the specifications for your slide show, so

- ❏ Choose one of the following: **M** View/Slide Show... or **W** Window/Slide Show....

- ❏ For pages 1, 7, 8, and 9, leave opaque 🔳.

- ❏ For pages 2–6, set to transparent 🔲.

- ❏ The following options should be selected: Fit to screen, Center, Show cursor, Fade.

- ❏ Background and Border should be set to black.

Run your presentation by clicking the Start button. If you need to make adjustments to the objects on the pages, you can do so at this time or later. Be sure to save your document so that you have the most recent changes you have made. You've now completed your second slide show.

STARTING WITH THE ASSISTANT Another way to prepare a presentation is to begin with the Assistant. To use the Assistant,

- ❏ Choose File/New.... When the New Document window (Figure 3.9) appears, click the Use Assistant or Stationery button.

❏ Scroll down until you see Presentation; click it to select it; then click OK.

❏ The Welcome screen (Figure 3.10) will appear. Click the Next button, and

❏ The next screen appears (Figure 3.11); you will need to make two choices on this page. You must choose the mode of presentation (Computer Screen, Black/White Overheads, or Paper Distribution), and you must choose from among five types of Background styles. Then click the Next button, and

❏ The next screen appears (Figure 3.12); you must select from among seven types of presentation content. When you have made your choice, click the Next button, and

❏ You see the next screen (Figure 3.13), in which you can choose (or not) to have hints included and choose footer options. When you have made your choice, click the Create button, and

❏ The computer will take a few seconds to create your presentation template; then the template will appear on the screen (Figure 3.14).

Figure 3.9
Click Use Assistant or Stationery to begin a presentation or slide show with the Assistant.

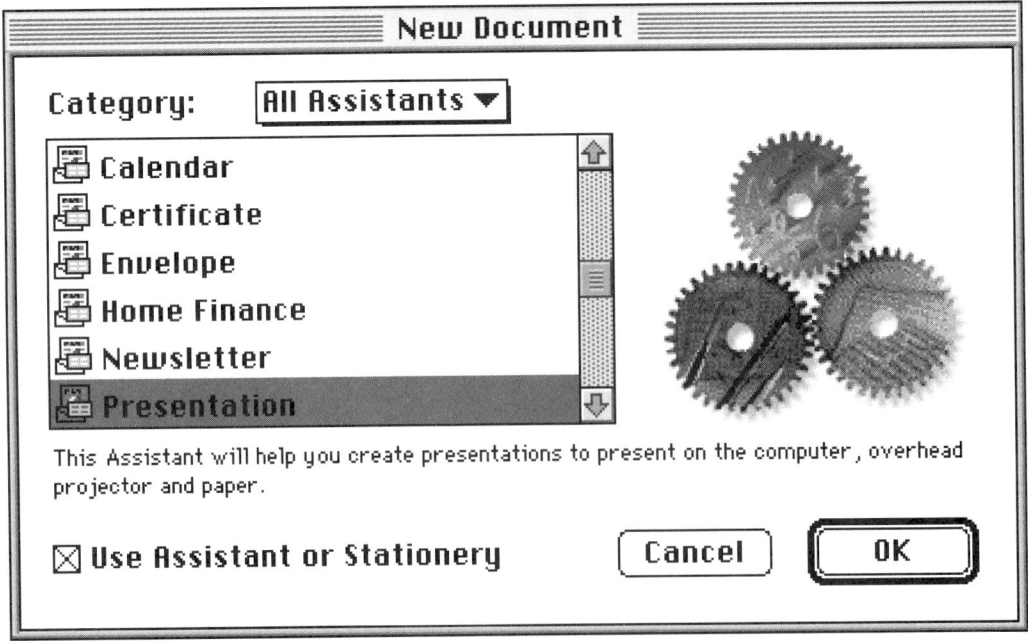

Figure 3.10
When the Welcome screen appears, click the Next button

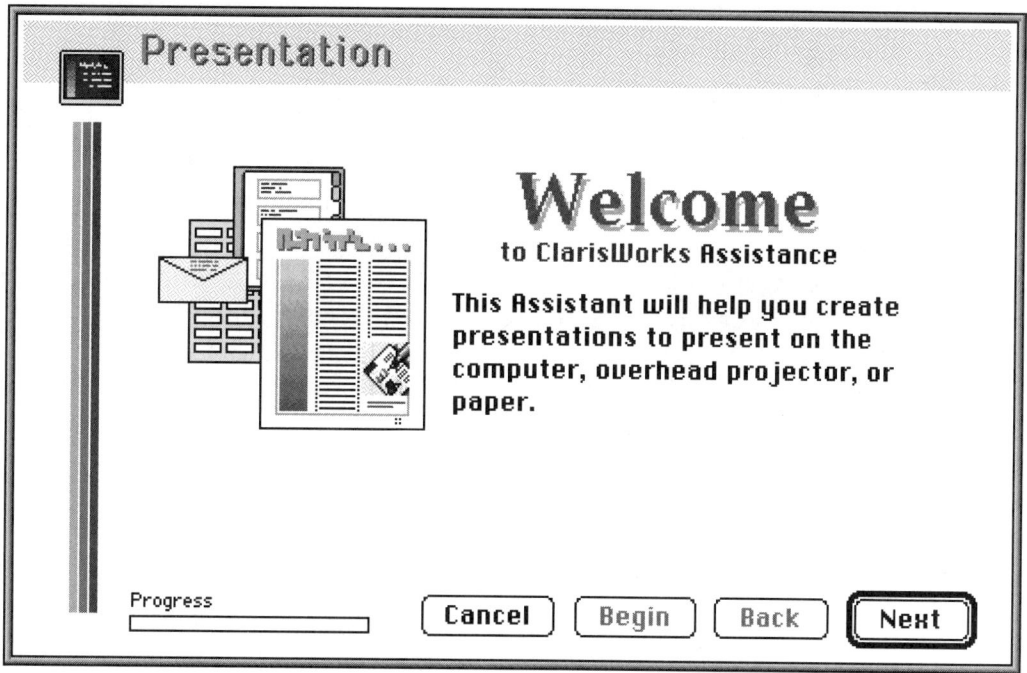

Figure 3.11
One of the first steps in creating a presentation with the Assistant

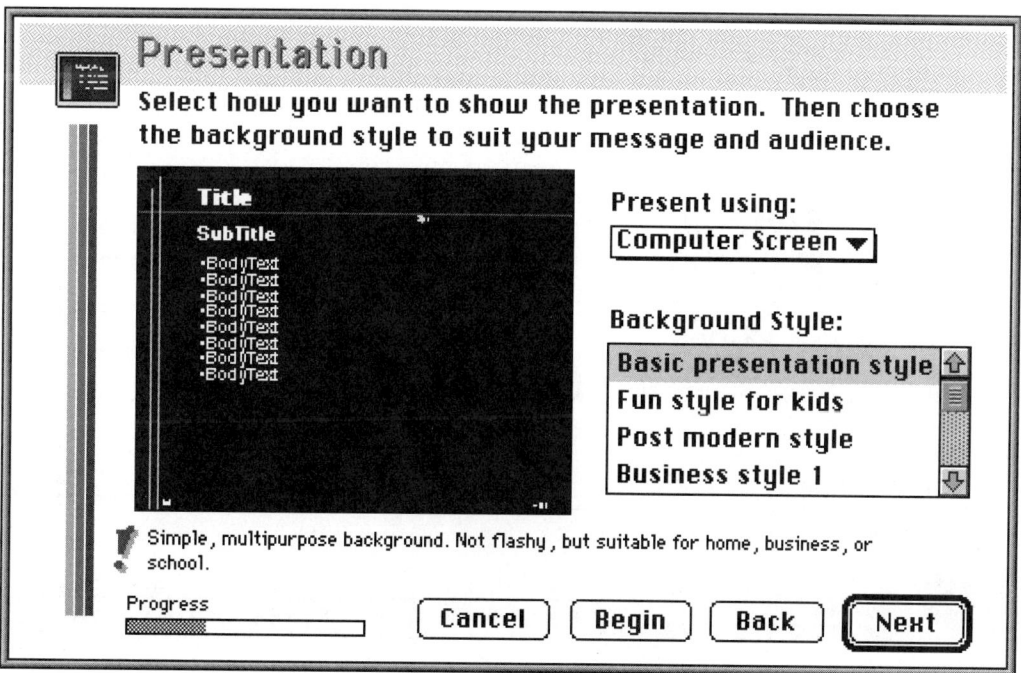

Figure 3.12
Next step in creating a presentation with the Assistant—selecting presentation content style

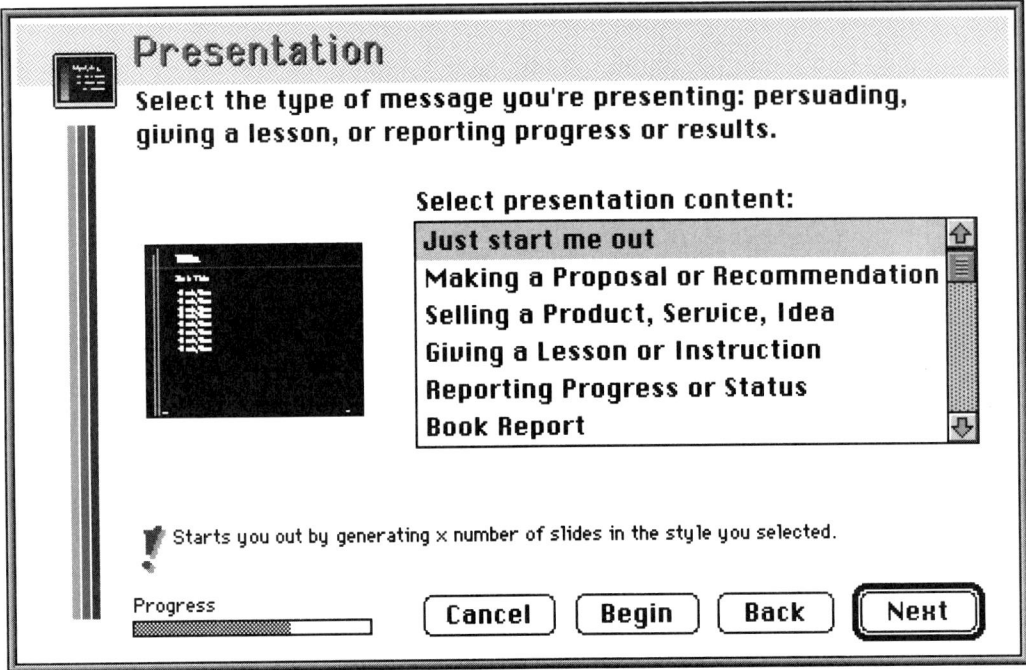

Figure 3.13
Next step in creating a presentation with the Assistant—selecting footer options and hints

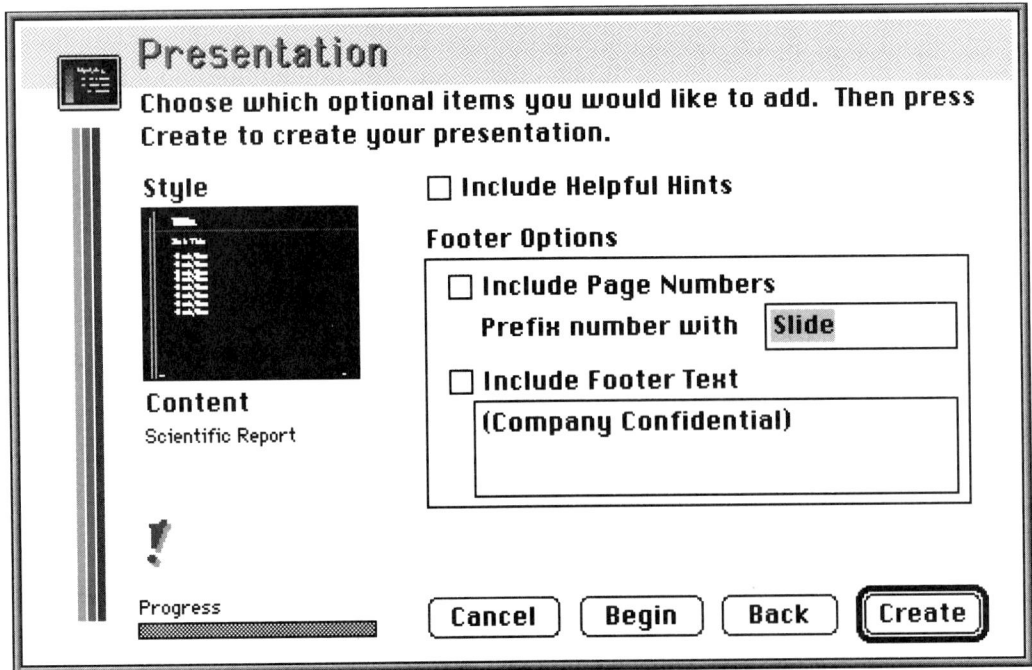

Figure 3.14
Presentation document created with the help of the Assistant

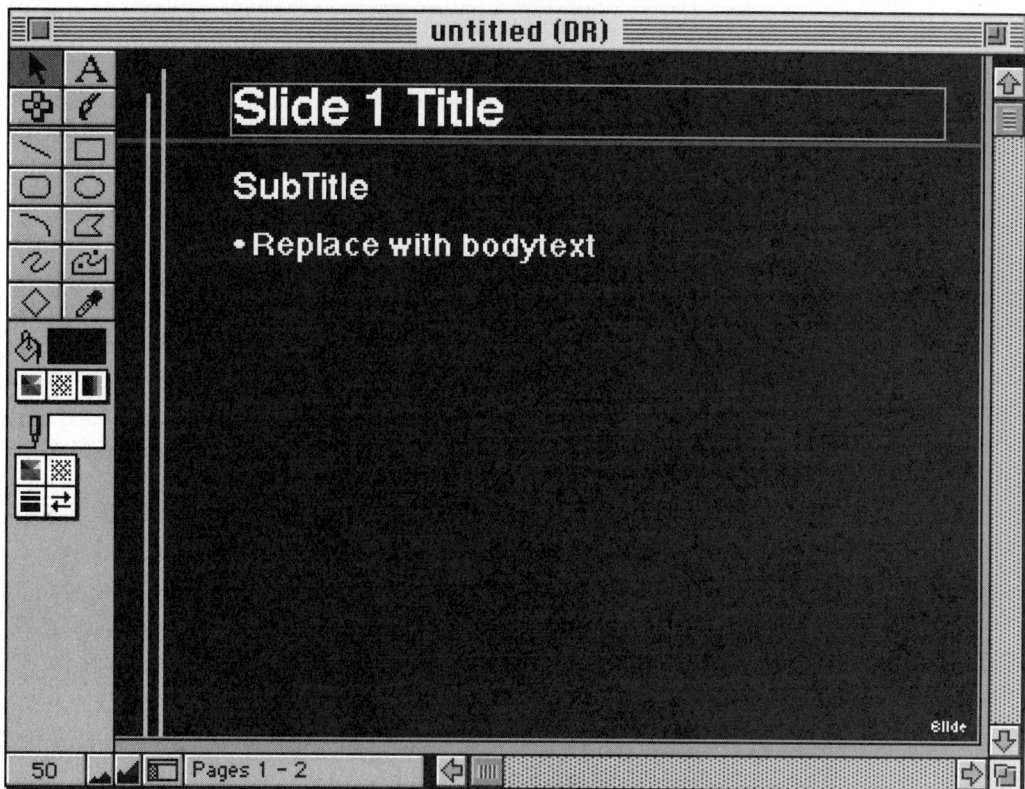

You now have a template for a new slide show. You may have to make some adjustments to items in the template, but this method is a quick way to get started.

Questions and Answers

Q1: **How can I ensure that I can make an overhead transparency, a slide show, and a handout from the same slide show document?**

A: Set the margins of your document large enough so that you will not have any problems printing it (.4 inch to 1 inch). If you plan to use the same document for all three purposes, either don't use a colored background on the master page or make the background transparent when you print the document for a transparency or a paper handout.

Q2: **Sometimes when I am showing a slide show, the previous slide shows through on the current slide. Why does this happen?**

A: When this occurs, it means that the current slide has been set to transparent ⊞; therefore, the previous slide will also appear on the current slide. If you don't want this to occur, go to the slide show options dialog box and click on the icon just to the left of the page number of the slide you were viewing until it is set to opaque ⊡.

Q3: **Is there an easy way to rearrange the order of the pages that will be shown on a slide show?**

A: To rearrange the order of slides or pages presented in a slide show, go to the slide show options dialog box and hold the mouse button down while over the page number you want to rearrange. Then pull up or down until you have repositioned the slide.

Q4: **Is there a way that I can skip a slide or page that I don't want to use without deleting it from the document?**

A: Go to the slide show options dialog box and, just to the left of the page number of the slide you want to hide, click the icon until it is set to hidden ⠿ .

Q5: **What order does the computer use to show the slides in a draw document?**

A: The computer presents all the slides in the first row, then the second row, and so forth, unless you rearrange the page order in the slide show options dialog box.

Q6: **Do you have to use a draw document to prepare a slide show?**

A: You don't have to use a draw document, although it is the most versatile and the easiest to use. You can also use any of the following document types: word processing, paint, database, and spreadsheet. Note that while you can use a paint document, you may find that it takes up too much memory, so you may want to choose a different document type. For a slide show prepared in a database document, see the file `Making a Presentation`, which is available when you go to start a new document. Click on `Use Assistant` or `Stationery` and then click `Category: All Stationery`; then scroll down to `Making a Presentation`.

Q7: **Can I show part of a graphic in one slide and another part of the same graphic in another slide without copying and pasting?**

A: You can use frame linking (`Options/Frame Links`) with paint frames, word processing frames, and spreadsheet frames to present their contents in smaller chunks.

Q8: **I prepared a short slide show with several paint frames in it. It would not fit on my floppy disk. Why?**

A: The reason your file was so large is that paint takes a great deal of memory even for small pictures. If you need to use paint graphics in a slide show, either use them sparingly or change them to draw format (see Chapter 2) before you insert or paste them into your slide show.

Q9: Ⓜ **Can I use a digitized movie in my slide shows?**

A: You can use digitized movies in a slide show on the Macintosh version of ClarisWorks. On the slide show dialog box, there are two options for controlling QuickTime movies (see Table 3.1 and Figure 3.1). The movies are not saved as a part of the slide show, so if you share your slide shows with colleagues, you need to remember to include any digitized movies that are part of the slide show.

Activities

1. Use the Assistant to prepare a slide show template with the following styles:
   - ❏ Basic presentation style
   - ❏ Fun style for kids
   - ❏ Post-modern style
   - ❏ Business style 1
   - ❏ Business style 2

   Compare them and list the basic advantages and disadvantages of each. Is one style more appropriate for a particular type of presentation than the others?

2. Use the Assistant to prepare a slide show template to accomplish the following tasks:
   - ❏ Make a proposal or recommendation
   - ❏ Sell a product, service, or idea
   - ❏ Give a lesson or instruction
   - ❏ Report progress or status
   - ❏ Make a book report
   - ❏ Present a research or scientific report

3. Start from scratch to prepare a template for teaching a concept, rule, or idea in an academic area of interest to you. Consider providing both examples and nonexamples on each page of the slide show if you are teaching a concrete concept or idea.

4. Start from scratch to prepare a template for giving a quiz from a slide show that will be projected for the entire class to see.

5. Prepare a slide show template for a test or quiz in which there is a sequential and logical sequence of events or operations (such as the stages of mitosis) in which the student must rearrange the sequence of the slide presentation.

6. Prepare a list of five ways that you could use a slide show in your classroom to teach something to students.

7. Prepare a list of five noninstructional ways you could use a slide show.

8. Prepare a list of five purposes for which your students could use a slide show.

9. Open the file `Story_Bd` and print out a copy of the document. The objective of this document is to encourage you to plan your slide shows rather than just jumping in on a new one. Make any changes you would like to make in the layout of the storyboard and save it as a stationery file for your own template.

Summary

The slide show is a versatile technique for students and teachers to prepare lessons, handouts, and overhead transparencies for both instructional and noninstructional purposes. The most versatile and easiest document to use to prepare a slide show is the draw document, but you can also use a word processing, paint, database, or spreadsheet document.

You and your students may be tempted to begin your slide shows without planning. You can save a tremendous amount of time and possibly heartache by preparing a storyboard of your slide show before you begin authoring your show. A storyboard is much easier to edit than a slide show! In addition, if you encourage or require your students to prepare a storyboard of their slide shows, you will be giving them practice in planning in addition to the subject matter content of your course.

Key Terms

Master Page 75

slide show 72

References

Anderson, M. A. (1995). The easy way to create computer slide shows. *Technology Connection, 2*(3), 16–17.

Chilcoat, G. W. (1991). The illustrated song slide show as a middle school history activity. *Social Studies, 82*(5), 188–190.

DiLella, C. A. (1992). *Popcorn story frames.* (ERIC Document No. ED 344184)

Head, J. (1992). New directions in presentation graphics: Impact on teaching and learning. *New Directions for Teaching and Learning, 51 (Teaching in the Information Age: The Role of Educational Technology),* 17–31.

Krebs, C., & Nichols, C. (1994). *Sonnets, high tech, Haiku: Teaching poetry in the CAI classroom.* (ERIC Document No. ED 382997)

Taylor, H. G., & Stuhlmann, J. M. (1995). Creating slide show book reports. *Learning and Leading with Technology, 23*(1), 8–10.

Vidor, C. (1993). Using Write-On slides with research skills. *School Library Media Activities Monthly, 9*(9), 36–39.

Desktop Publishing

O B J E C T I V E S

Design layouts from scratch and with the Assistant.

Prepare lesson supplements and curriculum materials with layouts.

Prepare newsletters and pamphlets.

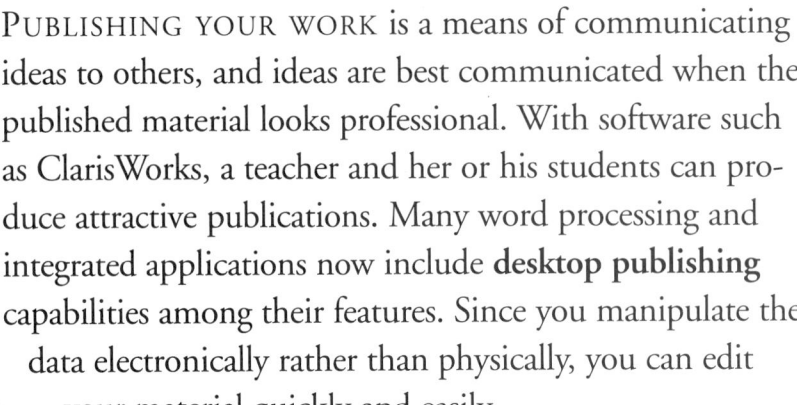

PUBLISHING YOUR WORK is a means of communicating ideas to others, and ideas are best communicated when the published material looks professional. With software such as ClarisWorks, a teacher and her or his students can produce attractive publications. Many word processing and integrated applications now include **desktop publishing** capabilities among their features. Since you manipulate the data electronically rather than physically, you can edit your material quickly and easily.

Students can publish their stories individually or as a team. They can prepare and publish a school newsletter based upon a particular issue. Students in foreign language classes can publish articles in that language. Social studies students can produce a newspaper as it might have appeared during the era or country they are studying (Figure 4.1).

Teachers can publish lesson supplements, parent newsletters, brochures, programs, handbooks, and curriculum materials with the desktop publishing or **layout** capabilities of an application such as ClarisWorks.

Figure 4.1
Civil War Newsletter (1994) downloaded from America Online, Dana K. Dabov (Editor)

The Union Press

Motto: With Malice Toward None and Charity for All
Volume 1 Issue 5   1994

Cattle and Horses?

"Fourscore and seven years ago our fathers brought forth on this continent a new nation, conceived in liberty, and dedicated to the proposition that all men are created equal.

Now we are engaged in a great civil war, testing whether that nation, or any nation so conceived and so dedicated, can long endure."

These are the words of our great President, Abraham Lincoln. All the fighting that has occurred has been because of a difference -- mostly, a difference of color.

In 1861, Texas, Arkansas, Louisiana, Mississippi, Alabama, Georgia, Florida, South and North Carolina, and Virginia felt that there was nothing wrong with having negroes as slaves. Down South, the going price for a strong young black man in good health is $1800!

Our Chief General views slavery as an evil. Our own brothers and sisters, regardless of skin tone, should not be put on the auction block to be sold like horses, cattle and hogs. Please with your support help us to end this campaign.

Who is Bobby Lee?

He was born Robert Edward Lee on January 19, 1807, at his family's home "Stratford," in Westmoreland County, Virginia. His father, Henry, "Light Horse Harry," Lee, had been a cavalry officer during the American Revolution and a close friend of George Washington. His father also was known as a compulsive gambler and lost most of the family fortune in land speculation prior to his death in 1818. Thus, Robert grew up in genteel poverty, in Alexandria, Va. Bobby excelled as a student graduating from West Point in 1829. In 1831, Lee married the great-granddaughter of Martha Washington, Mary Ann Randolph Custis. The Lee's make their home in Arlington.

A moderate, Lee was dismayed by the extremists on both sides of the North-South controversy. In the 50's, He does not believe in slavery, any more than President Lincoln. In fact, long before the War started, Lee set free all the slaves which he had inherited, believing that human slavery is wrong.

When war was declared, Lee held a high office in our United States Army. President Lincoln offered him the command position of our Federal troops, but Lee could never lead troops against his beloved and native Virginia, against his friends and relatives; and though he loved our Union dearly, and did not want to see it severed; and though he knew that there was little hope for the success of the cause of the South; *CONTINUED-PLEASE SEE "LEE" ON PAGE 2*

G-E-N-E-R-A-L

How at my superstitious I've always been when I started to go anywhere, or to do anything concerning cornbread or to stop and the thing thwarted was unexplained
-- Ulysses S. Grant

Getting Started

Desktop publishing involves the integration of text, graphics, and columns. Which of the environments in ClarisWorks should you use for preparing a publication? Your first impression might be word processing. However, it's much easier to begin with a draw document and then to prepare your layout with text frames and graphics. In this chapter, you will have the opportunity to insert text and graphics into an existing layout, to prepare a publication from a template, to prepare a layout from scratch, and to prepare a publication with the help of the Assistant. When you choose the help of the Assistant for designing a layout, you are asked to make several choices involving the appearance of your layout. Then the computer and the software use that information to prepare a template.

Using an Existing Layout

💾 We have saved a layout named `Remember`, in which two teenage sisters have recalled the summer of 1988 based upon the notes they had taken during that trip. They entered the notes into a word processor and saved them as **text files.** Both the layout template and the text files are located in the `Tools` folder.

You are going to open the file, insert text from the text files into the appropriate text frames, and then place two graphics on the page. If you have not already started ClarisWorks, you need to start it now. Open the file `Remember` with `File/Open...`. The layout (see Figure 4.2) for this document consists of five text frames: the name of the publication *(Remember When)*, a **headline** for the first article, a text frame for the first article, a headline for the second article, and a text frame for the second article, along with three graphic objects (the vertical line on the left side and the two **place holders** for graphics).

Figure 4.2
Layout for a summer tale of two sisters

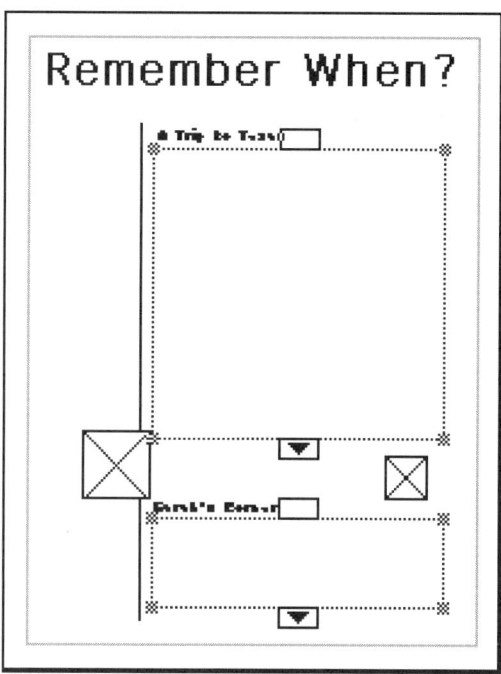

With the Text tool, click within the upper text frame provided for the first article (below the headline). The insert cursor should be in the upper left corner of the text frame. You're now ready to insert text from a text file.

❑ Choose `File/Insert...` and locate the file **M** `Trip` or **W** `Trip1`.

❑ With the name of the file selected, click `Insert`.

The text from the file will flow into the text frame in which the insertion cursor is located. Now you're ready to insert text into the text frame (for the second article) just below the heading `Sarah's Corner`. Click within this text frame (below the headline) with the Text tool and follow the exact procedure as with the first text frame, except this time insert the contents of the text file **M** `Corner` or **W** `Corner1`.

Now you will place the graphics on the layout in place of the graphic place holders.

❑ To remove the graphic place holders, select them with the pointer and then unlock them with `Arrange/Unlock`.

❑ Delete the place holders with `Edit/Cut` (or `Clear`).

Depending upon the computer you are working on and the fonts you choose for the following activities, you may have to adjust the size of the text frames or the font size of the text to display all the text in an appropriate manner.

❏ Use File/Insert... (with the pointer selected) to place the following two graphics on your layout: Car (on the right side) and Map (on the left side). Overlap the map graphic over the text area of the lower left corner of the first article (Figure 4.2).

❏ To ensure that text will wrap around the graphics (should you place the graphic over any text), click the graphic object with the pointer and choose Options/Text Wrap.../Regular/OK. If you have overlapped a graphic over a text area, you may need to adjust the position of the graphic so that you can see all of the text.

That's it, your first newsletter! Save your newsletter, print a copy of it, and then close the document.

💾 Now you're going to prepare a publication in which you will use an existing layout but will have to flow text from one text frame to another frame. Open the file Free (see Figure 4.3). This layout consists of one page with room for two articles. You will insert text from a file into the text frame below the header What is Shareware? When you have inserted the text into the first article body and inserted the graphics, you will type in your own comments for the second article body.

Figure 4.3
Layout for Freeware newsletter

❑ Highlight the words `Article 1 Body` (with the Text tool) in the text frame on the left side of the layout document (Figure 4.3).

❑ 💾 Choose `File/Insert…`, locate the text file named `Free-ware`, and click **M** `Insert` or **W** `Open`.

❑ With the insert cursor located in the text frame, select all the text and change the font to **M** Times or **W** MS Serif 12 point. Locate the bottom of this text frame and notice the ⊠ symbol in the lower right corner. This **text overflow indicator** ⊠ means that there is more text than there is room in the text frame.

❑ Now select the same text frame with the pointer. Note the **continue indicator** ▼ at the bottom center of the text frame. The continue indicator can be used to flow the extra text from this frame into another text frame. First, however, you need to unlock the frame with `Arrange/Unlock`.

❑ To flow the additional text into another text frame, click the continue indicator ▼ with the pointer. The cursor now looks like �. Move the cursor to the lower right side of the layout. Hold the mouse button down and drag the mouse for about an inch. When you release the mouse, you should see a new text frame.

❑ With the new text frame selected, point to `Options/Object Info…`. When the `Info` palette appears on the screen, use the following data to size and place the new text frame more precisely:

❑ Enter 4.76 into the width box ↔ ; then press tab.

❑ Enter 4.79 into the height box ↕ ; then press tab twice.

❑ Enter 2.75 into the left edge box ⊢ ; then press tab.

❑ Enter 5.15 into the top edge box ⊤ . The right and bottom edge values should be 7.51 and 9.94, respectively.

❑ Select and lock the frames to avoid accidentally moving them.

Your new text frame is now in appropriate position on the layout.

❑ Remove the graphic place holders. (Remember, you will need to unlock them first.)

❑ Insert the graphics `Burst` (lower left) and `Computer` (upper right) (Figure 4.3) in place of the place holders.

❑ Set text wrap of these objects to regular. Adjust the placement of the graphics so that the text can be read easily.

We don't want the words `Article 1 Body` *to remain in the text frame, so by selecting it and inserting more text, the original text is removed. The only purpose of the original text is to show there is a text frame at that location and to identify the basic purpose of the frame.*

The top-of-frame indicator ▭ *on a text frame identifies the top of a text frame where the text originates. At the bottom center of such a frame there will be either a continue indicator* ▼ *or a link indicator* ⊠⊠ *. This link refers to an electronic connection between two text frames. If frame A is linked to frame B, then when frame A is filled with text, the overflow text will flow to frame B.*

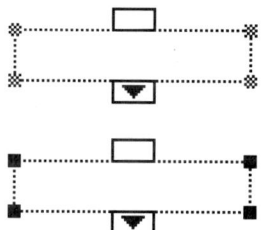

The upper text frame is locked; note the ghosted handles. The lower text frame is unlocked.

When you flow text into a new text frame, you will see the link indicator ⊠⊠ *at the bottom of the linked-from frame and at the top of the linked-to frame.*

You may want to go to 100% view to type the text into the frame.

❑ Now type in your own personal comments in the remaining text frame (below the title, *Is it Free?*).

❑ Save the newsletter and print a copy.

Starting from Scratch

Usually, the most difficult part of publishing is preparing your own layout. It's possible that you may never design your own layouts; perhaps you will choose to use existing templates or the Assistant in ClarisWorks. Or you may prefer to wait until you have more experience with existing layouts before you work up the courage to prepare your own. Why, then, do we have a section on preparing a layout? You may elect to begin with existing layouts but will soon discover at least two problems. First, you will normally have to edit existing layout templates to fit your text and graphics for a particular publication; therefore, you need to have a basic understanding of layouts. Second, there may be no available template that fits what you want to do with a particular publication.

To begin your layout, close any open documents and choose

❑ `File/New.../Drawing/OK`.

❑ Choose one of the following: **M** `View/Page View` or **W** `Window/Page View` so that you can observe the appearance of the page as it will appear when printed.

❑ Go to 33% or 50% with the `Zoom Percentage` box so that you can see the entire page without scrolling the screen. This percentage is just a suggestion; you may select the one with which you are most comfortable, and you may want to change back and forth, perhaps having several views of the document open at various percentages.

❑ Choose `Format/Document...` and set all four margins to .5 inch.

❑ Choose `Format/Rulers.../Graphics` to place a ruler at the top and left side of your document.

The approach we will use to introduce you to preparing a single-page newsletter layout will allow you to take a mechanical approach, a more artistic approach, or a combination of these. The art of preparing layouts will come with a great deal more experience. Look at Table 4.1. These data may appear to be overwhelming to you initially, but you will learn that you can very quickly prepare a layout by using them. These specifications or numbers are a precise description for a single-page newsletter layout (Figure 4.4); by following them, you can experience the feel of preparing a layout. However, you may simply ignore the num-

You may be asking yourself, "Where did these numbers come from?" We prepared the layout and then recorded the numbers from the completed layout. Henceforth, you will probably not use dimensions in this manner to prepare your layouts. The numbers are a teaching device so that while you are learning to prepare a layout, it will be easier for you to place the various objects in your layout in a professional-looking manner. However, you don't have to use the numbers; they are provided as an option.

bers and instead use Figure 4.4 as a visual guide, or you may use a combination of the two approaches. The same approach to preparing a layout doesn't work for everyone, so select the approach to preparing a layout that works best for you.

Table 4.1

Specifications for Preparing a Layout from Scratch

Object	1 Name of Publication (Center)	2 Issue #	3 Date (Right Align)	4 Horizontal Line	5 Vertical Line	6 Headline Article 1	7 Article Body 1 (Frame Link)	8 Graphic Place Holder	9 Article Body 1 (Link from 7)	10 Headline Article 2	11 Article Body 2 (Frame Link)
Object Type	Text Frame	Text Frame	Text Frame	Line (Draw)	Line (Draw)	Text Frame	Text Frame	Rectangle (Draw)	Text Frame	Text Frame	Text Frame
Left Edge	0.00	0.09	5.13	0.04	3.82	0.09	0.09	0.08	0.09	3.93	3.93
Top Edge	0.00	1.00	1.00	1.25	1.25	1.38	1.81	4.51	7.45	1.38	1.81
Right Edge	7.38	2.34	7.38	7.47	3.82	3.59	3.59	3.67	3.59	7.43	7.43
Bottom Edge	1.00+	1.19+	1.19+	1.25	9.92	1.73+	4.18	6.94	9.75	1.73+	9.75
Width	7.38	2.25	2.25	7.43	0.00	3.50	3.50	3.59	3.50	3.50	3.50
Height	1.00+	0.19+	0.19+	0.19+	8.67	0.35+	2.37	2.43	2.30	0.35+	7.94
Font and Size M	Helvetica	Helvetica	Helvetica			Helvetica	Times		Times	Helvetica	Century Schoolbook MS Serif
	72	12	12			24	12		12	24	12
W	Arial or MS Sans Serif	Arial or MS Sans Serif	Arial or MS Sans Serif			Arial or MS Sans Serif	Century Schoolbook MS Serif		Arial or MS Sans Serif	Century Schoolbook MS Serif	Times
	72	10–12	10–12			20–24	10–12		10–12	20–24	12
Border	none	none	none	1 pt; black	1 pt; black	none	none	1 pt; black	none	none	none

Figure 4.4
Layout to be developed from scratch. 1 = name of publication, 2 = issue number, 3 = date, 4 = horizontal line, 5 = vertical line, 6 = headline for article 1, 7 = article 1 body, 8 = graphic place holder, 9 = continuation of article body 1, 10 = headline for article 2, 11 = article 2 body

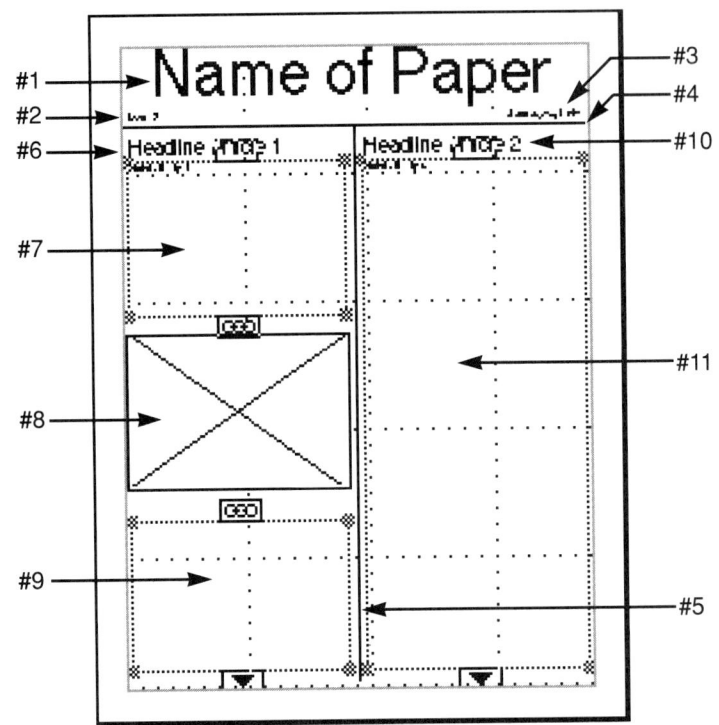

There will be eleven objects on your page layout (Table 4.1 and Figure 4.4). The first object you will place on the layout is a text frame for the name of the publication. We will describe the steps necessary for the creation of each object; our intent is that after creating the first two or three objects, you will not need to use the steps for the remaining objects but can simply use the information provided in Table 4.1 and Figure 4.4 as you gain confidence.

1. TEXT FRAME FOR NAME OF PUBLICATION This frame will be placed at the top of the document. Frame Links under Options should be off (not selected).

- ❑ With the Text tool, draw a text frame about 7.5 inches wide and about an inch high.

- ❑ Use the Text tool to type a short name for your publication in the new text frame.

- Select the text and change the font size to 72 point 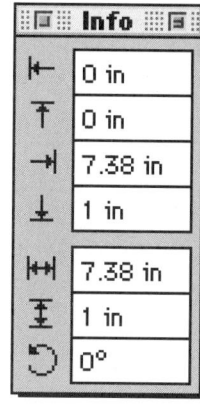 M Helvetica or W Arial or MS Sans Serif. Center the text in the text frame.

- Resize and reposition the text frame with the mouse and the keyboard arrow keys so that it is at the top of the document, centered between the right and left margins (Figure 4.4).

- If you desire to have a more precise placement of the frame, select the frame and point to `Options/Object Info...`. The `Info` dialog box will appear on the screen. Enter the information from Table 4.1 into the dialog box. It may be more efficient to begin with the dimensions for the width and the height and then proceed with the left edge and top edge.

- Lock the frame (select it and choose `Arrange/Lock`) when you have it sized and positioned to your liking. By locking the frame, you prevent accidental movement of the frame while you are working with another object.

2. TEXT FRAME FOR THE ISSUE NUMBER OF THE PUBLICATION This frame will be located on the left side just below the text frame containing the name of the publication. The size of the frame should be about 2.25 inches wide and about .25 inch tall. `Frame Links` under `Options` should be off.

- Draw the text frame with the Text tool and type `Issue #1` into the frame.

- Set the font to M 12 point Helvetica or W 10 or 12 point Arial or MS Sans Serif.

- Place the frame just below the name of the publication, flush against the left margin.

- If you desire to have a more precise placement of the frame, select the frame and point to `Options/Object Info...`. The `Info` dialog box will appear on the screen. Enter the information for item 2 from Table 4.1 into the dialog box. It will be more efficient to begin with the dimensions for the width and the height and then proceed with the left edge and top edge.

- Lock the frame.

3. TEXT FRAME FOR THE DATE OF THE PUBLICATION This frame will be located on the right side just below the text frame containing the name of the publication. The size of the frame should be about 2.25 inches wide and about .25 inch tall. `Frame Links` under `Options` should be off.

To center align, click the text frame with the pointer and then choose `Format/Alignment/Center`.

Data for sizing and locating the name of your publication.

Data for sizing and locating the issue number of your publication.

❏ Draw the text frame with the Text tool (or use Duplicate to make a copy of the issue number text frame), and type the date into the frame.

❏ Set the font to **M** 12 point Helvetica or **W** 10 or 12 point Arial or MS Sans Serif.

❏ Right justify the text.

❏ Place the frame just below the name of the publication, flush against the right margin.

❏ If you desire to have a more precise placement of the frame, enter the information from Table 4.1 (for object 3) into the `Info` dialog box while the frame is selected.

❏ Lock the frame.

4. HORIZONTAL LINE This line separates the name of the publication from the body of the publication. The length of the line should be about 7.5 inches.

❏ Choose the Line tool.

❏ Choose a point size of 1 and a line color of black.

❏ Hold the <shift> key down as you draw the line to make a perfectly straight horizontal line.

❏ Place the line just below the issue number and the date, centered between the right and left margins.

❏ For a precise placement of object 4, use the information in Table 4.1.

❏ Lock the line.

5. VERTICAL LINE This line separates the right and left text columns of the publication. The length of the line should be about 8.5 inches.

❏ Choose the Line tool.

❏ Choose a point size of 1 and a line color of black.

❏ Hold the <shift> key down as you draw the line to make a perfectly straight vertical line.

❏ Place the line in the **alley** between the right and left text columns.

❏ For a precise placement of object 5, use the information in Table 4.1.

❏ Lock the line.

6. TEXT FRAME FOR THE HEADLINE OF ARTICLE 1 This text frame will contain the headline for the first article on the page and will be about 3.5 inches wide and less than .5 inch tall, positioned on the left side, just below the text frame for the issue number and the horizontal line. `Frame Links` under `Options` should be off.

❏ Draw the text frame with the Text tool and enter the words Head-line, article 1.

❏ With the text frame selected or the text inside the text frame selected, set the font to **M** 24 point Helvetica or **W** 20 or 24 point Arial or MS Sans Serif.

❏ Place the frame just below the horizontal line (object 4) on the left side of the document, flush against the left margin.

❏ Use the data in Table 4.1 to make precise adjustments to the size and placement of object 6.

❏ Lock the frame.

7. TEXT FRAME FOR ARTICLE 1   This text frame will contain the text of the first article and will be about 3.5 inches wide and about 2.5 inches tall, positioned on the left side, below the headline text frame you just completed.

❏ Choose Options/Frame Links. You will be linking this frame, so you must have frame links on.

❏ Draw the text frame with the Text tool.

❏ Set the font to **M** 12 point Times or **W** 10 or 12 point Century Schoolbook or MS Serif.

❏ Position the frame just below the headline text frame (object 6).

❏ Adjust the size and placement of the frame (object 7) with the data in Table 4.1.

❏ Do *not* lock this frame.

8. PLACE HOLDER FOR GRAPHIC   This draw object will be placed below the text frame you just drew. It will be about 3.5 inches wide and 2.5 inches tall.

❏ Use the Rectangle or Rounded Rectangle tool to draw the rectangle, with or without fill, and with or without lines across the rectangle.

❏ Position the rectangle below the text frame for the first article (object 7).

❏ Adjust the size and position of the object (8) with the data from Table 4.1.

❏ Lock the object.

9. TEXT FRAME FOR CONTINUATION OF ARTICLE 1   This text frame will provide for the overflow text from the first article body. It will be about 3.5 inches wide and about 2.5 inches high.

❏ If the frame for article body 1 (object 7) is locked, unlock it.

You may want to enter a phrase such as Article Body 1 into the text frame so you have a visual cue that a text frame does exist in that location.

If the frame appears to disappear, click it with the pointer tool, and you can see it again.

❑ To handle the overflow text from the text frame of article 1, click the continue indicator ▼ of that text frame with the pointer. The cursor should now appear as ⌐. Move the cursor to the lower left side of the layout just below and to the left of the graphic place holder. Hold the mouse button down and drag the mouse diagonally until the frame is about 3.5 inches wide and 2.5 inches high. When you release the mouse, you should see a new text frame.

❑ Use the data in Table 4.1 to adjust the size and position of the new frame (object 9) more precisely.

❑ Lock both text frames (7 and 9).

10. TEXT FRAME FOR HEADLINE OF ARTICLE 2 This text frame will contain the headline for the second article on the page and will be about 3.5 inches wide and less than .5 inch tall, positioned on the right side, below the text frame for the date and the horizontal line. Frame Links under Options should be off.

❑ Draw the text frame with the Text tool and enter the words Headline, article 2 (or duplicate object 6).

❑ With the text frame selected or the text inside the text frame selected, set the font to **M** 24 point Helvetica or **W** 20 or 24 point Arial or MS Sans Serif.

❑ Place the frame just below the horizontal line on the right of the document, flush against the right margin.

❑ Use the data in Table 4.1 to make precise adjustments to the size and placement of the frame (object 10).

❑ Lock the frame.

11. TEXT FRAME FOR ARTICLE 2 This text frame will contain the text of the second article and will be about 3.5 inches wide and about 8 inches tall, positioned on the right side, below the headline text frame.

❑ If Frame links is not selected, choose Options/Frame links.

❑ Draw the text frame with the Text tool.

❑ Set the font to **M** 12 point Times or **W** 10 or 12 point Century Schoolbook or MS Sans Serif.

❑ Position the frame just below the headline text frame on the right.

❑ Adjust the size and placement of the frame (object 11) with the data in Table 4.1.

❑ Lock the frame.

You now have a newsletter template that you can use for a one-page newsletter and the beginnings of a multipage newsletter. You may want to practice inserting text; first, however, you should save your template as a stationery file. Then close the document and open a copy of the stationery file.

Starting with the Assistant

If you want to get a quick start on preparing a publication, then you may want to try the ClarisWorks Assistant. The Assistant provides practice with desktop publishing before you have much experience in preparing your own layout. With the Assistant, you can prepare a wide variety of instructional and news layouts (Figure 4.5) by choosing from among a variety of options. For instance, with six basic types of layouts, you can choose from among the following options and the Assistant will place these features in the appropriate place on the final layout: the title, the date, the issue, the number of pages, whether or not you want a table of contents, whether or not you want an editorial, and whether or not you want a blank space for labels. These options do not cover every conceivable publication or style you may be interested in, but there are enough options to get you and your students started.

To use the Assistant in preparing a publication,

❑ Choose `File/New…`.

❑ Click `Use Assistant or Stationery`, then click `Newsletter`, and then click `OK`.

Follow the directions on the screen, and the Assistant will guide you through the appropriate steps and will request information from you. The last choice you will make, prior to clicking the `Create` button, is whether you want the Hints and Tips Document. If you don't de-select the choice, it will prepare a copy of that document each time you use the Assistant. The computer will take a few seconds to prepare your layout, and then your layout will appear on the screen. Even though the computer will prepare a basic layout, you will still have to make decisions about the size of text frames so you get a match between the initial layout, the amount of text you use, and the number and placement of graphics. Figures 4.6 through 4.14 will give you an idea of the basic types of publications that the Assistant can prepare.

To save a document as a stationery file,
❑ *Choose* `File/Save…`.
❑ *When the save dialog box appears, choose* `Stationery`.
❑ *Then enter the name you want the file to have and save the file as usual.*

Figure 4.5
Choices for preparing a layout with the Assistant

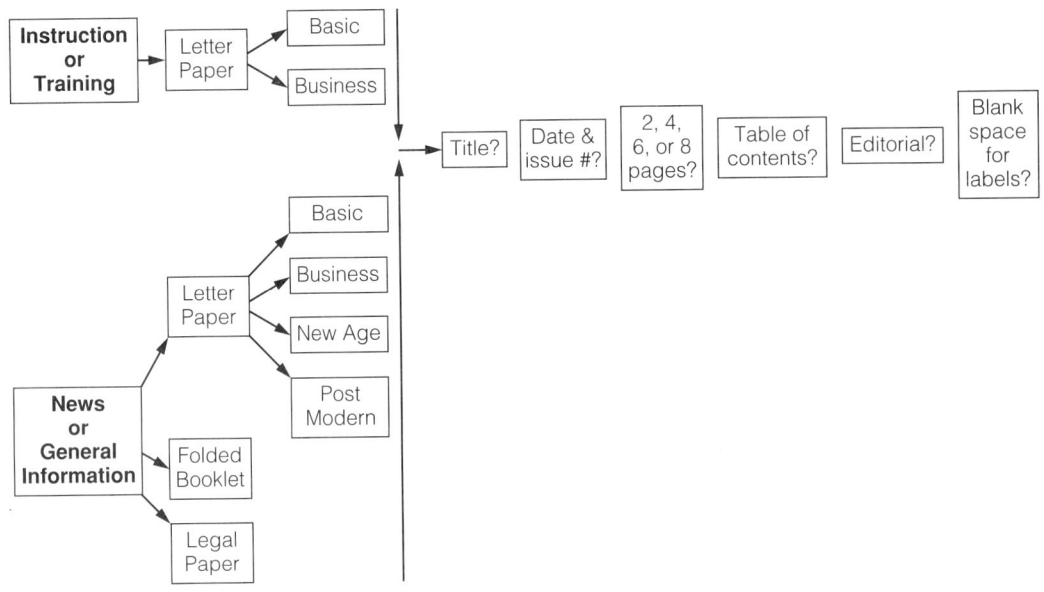

Figure 4.6
Using the Assistant to prepare a newsletter layout

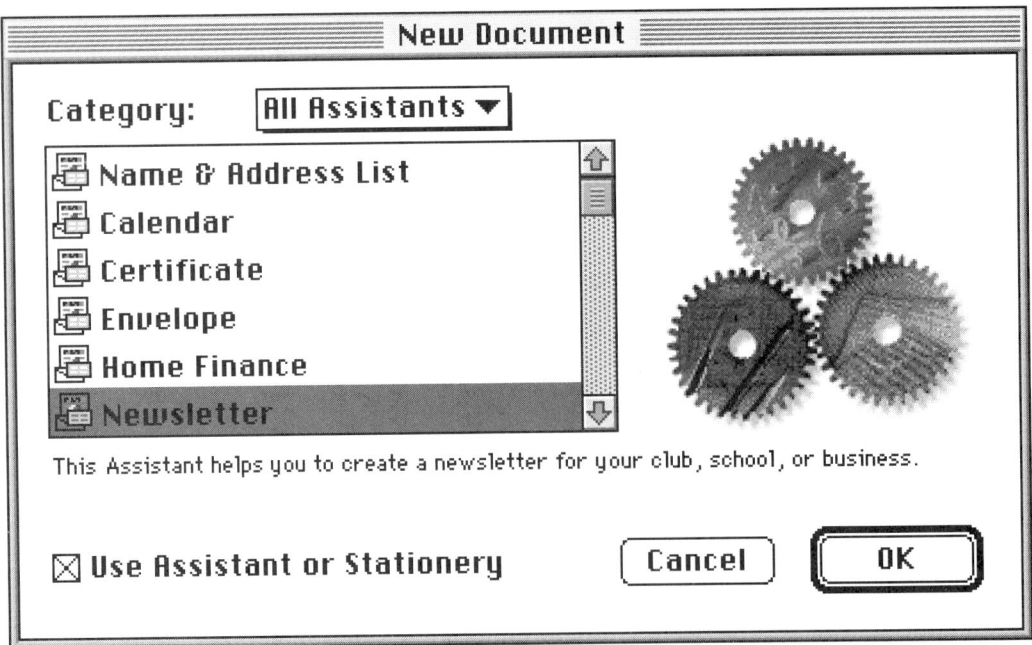

Figure 4.7
Instructional Basic Layout

Figure 4.8
Instructional Business Layout

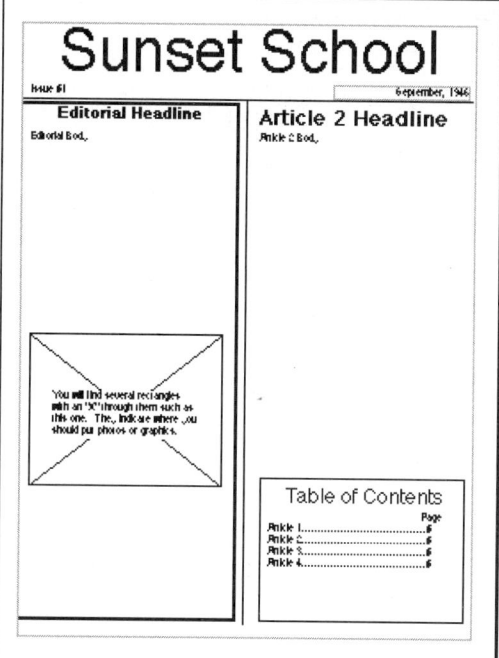

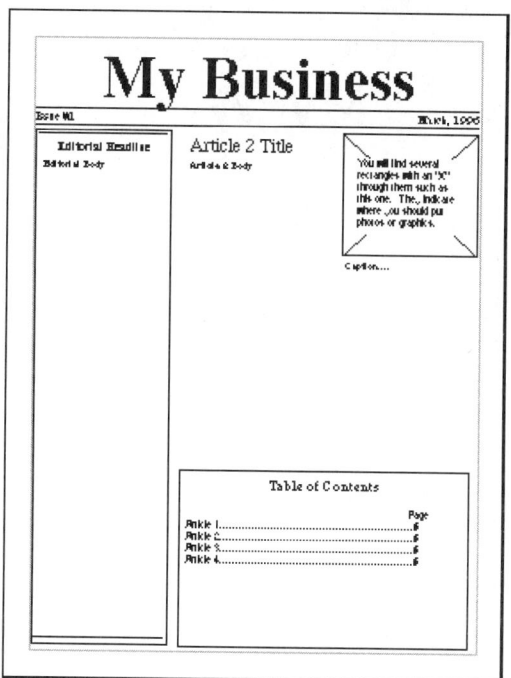

Figure 4.9
News Basic Layout

Figure 4.10
News Business Layout

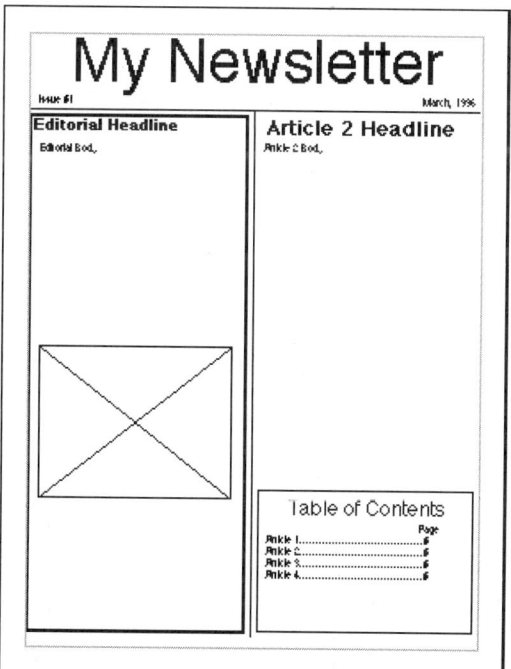

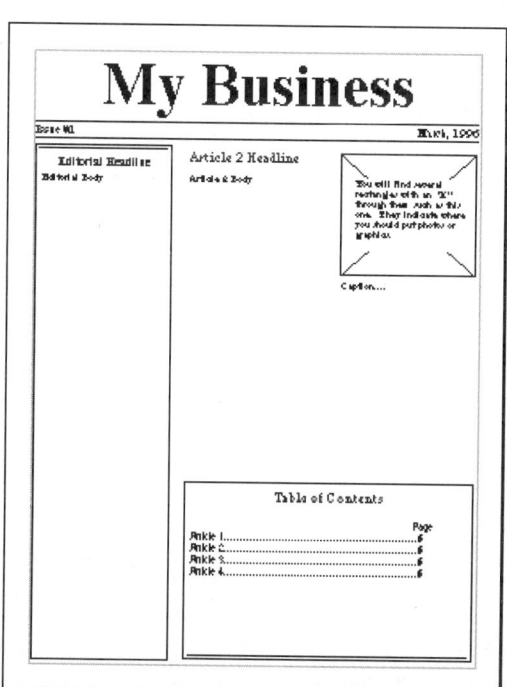

Figure 4.11
News New Age Layout

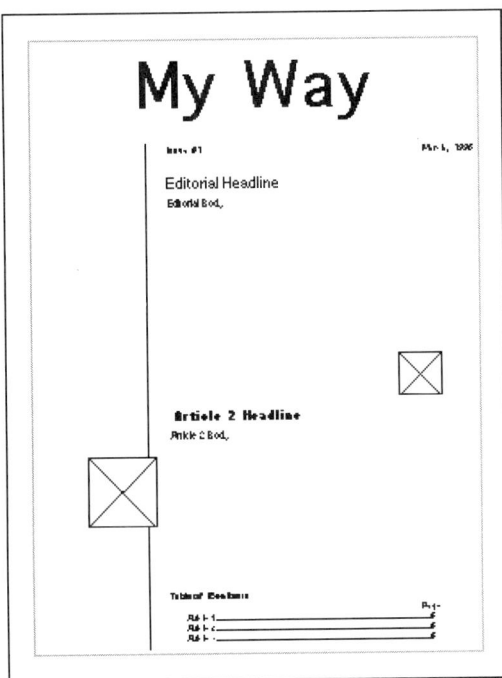

Figure 4.12
News Post-Modern Layout

Figure 4.13
News Folded Booklet Layout

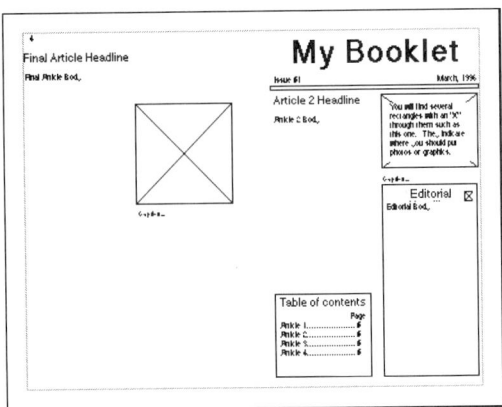

Figure 4.14
News Legal Layout

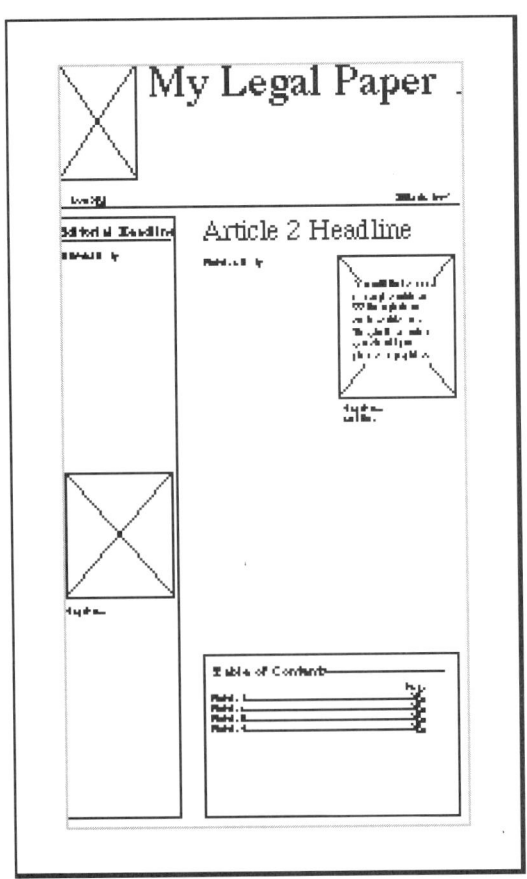

Basic Design Guidelines

The following guidelines are certainly not absolute but exactly that, guidelines. They are meant to guide you and not to be restrictive. With experience, you will begin to get the feel of what appeals to you and your students.

❏ For headlines, use a **sans serif** font such as Geneva or Helvetica on the Macintosh and Arial or MS Sans Serif on a Windows computer.

❏ For body text, use a **serif** font such as Times or New York on the Macintosh and Century Schoolbook or MS Serif on a Windows computer.

❏ Be generous in the use of **white space;** white space is good! Ways to increase the amount of white space in your documents include indenting paragraphs, using wider margins, using ragged-right (left-aligned) text, and double spacing text.

❏ Use **drop shadows** to draw attention to graphics.

❏ Overlay graphics give a three-dimensional effect to your graphics.

❏ For body text, left-aligned text is easier to read than fully justified text.

❏ Use oversized first letters to emphasize the first sentence of an article.

❏ Use *italics* rather than <u>underlining</u> for emphasis.

Graphic with a drop shadow.

Overlaid graphics.

Oversized first letter.

In the Classroom

1. Have your students prepare a newsletter in which they present their own poems, essays, or descriptive writing.

2. Students can prepare their science laboratory reports in a layout template. You can have graphics libraries available that are complementary to the lab activity so that students can illustrate their reports with graphics.

3. Have students prepare historical perspectives on significant events, persons, and places they are studying, such as

   ❏ The first controlled nuclear explosion

   ❏ Sojourner Truth

   ❏ The first fifty years in the life of a city: Chicago

   ❏ Thomas Jefferson

   ❏ George Washington Carver

   ❏ Oklahoma in the Dust Bowl days/Oklahoma today

   ❏ Plants we hate to love

   ❏ Animals we love to hate

   ❏ The politics of war

   ❏ The first settlers of California

   ❏ The presidential election of 2000

   ❏ Chemicals I found in my house

4. Have students write an alternate ending to a story or book they have heard or read.

5. Have students enter into a layout template their reactions to a story or book they have had read to them or that they have read themselves.

6. Have students compare the cost of food items and/or other items for a range of time, such as 1900, 1910, 1920, 1930, 1940, 1950, 1960, 1970, 1980, 1990, today.

7. Have students interview one of the following individuals on a topic related to a class and report the results in a layout template:

   ❏ Mayor

   ❏ Judge

- ❏ County commissioner
- ❏ Business person
- ❏ Juror
- ❏ Individual running for a political office

8. Students can "interview" someone from the past (such as Susan B. Anthony or Cleopatra) and write up the results in a newsletter format.

9. Interview parents, grandparents, or any older adults for their views and memories of

- ❏ World War I or II
- ❏ 1947 in the New Mexico Desert: UFO?
- ❏ The *Andrea Doria,* the *Titanic,* the *Lusitania,* the *Hindenburg*
- ❏ Vietnam
- ❏ The March on Selma
- ❏ Assassination of JFK
- ❏ The Crash of '29

10. Have students, individually or in groups, summarize a unit of instruction that the class has completed.

11. With the use of layouts, the teacher could

- ❏ Introduce a unit
- ❏ Summarize a unit
- ❏ Present a complete unit in a series of newsletters
- ❏ Prepare a worksheet for student practice
- ❏ Post classroom rules
- ❏ Present the syllabus or outline of a course of study
- ❏ Prepare a lab manual
- ❏ Prepare a newsletter to parents

Questions and Answers

Q1: **Why is it that sometimes I can import text I have prepared with ClarisWorks and sometimes I can't?**

A: In ClarisWorks, you cannot insert files saved as a ClarisWorks file, although you can insert files saved with applications such as Word-Perfect and Word. If you save your document as a text file or as an RTF file in ClarisWorks, then you can insert the contents of that file.

Q2: **Are insert and copy/paste the only ways I can get text into a layout?**

A: You can also type directly into a text frame.

Q3: **Occasionally, I draw a text frame, and then it disappears. Am I doing something wrong?**

A: If Frame Links is turned off and if you have not entered any text into the frame, then the frame does disappear when you click else-where in the document. If you will type at least one letter or symbol into the text frame, then it will not disappear.

If Frame Links is selected when you draw the frame, then the frame is still there. You may want to enter a small amount of text into the frame or change the color of the frame border to a dark color so you can still see the outline of the frame even when it is not selected.

Q4: **Sometimes when I paste a graphic into a page layout, it acts as though it were text and I can't seem to select it. What's wrong?**

A: When you pasted (or inserted) the graphic into your layout, you prob-ably had the Text tool selected. In this case, the graphic is treated as inline text. It can be selected, but it has a different appearance than if it were a graphic object selected with the pointer. If you don't want a graphic to be treated as an inline graphic, then choose the pointer tool before you paste or insert the graphic.

Q5: **Sometimes I can't select a graphic that I have inserted into my newsletter. Why can't I select it?**

A: If you can't select a graphic object with the pointer, it may be because the graphic is behind another object, such as a text frame. If this is the case, select the text frame and move it to the back with the `Arrange` menu. Then you should be able to select the graphic.

Q6: **Sometimes I can't find a graphic (that I have prepared with ClarisWorks) when I try to insert it. What am I doing wrong?**

A: If you will save your graphics as Macintosh Picture (PICT or PCT) files, then you should be able to insert them. The graphics that you cannot find were probably saved as a ClarisWorks file, and they cannot be inserted. However, it's simple to open them and save them as PICT files. Then you can insert them, or simply open the file and use copy/paste or drag-drop to place them into your layout.

Q7: **Occasionally, I attempt to paste text into a page layout, and it seems to have a mind of its own; it doesn't go where I want it to. Is there something wrong with my layout?**

A: Assuming that you have a text frame in your layout, you are probably not clicking inside that text frame with the Text tool prior to pasting the text. In you have not clicked inside the frame, then the text may appear to be placed randomly on the screen. If this occurs, select the misbehaving frame that contains the text, delete it, and start over.

Activities

1. Use the Assistant to design a layout for the following purposes:

a. A two-page newsletter layout with a table of contents to present students with an introduction to figures of speech.

b. A two-page template with an editorial so your students can prepare a newsletter on their most and least favorite summer activities.

c. A folded booklet explaining the policy of your school on homework.

d. A four-page template with a title, table of contents, and space for a label for a topic related to something the students are currently studying.

e. A two-page newsletter with a post-modern design and table of contents for a student newsletter to be sent home to parents or guardians.

2. Open `Layout1` and link the right column of page one to the right-hand or second column of page two so that text from the first page of the newsletter will flow into the second column of the second page. Insert text into the left column of the first page to observe how well you did.

3. Open the file `Layout2` and place text frames in the indicated places. Save the file under a different name when you have made the changes.

4. With the file from the previous activity, change the layout to a two-page newsletter. Preserve the look and feel of the first page.

5. Enter the information for a table of contents for the file `Layout3`.

Summary

Desktop publishing consists of combining text and graphics in column format. Teachers and students can prepare a wide range of publications both for instructional purposes and for more general purposes. The teacher can either prepare or locate appropriate templates for her or his class and then customize them for student use. In some cases, it may be appropriate for the students themselves to prepare their own templates.

By incorporating the use of newsletters and layouts into your curriculum, you are helping your students gain experience in planning and writing, in addition to the primary subject matter they are working with in your class.

Key Terms

alley 104

continue indicator 99

desktop publishing 94

drop shadow 111

headline 96

layout 94

link indicator 99

place holder 96

sans serif 111

serif 111

text file 96

text overflow indicator 99

top-of-frame indicator 99

white space 111

References

Anderson, D., & Newton, R. (1993). Putting students in the picture. *Education for Information, 11,* 331–337.

Electronic publishing. (1995). *Technology learning activity. Teacher edition. Technology education series.* (ERIC Document No. ED 380592)

Tharp, M., & Zimmerman, D. (1992). Using desktop publishing in an editing class—The lessons learned and students' assessments. *Technical Communication Quarterly, 1*(2), 77–92.

5

Developing Inquiry Skills with Databases

O B J E C T I V E S

Search, sort, and print reports from a database.

Design and fill a new database.

Use a database to find information, look for relationships, and test hypotheses.

Prepare lessons using databases.

WE ARE LIVING IN the Information and Communications Age, a time when the amount of accumulated information doubles in fewer than five years. No one can easily keep up with this information explosion, even within a particular field of expertise. Knowing how to find and interpret information may be as important as knowing facts. Students today need to develop inquiry skills to help them organize, access, manipulate, and evaluate information, whether they collect the information themselves or access and manipulate information gathered by others.

The computer, with its powerful memory and speed, is an excellent tool for storing information in an organized manner and accessing that information quickly. This information can be stored in a **database.** A database is simply an organized collection of information. Your address book, the telephone book, and a catalog are examples of databases. Before computers became widespread, databases were usually stored in filing cabinets, but now most of them are computerized and stored on disks or some other type of electronic storage device. In many libraries the card catalog is now on computer.

In the classroom, students are using databases, both those that have been prepared for them and those that they develop themselves, as tools to develop critical thinking skills. Computerized databases make it easy to search and sort through large amounts of information in order to find patterns and identify trends. For example, with a database containing sociological information about Native American tribes, a teacher might ask students to find a relationship between the kind of clothing the Indians wore in the eighteenth and nineteenth centuries and the geographical location of the tribe, or the teacher might ask students to test the hypothesis that Indians who ate acorns also used mortars and pestles as tools. After establishing a variety of patterns and trends, the teacher could give students selected attributes of an unknown tribe (such as "they wore little clothing") and have them make inferences about related attributes based on the established patterns (such as "they must have lived in a warm climate") (Pon, 1984). Used in this way, databases help students develop higher-order thinking skills involving analysis, synthesis, and evaluation. The overall goal for the use of databases in the classroom should be that they are used as inquiry tools to reason about and experiment with data and ideas.

What Is a Database?

In its simplest form, a database is an organized collection of information. Suppose you have written the name, address, phone number, and birthday of each of your friends on a different 3" x 5" card. This collection of information is a database. The **categories** of information in your "Friends" database are Name, Address, Phone, and Birth. Another name for *category* is **field.** Therefore, there are four fields in our database of friends.

Let's fill in one of the cards in our database:

```
Name: Sarah Land

Address: 4505 Tobago

Phone: 689-4139

Birth: 5/23/81
```

We have placed information in each category or field; this collection of information is referred to as a **record.** A record is a collection of fields (or categories) with data or information entered in one or more of those categories. In the case of our Friends database, the card with the information about Sarah Land represents one record in our database. Two or more related records make up a database **file** of information (Figure 5.1).

Figure 5.1
A collection of related records constitute a database file

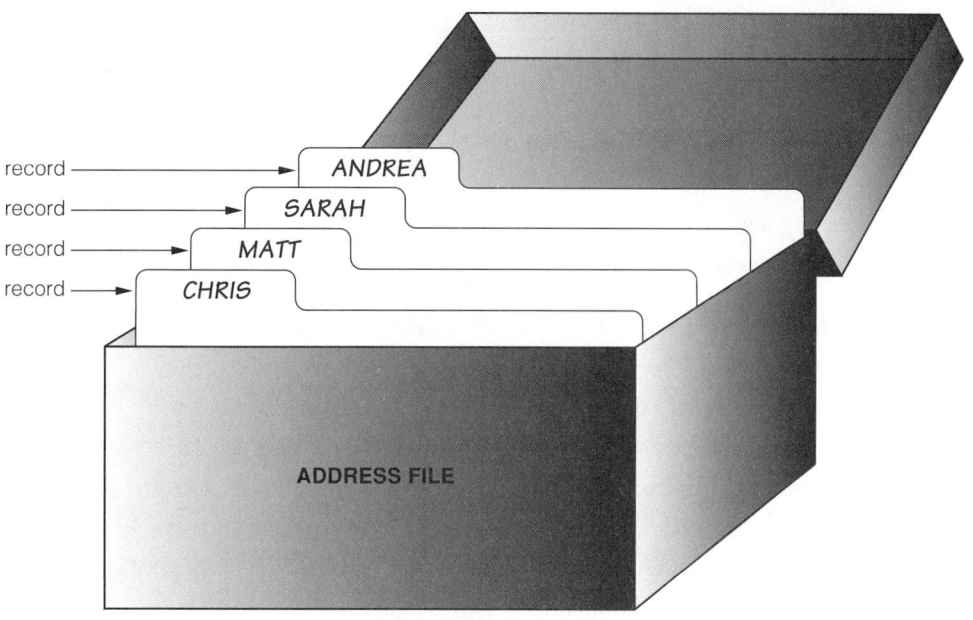

In summary, a group of fields or categories constitutes a record, and a collection of related records constitutes a database file.

Working with an Existing Database

If you have just started ClarisWorks, you may have to click Cancel before you can choose from File.

Now let's look at a computerized **database application.** A database application, such as that found in ClarisWorks, allows you to work with electronic databases. We are going to look at an existing database located in the 05 db folder. If you have not started ClarisWorks, you need to do so at this time.

❑ Choose File/Open.

💾 ❑ Locate and highlight the file Africa; then click Open.

The database Africa should now be showing on your screen (Figure 5.2). It contains fifty-four records of twelve fields each, but you can see on the screen only part of the database document at a time. If you want to see other records, scroll down the document by clicking on the scroll area on the right side of the document. If you want to see more fields, use the scroll bar at the bottom of the window to see the additional fields to the right.

Figure 5.2
Africa database showing data on more than one country

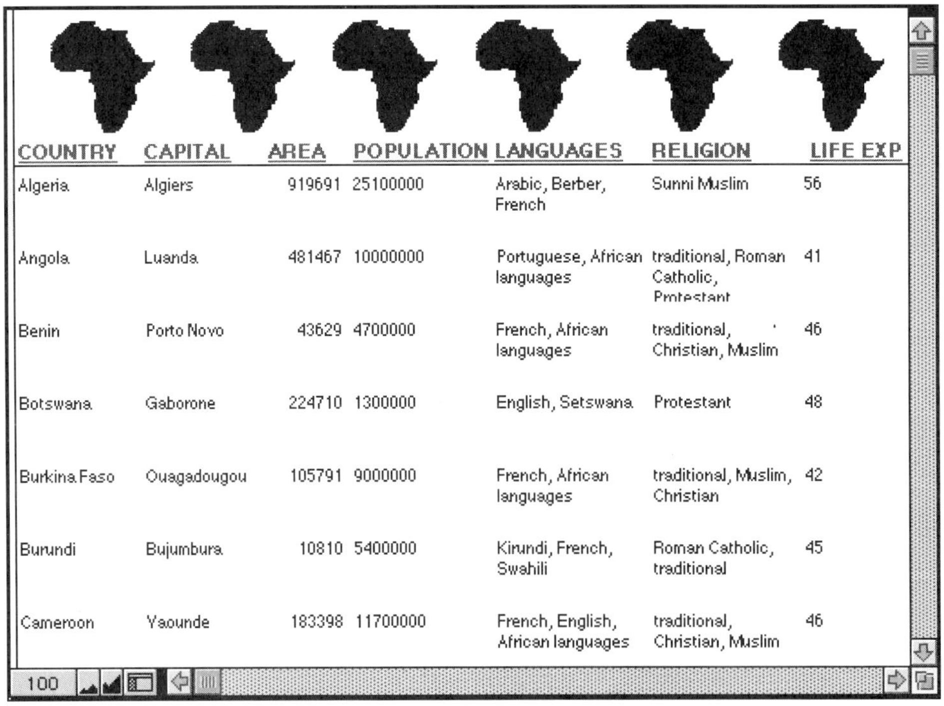

COUNTRY	CAPITAL	AREA	POPULATION	LANGUAGES	RELIGION	LIFE EXP
Algeria	Algiers	919691	25100000	Arabic, Berber, French	Sunni Muslim	56
Angola	Luanda	481467	10000000	Portuguese, African languages	traditional, Roman Catholic, Protestant	41
Benin	Porto Novo	43629	4700000	French, African languages	traditional, Christian, Muslim	46
Botswana	Gaborone	224710	1300000	English, Setswana	Protestant	48
Burkina Faso	Ouagadougou	105791	9000000	French, African languages	traditional, Muslim, Christian	42
Burundi	Bujumbura	10810	5400000	Kirundi, French, Swahili	Roman Catholic, traditional	45
Cameroon	Yaounde	183398	11700000	French, English, African languages	traditional, Christian, Muslim	46

100

The twelve categories or fields in the `Africa` database are Country, Capital, Area (in square miles), Population, Languages, Religion, Life Exp (life expectancy), Literacy (percent of population), Industry, Exports, Income (per capita), and GNP (gross national product). To see all twelve fields for a particular country, select `Layout/Single Records`. The first record consists of information on Algeria. To get back to a layout showing multiple records, select `Layout/ Multiple Records`.

Under `Layout`, *the four layouts labeled* `Multiple Records`, `Area-Pop-Life-Liter`, `Single Records`, *and* `Two Across` *were prepared by the authors for these particular data.*

Sorting Records

The records in the `Africa` database are currently arranged in alphabetical order by name of country. Suppose that you want to know which are the least populous countries in Africa. To **sort** (or arrange) the records in increasing order of population,

❏ Select `Organize/Sort Records...` and release the mouse button (Figure 5.3).

❏ Click `Clear` to clear the previous sort.

❏ Click `Population`; then click the `Move` button. `Population` now appears in the `Sort Order` window.

❏ Click the `OK` button to see your sort.

Figure 5.3
When you point to `Organize/Sort Records...`, this dialog box appears

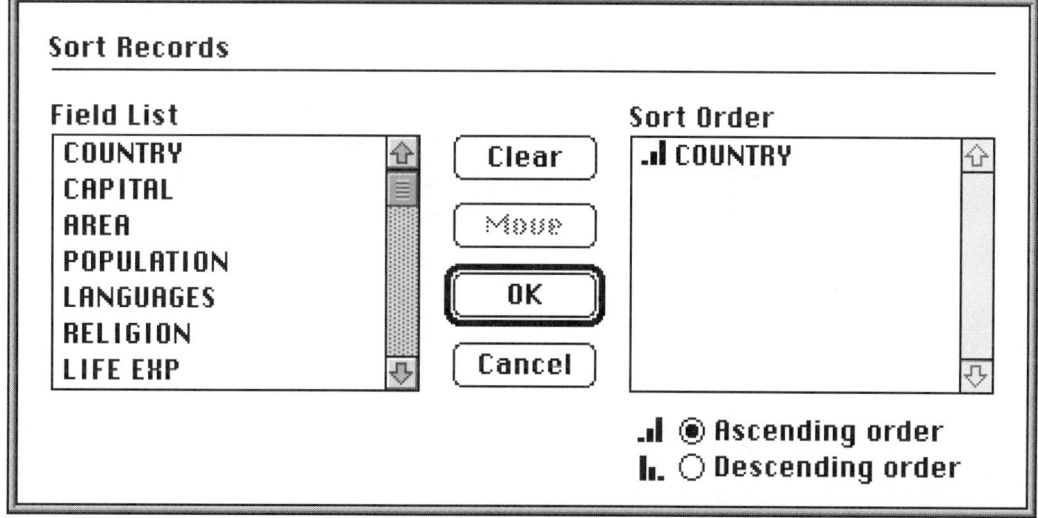

The records are now arranged in order from the least populous country to the most populous country.

Searching on the Basis of One Criterion

Let's find all of the African countries whose areas are larger than 500,000 square miles. Stated another way, let's **search** our database document on the basis of a criterion associated with the field Area to find the countries with an area greater than 500,000 square miles. There are two ways you can conduct your search. First,

❑ If your Shortcuts palette is not showing, point to File/Short-cuts/Show Shortcuts.

❑ Choose Layout/Find and release the mouse (or click ⊞).

❑ Click the rectangle below the field label Area.

❑ Enter >500000 (or >500,000) (Figure 5.4).

Figure 5.4
Enter >500,000 into the field Area under the label Area.

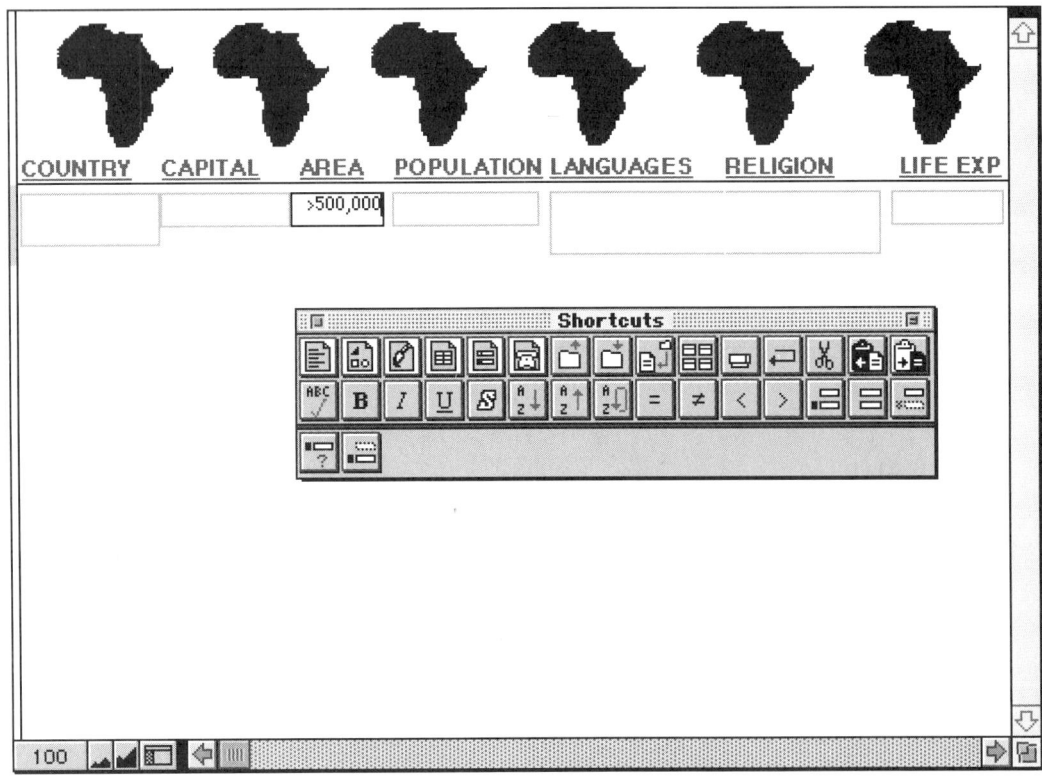

❑ Choose one of the following: **M** View/Show Tools or
W Window/Show Tools.

❑ The All button is selected by default, so click Find.

The four countries matching your selection criterion should be the only countries showing.

Here's a second way to search with the same criterion. First, however, show all records with Organize/Show All Records (or ▤).

❑ Point to Organize/Match Records... and release the mouse.

❑ Click the field Area.

❑ Click the > symbol.

❑ Enter 500000 (*not* 500,000) (Figure 5.5).

❑ Click the OK button.

❑ To show only the selected countries, point to Organize/Hide Unselected (or ▤). You may have to scroll up the document to see the selected items.

The countries selected should be the same ones as with the previous search.

Figure 5.5
When you point to Organize/Match Records..., this dialog box appears. Click on the field Area and then the symbol >. Enter 500000 in the Formula rectangle.

Enter Match Records Condition

Fields	**Operators**	**Function**
COUNTRY	+	ABS(number)
CAPITAL	–	ACOS(number)
AREA	*	AND(logical1 ,logical2 ,...)
POPULATION	/	ASIN(number)
LANGUAGES	=	ATAN(number)
RELIGION	>	ATAN2(x_number ,y_number)
LIFE EXP	<	AVERAGE(number1 ,number2 ,...)

Formula

'AREA'>500000

Cancel   OK

We could show all records with
*Organize/Show All
Records* (or 🗐), but this
search will work properly
without performing this
procedure.

*While your entry looks like this:
'Area' >500000, it is
permissible to enter spaces like
this: 'Area' >500000 to
facilitate reading.*

Searching on the Basis of Multiple Criteria

Now let's perform the following search: locate all the countries in Africa with a population greater than 5 million that also export coffee. How many search criteria are implied? There are two; the first is concerned with the field `Population`, and the second is concerned with the field `Exports`.

❏ Point to `Layout/Find` (or 🖼️).

❏ Enter `>5000000` into field `Population`.

❏ Scroll over to field `Exports` and enter `coffee`.

❏ Click the `Find` button.

You should see the names of twelve countries. You can't see all the countries selected in the current layout, but you can if you choose `Layout` and scroll down to `Area-Pop-Life-Liter`. These countries have a population greater than 5,000,000, and they export coffee.

Now let's try a search with three criteria. Which African countries have a population with a life expectancy greater than forty years, a literacy rate greater than 60 percent, and English as one of the languages spoken? We will be working with the following fields: `Literacy`, `Life Exp`, and `Languages`. First, however, because the current layout does not show all of the fields that we need to work with, choose `Layout/Multiple Records`.

❏ Point to `Layout/Find` (or 🖼️).

❏ Enter `English` into field `Languages`.

❏ Enter `>40` into field `Life Exp`.

❏ Enter `>60` into field `Literacy`.

❏ Click the `Find` button.

Five countries meet the criteria.

Printing

When you are ready to print a copy of a search or a report, the search or report should be showing on the screen.

❏ Choose `File/Print`.

❏ Click the **M** `Print` or **W** OK button.

That's it, assuming, of course, that your computer is connected to a printer and the printer is on! Only the countries that meet all of the criteria will be printed.

Starting a Database from Scratch

Now that you have begun to learn how to use a database to find information and to search and sort, let's develop a database about dinosaurs with the information from Table 5.1. As shown in Table 5.1, your database will consist of information on fourteen dinosaurs with seven fields or categories of information for each dinosaur record. The fields will be named Name, Nickname, Food, Habitat, Claws?, Feet, and Armored?

To begin your new dinosaur database,

❏ Choose File/New.../Database/OK. A dialog box (Figure 5.6) will appear, prompting you for the name of the first field for your database. The first field name you will enter is Name and is of type text. Note that text is the default field type, so you don't have to choose the field type on this field.

Figure 5.6
Dialog box after the first field has been named

```
┌─────────────────────────────────────────────────────────────┐
│ ═══════════════ Define Database Fields ═══════════════        │
│                                                               │
│  Field Name                      Field Type                   │
│  ┌──────────────────────────────────────────────────────┐ ⬆ │
│  │                                                        │   │
│  │                                                        │   │
│  │                                                        │   │
│  │                                                        │   │
│  │                                                        │ ⬇ │
│  └──────────────────────────────────────────────────────┘   │
│                                                               │
│  Field Name │Name            │   Field Type │Text ▼│          │
│  ┌────────────┐  ┌──────────┐  ┌──────────┐  ┌──────────┐    │
│  │  Create    │  │  Modify  │  │  Delete  │  │ Options...│    │
│  └────────────┘  └──────────┘  └──────────┘  └──────────┘    │
│  Select Create to make a new field or press Modify to rename or change  ┌──────────┐ │
│  the type of an existing field.                               │  Done    │ │
│                                                               └──────────┘ │
└─────────────────────────────────────────────────────────────┘
```

Table 5.1
Data for Dinosaurs Database

Field Type	Text	Text	Text	Text	Check Box	Radio Button	Popup Menu
Field	**Name**	**Nickname**	**Food**	**Habitat**	**Claws?**	**Feet**	**Armored?**
	Ankylosaurus	Curved Lizard	plants	land	no	4	yes
	Brachiosaurus	Giant Lizard	plants	swamps, water	no	4	no
	Corythosaurus	Helmet Lizard	plants	swamps, water	no	2	no
	Diplodocus	Double Beam	plants	swamps, water	no	4	no
	Iguanodon	Tooth Lizard	plants	land	no	2	no
	Proceratops	First Horn Face	plants	land	no	4	yes
	Trachodon	Duck Bill	plants	water	no	2	no
	Triceratops	Three Horn	plants	land	no	4	yes
	Allosaurus	Other Lizard	meat	land	yes	2	no
	Brontosaurus	Thunder Lizard	plants	swamps, water	yes	4	no
	Coelophysis	—	meat	land	yes	2	no
	Gorgosaurus	Terrible Lizard	meat	land	yes	2	no
	Stegosaurus	Covered Lizard	plants	land	yes	4	yes
	Tyrannosaurus	Tyrant Lizard	meat	land	yes	2	no

Source: Information from D. Lambert, *A Field Guide to Dinosaurs* (New York: Avon, 1983).

❏ Type in Name.

❏ Click the Create button, and you will be prompted for the name of the next field. Since the next three fields (Nickname, Food, Habitat) are also of type text, you will enter them exactly as you did for field Name. You should enter the information for these three fields now.

When you have entered the first four field names, the dialog box on your screen should look similar to Figure 5.7. The next field name you will enter is `Claws?` Note in Table 5.1 that its field type is `Checkbox`.

Figure 5.7
Dialog box showing the names of four fields entered

Variations of the Checkbox button:

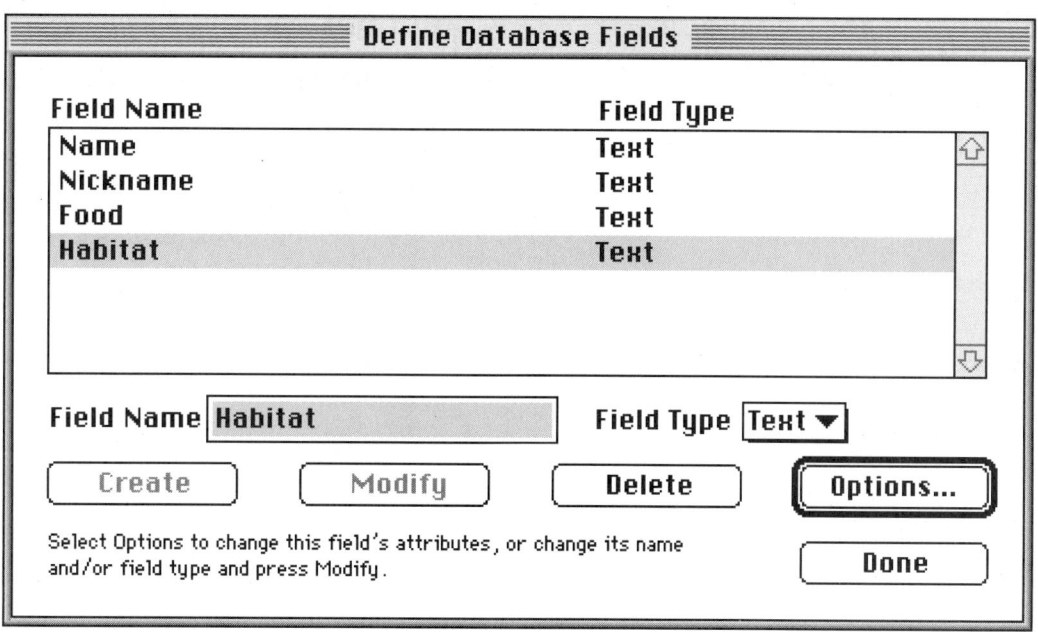

❏ Enter the field name `Claws?`

❏ Choose field type `Checkbox` by clicking the selection rectangle to the right of `Field Type`, pulling down to `Checkbox`, and then releasing the mouse button.

❏ Click `Create`.

❏ Click `Options`. At the `Options` dialog box (Figure 5.8) you can change the label for the checkbox and select whether or not you want the default value to be initially checked or not. Since we don't want to change the label and we do want the default value to be checked, click `OK`.

Figure 5.8
Dialog box to change name of label on Checkbox field and display whether the default value is initially checked

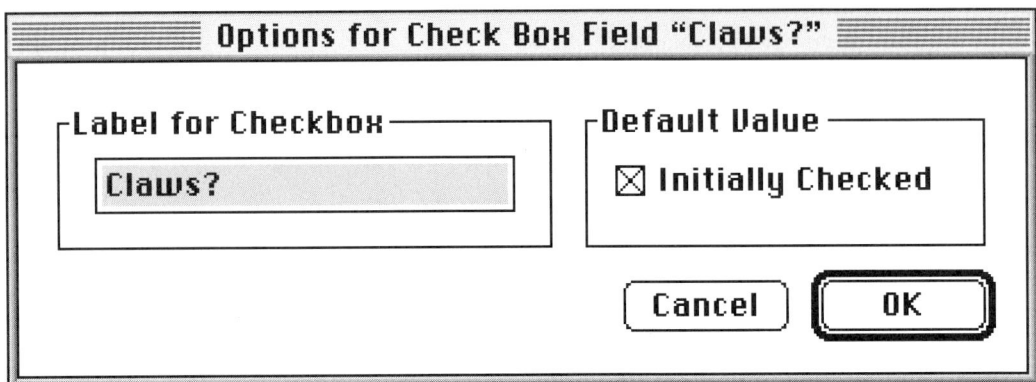

Variations of the Radio Button:

The next field Feet is of type Radio Button, so

❏ Enter the name of the field Feet.

❏ Change field type to Radio Buttons.

❏ Click Create.

❏ Enter 2 into Item Label to replace Item1 (Figure 5.9).

❏ Click Modify.

❏ Now enter 4 into Item Label to replace Item2.

❏ Click Modify.

Figure 5.9
Dialog box to change the Radio Button items, which items show automatically, and the label

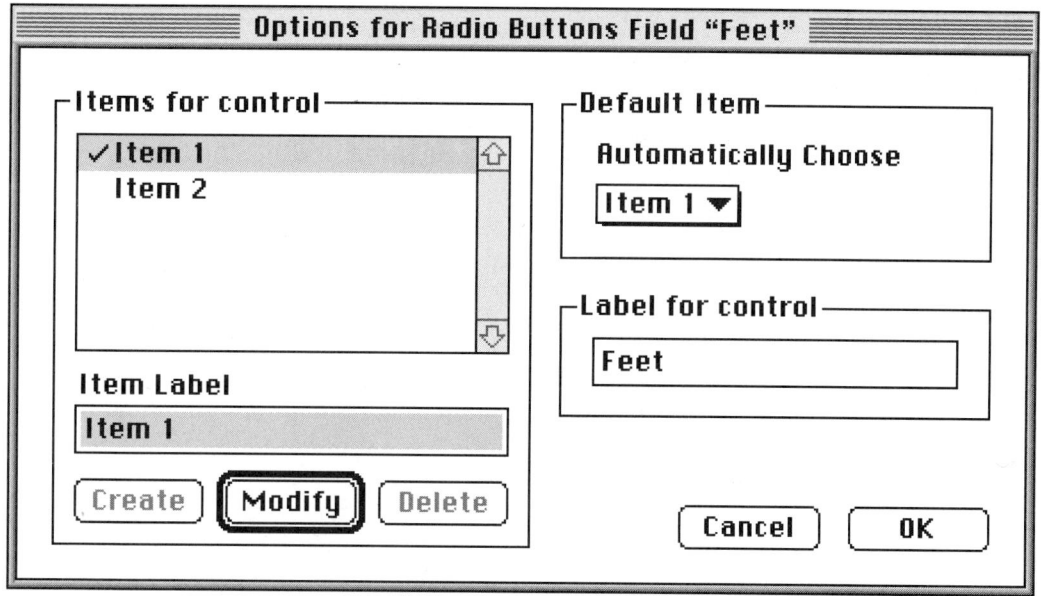

For each new record, we want the default item to be 2 and the label to be Feet, so we will not change the default item or the label; therefore, click OK.

You are now ready to enter the name of the last field Armored?, which is of type Popup Menu.

Variations of the Popup Menu:

Armored? [yes ▼]
Armored? [no ▼]

❑ Enter the name of the field Armored?

❑ Change field type to Popup Menu.

❑ Click Create.

❑ Enter yes for Item Label to replace Item1 (see Figure 5.10).

❑ Click Modify.

❑ Now enter no into Item Label.

❑ Click Create.

Since we do not want to change the default item or the control label,

❑ Click OK.

❑ Click Done.

Figure 5.10
Dialog box to change names of items on Popup Menu field, the default item to be chosen, and the label for the menu

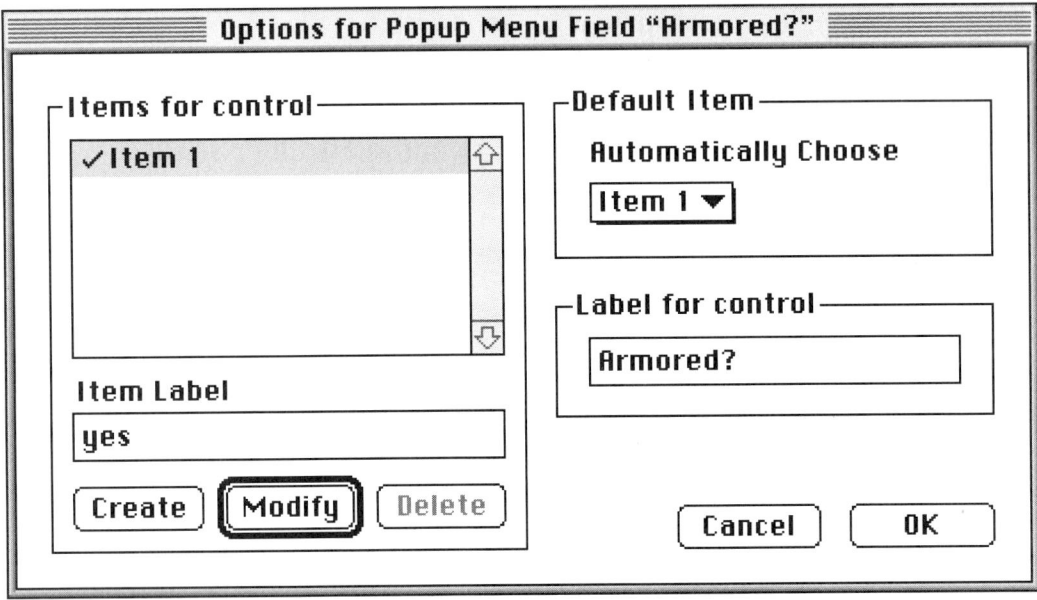

Now you're ready to enter the data for the first dinosaur into the first record. With the database showing on the screen,

❏ Type in the name of the first dinosaur from Table 5.1.

❏ Press the <tab> key to go to the Nickname field.

❏ Enter the nickname of the dinosaur.

Use the procedure above to enter the data for the remaining five fields for the first dinosaur.

When you have entered all of the data for the first dinosaur, you will need a new record. To get a new record, choose Edit/New Record. Then use the same procedure as you did for the information on the first dinosaur. Continue this procedure until you have entered the data for all fourteen dinosaurs; then save your new database with the name Dinosaurs.

You can also use **M**
⌘ -R (**W** *<ctrl>-R)*
or click
on the Shortcuts palette
for a new record.

Editing a Layout

Now you are going to change the appearance of the basic layout of your database (Figure 5.11). You are going to change the size and position of three of the fields (Claws?, Armored?, and Feet), and you are going to add a horizontal line so that it is easy to observe where the information for one dinosaur ends and another one begins.

Figure 5.11
Appearance of edited layout when finished

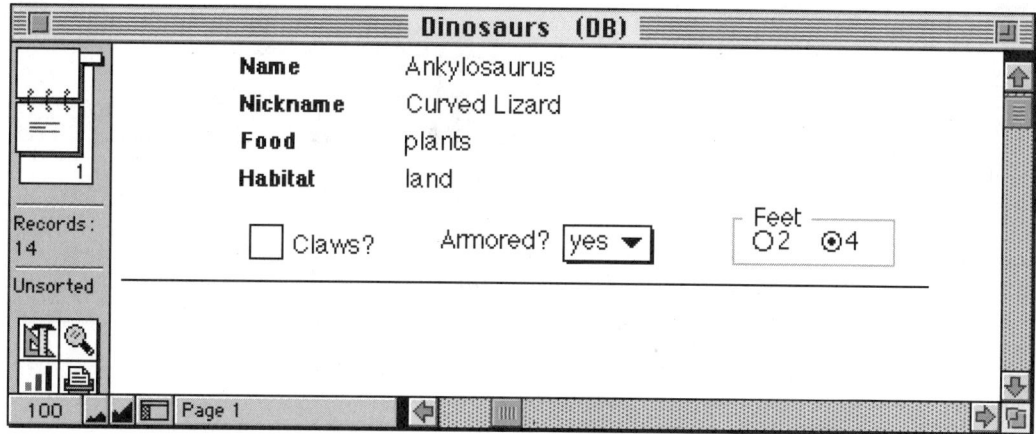

To get to Layout, point to Layout/Layout. Now you will be able to edit the information and objects in the layout. However, it would be helpful if you could instantly observe any changes you make in the layout. To do this, display another window of the database on the screen:

❏ Choose from **M** View/New View or **W** Window/New View. Your screen will show two windows of the same document. However, you need to be able to see both windows at the same time, so

❏ Choose from **M** View/Tile Windows or **W** Window/Tile or Cascade. Resize each of the two windows and place one on the top half of the screen and one on the bottom half.

Now you should have two windows of the same document showing on the screen (Figure 5.12). You will be working in the top window and observing in the bottom window, so click somewhere in the bottom window and

If you have another document open, close it now; it will be less confusing if you have only one document open at this time.

Figure 5.12
Upper window in Layout/Layout and lower window in Layout/Browse

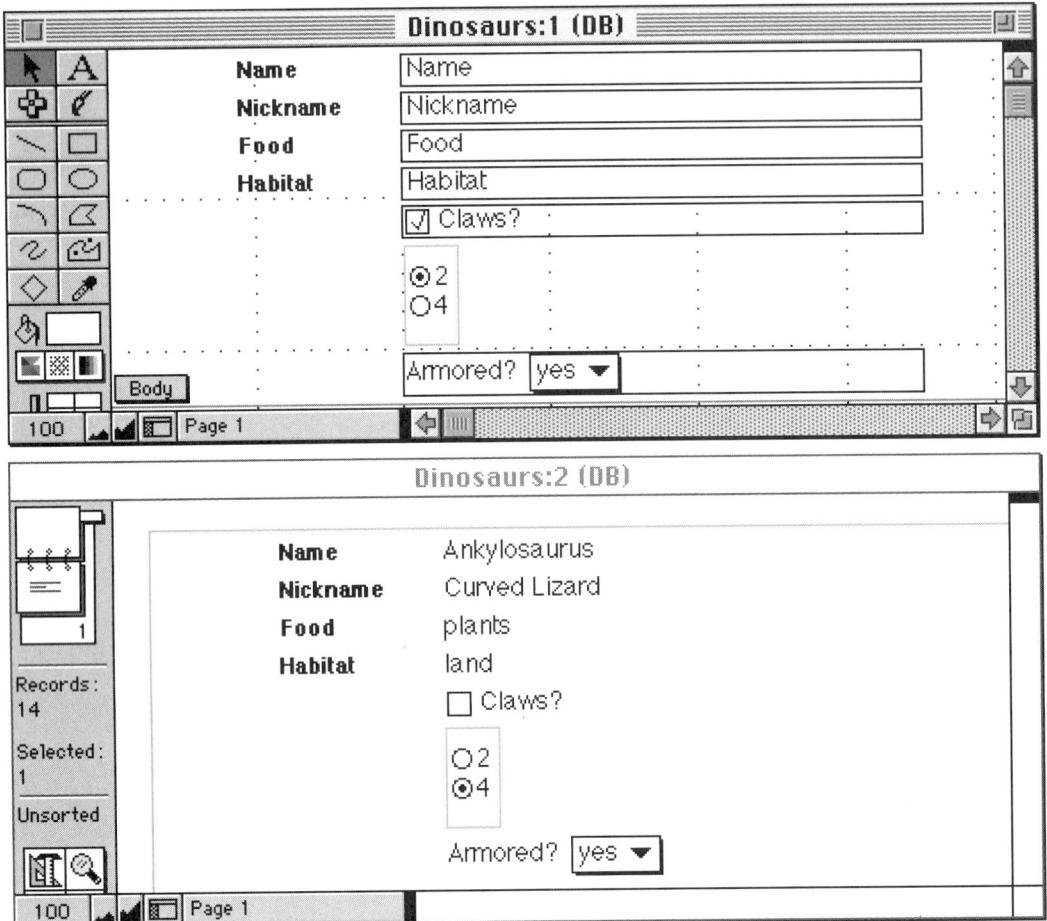

If the Tools panel is not visible, click the Show/Hide Tools control icon at the bottom left of the screen.

❑ Choose Layout/Browse. When you make a change in the top window, you will be able to see the results immediately in the bottom window.

❑ Click somewhere in the top window so you can begin editing the layout. Check to be sure you are in Layout/Layout.

You are going to decrease the width of the Claws? field to about 1 inch with a height of about .25 inch. With the pointer,

❑ Select the Claws? field and decrease the width of the field to about 1 inch and increase the height to about .25 inch. In a moment, you can check the exact measurements and make changes accordingly.

❏ Move the field so that it is located just below the field label Habitat (Figure 5.13). Now you're ready to resize and move two more fields.

❏ Resize the field Armored? until it is about 1 inch wide and about .25 inch high. Now move the field about .5 inch to the right of the Claws? field.

❏ Resize field Feet (the one with a choice of 2 or 4) until it is about 1.5 inches wide and about .5 inch high. Move it to a position about .5 inch to the right of the field Armored?

The bottom window showing on your screen should look similar to Figure 5.11. If you want to be more precise about the size and arrangement of the three fields you have just moved and resized, then continue with the following instructions.

❏ Choose Options/Object Info... to place the Info palette on the screen.

❏ See Table 5.2 for the dimensions to enter into the Info palette for each of the three fields to position them on the layout more precisely.

Table 5.2

Specifications for Fields That Were Resized and Moved

Field	Claws?	Armored?	Feet
Left edge	0.94	2.24	4.25
Top edge	1.19	1.19	0.99
Right edge	1.94	3.74	5.38
Bottom edge	1.45	1.45	1.45
Width	1	1.5	1.13
Height	0.26	0.26	0.45
Rotate	0	0	0

❑ Use the Line tool to draw a horizontal line about .25 inch below the field Armored?

❑ Point to Layout/Browse to return the upper window to the Browse view. Your edited document should look similar to Figure 5.13.

❑ Close the lower window and save your edited document.

Figure 5.13
Revised layout in Layout view (top) and Browse view (bottom)

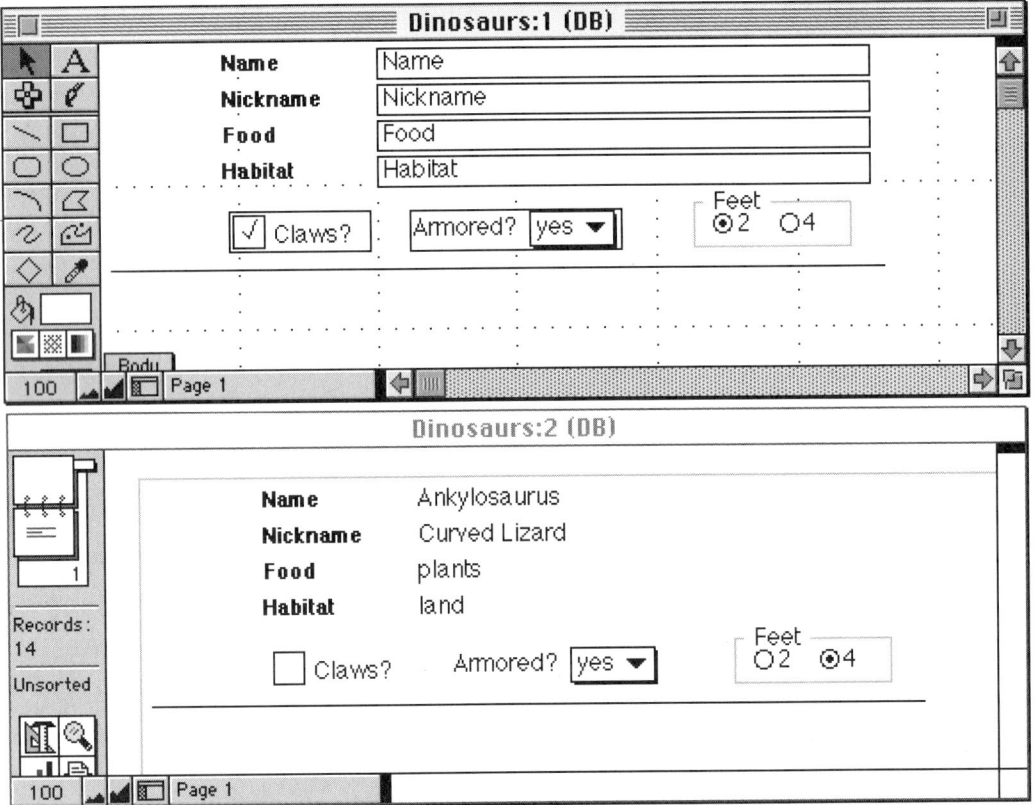

Preparing a New Layout

When you start a new database, the first layout in the database is named Layout 1 by default. However, you can prepare additional layouts. You are going to construct a new layout that will look similar to Figure 5.14. To begin your new layout,

Figure 5.14
New layout as seen in Layout/Browse

Name	Habitat	Food	Armored?	Feet	Claws?
Ankylosaurus	land	plants	yes ▼	○2 ◉4	☐
Brachiosaurus	swamps, water	plants	no ▼	○2 ◉4	☐
Corythosaurus	swamps, water	plants	no ▼	◉2 ○4	☐
Diplodocus	swamps, water	plants	no ▼	○2 ◉4	☐
Iguanodon	land	plants	no ▼	◉2 ○4	☐
Proceratops	land	plants	yes ▼	○2 ◉4	☐
Trachodon	water	plants	no ▼	◉2 ○4	☐
Triceratops	land	plants	yes ▼	○2 ◉4	☐
Allosaurus	land	meat	no ▼	◉2 ○4	☑
Brontosaurus	swamps, water	plants	no ▼	○2 ◉4	☑
Coleophysis	land	meat	no ▼	◉2 ○4	☑
Gorgosaurus	land	meat	no ▼	◉2 ○4	☑
Stegosaurus	land	plants	yes ▼	○2 ◉4	☑
Tyrannosaurus	land	meat	no ▼	◉2 ○4	☑

❏ Choose Layout/New Layout..., and the New Layout dialog box will appear on the screen.

❏ Choose Columnar report and click OK, and the Set Field Order dialog box will appear on the screen (Figure 5.15).

Another way to start a new layout is to point to the Layout Popup icon, click the icon in the upper left corner, and pull over to New Layout....

Figure 5.15
Set Field Order dialog box

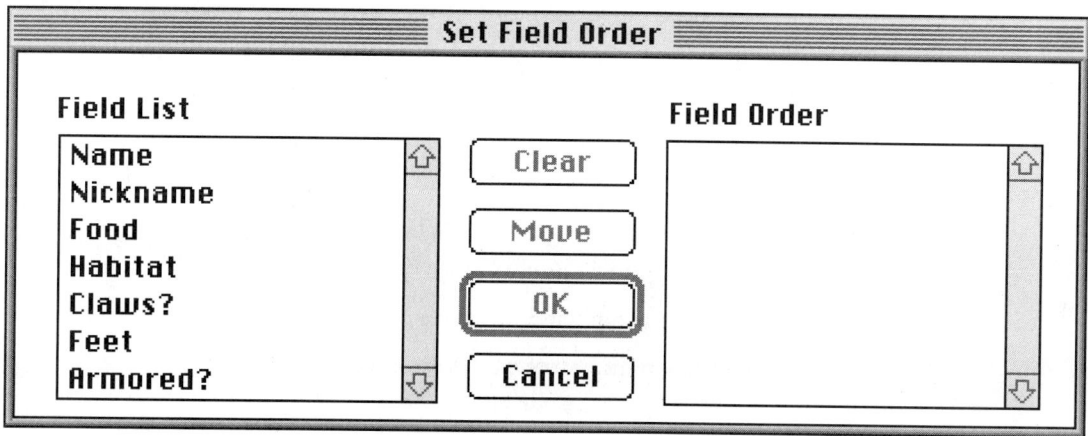

The field Nickname will not appear on this layout.

❏ In the Field List, click Name and then click the Move button to place Name in Field Order.

❏ Use the same technique for the following fields in the order indicated: Habitat, Food, Armored?, Feet, Claws?

❏ When you have moved all of the fields above to Field Order, click OK.

❏ The view on the screen now is in Browse mode (Figure 5.16); you need to be in Layout mode to edit the layout, so select Layout/ Layout.

Figure 5.16
Browse mode view

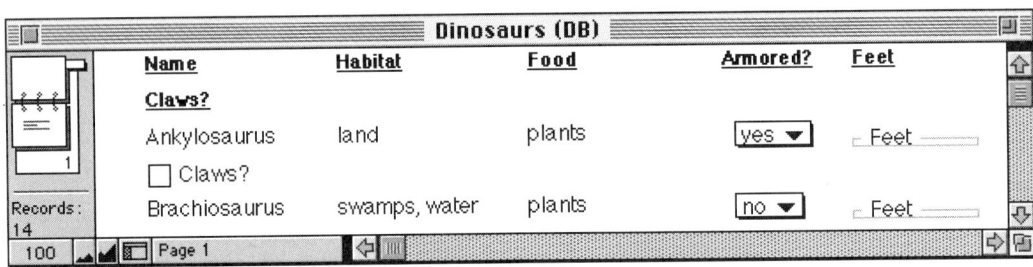

If you have any other documents open, close them now. You are going to display another window of your new database on the screen to help your editing. To accomplish this,

❏ Choose from **M** View/New View or **W** Window/New View. Your screen will show two windows of the same document. However, you need to be able to see both windows at the same time, so

❏ Choose from **M** View/Tile Windows or **W** Window/Tile or Cascade. Resize each of the two windows and place one on the top half of the screen and one on the bottom half.

Now you should have two windows of the same document showing on the screen. You will be working in the top window and observing in the bottom window, so click somewhere in the bottom window and

❏ Select Layout/Browse. When you make a change in the top window, you will be able to see the results in the bottom window.

❏ Click in the top window so you can begin editing the layout.

❏ Set all margins (Format/Document...) to .5 inch.

❏ Select all of the objects in the layout and change the font to **M** 12 point Times or **W** 10 point Arial.

❏ Use the `Info` dialog box to make the width of field `Claws?` .8 inch; make the width of all other fields and field labels 1.2 inch.

❏ Select field `Feet` and use the `Radio buttons style` dialog box (`Options/Field Format...`) (Figure 5.17) to de-select `Show Label`. Click `OK`.

❏ Select field `Claws?` and use the `Checkbox Style` dialog box (Figure 5.18) (`Options/Field Format...`) to select `Use` ✓ `mark`. Click `OK`.

Figure 5.17
`Radio buttons style` dialog box

Radio buttons style

Font [Times ▼]   Size [12 Point ▼]

☐ **Bold**   ☐ **Shadow**
☐ **Italic**   ☐ **Condense**
☐ **Underline**   ☐ **Extend**
☐ **Outline**   Color ■

☐ **Show Label**

(Cancel)   (OK)

Figure 5.18
Checkbox Style dialog box

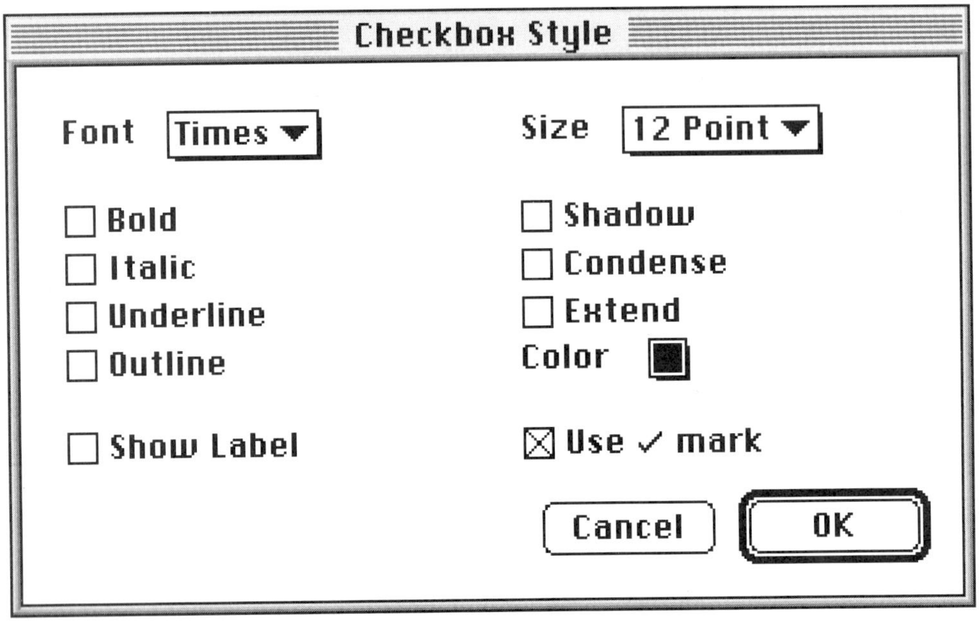

If field Claws? *appears at the bottom left of the layout, then move it and its field label to the top row on the right side.*

You may also want to Turn Autogrid Off *(*Options*) so that you can make finer adjustments using the keyboard arrow keys.*

❑ Select the field labels (not the fields themselves) with the pointer by drawing an imaginary line around the field labels; set alignment to center.

❑ Use the pointer, the arrows on the keyboard, Arrange/Align Objects..., and the Info dialog box (Options/Object Info...) to align the field labels and the fields as shown in Figure 5.14. The field labels in this layout are located in the header. In the process of editing the layout, the header delimiting line separating the header from the body (Figure 5.19) may not be snug against the bottom margin of the field names. To adjust the header, point to the horizontal header line, and the cursor will appear as ‡. When you get this cursor, hold the mouse button down and push the line up snug against the bottom margin of the field names.

Figure 5.19
Adjusting the header and body delimiting line

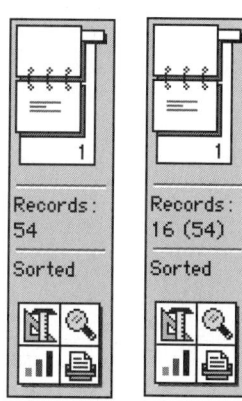

❑ Use the Line tool (with the <shift> key down) to draw a horizontal hairline just below the fields. Select a pattern that will show a dotted … or dashed — line.

❑ With the pointer, use the ↕ cursor to push the body delimiting line (Figure 5.19) snug against the bottom of the fields.

❑ Point to Layout/Browse to return the upper window to the Browse view.

❑ Close the lower window and save your edited document.

The Browse mode with the Tools panel showing. Look at the left side of the database document just below the Record Book, and you will see the number of records indicated. If a search has been performed, the total number of records will be shown in parentheses (above right).

Searches, Sorts, and Reports

You practiced searching and sorting in an earlier activity in this chapter. You used both Layout/Find and Organize/Match Records… to search and Organize/Sort Records… to sort data. Each time you prepared a search or a sort, however, you lost the previous search or sort. In this section you will prepare two searches and two sorts to be saved as a part of your database. Then you will combine a layout, a search, and a sort to prepare and save a **report.**

Open your Dinosaurs database; Layout 2 should be showing on the screen. If it isn't, then select Layout 2 by pointing to **Layout Popup** 📑 (or under the Layout menu). First, you are going to prepare two searches using **Search Popup** 🔍. These searches will become a part of your database. Your first search will be for all dinosaurs in your database that lived on land and were armored. To begin your search,

❏ Point to Search Popup 🔍, depress the mouse button, and pull over to New Search.... A dialog box will appear; enter a descriptive name for your search, such as Land & armored, and click OK.

❏ When prompted for search criteria (Figure 5.20), enter land in the Habitat field and click the Armored? field until yes appears. See Figure 5.21 for information about searching with Popup, Radio button, and Checkbox field styles.

Figure 5.20
Enter land into field Habitat and click on field Armored until yes appears

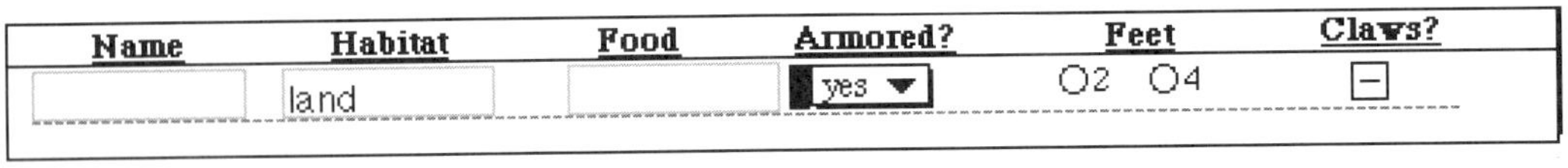

Figure 5.21
Searching with Popup, Radio button, and Checkbox field styles

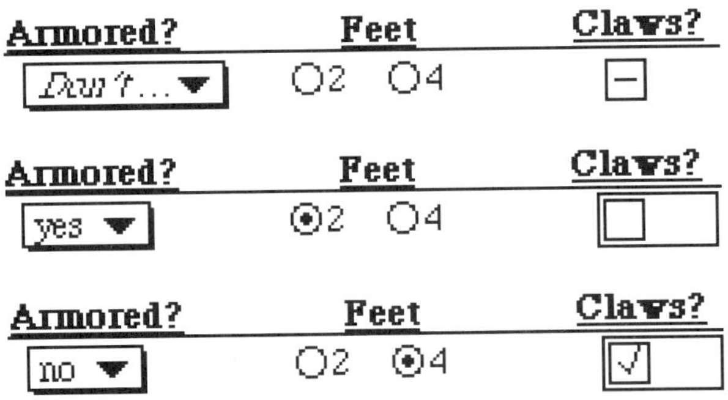

In this search, **Armored?**, **Feet**, and **Claws?** are set to the default settings.

In this search, **Armored?** is set to yes, **Feet** is set to 2, and **Claws?** is set to no.

In this search, **Armored?** is set to no, **Feet** is set to 4, and **Claws?** is set to yes.

❏ Click Store to store the results of your search.

Your next **stored search** will be for all the dinosaurs in your database that lived on land but were not armored.

❏ Point to Search Popup 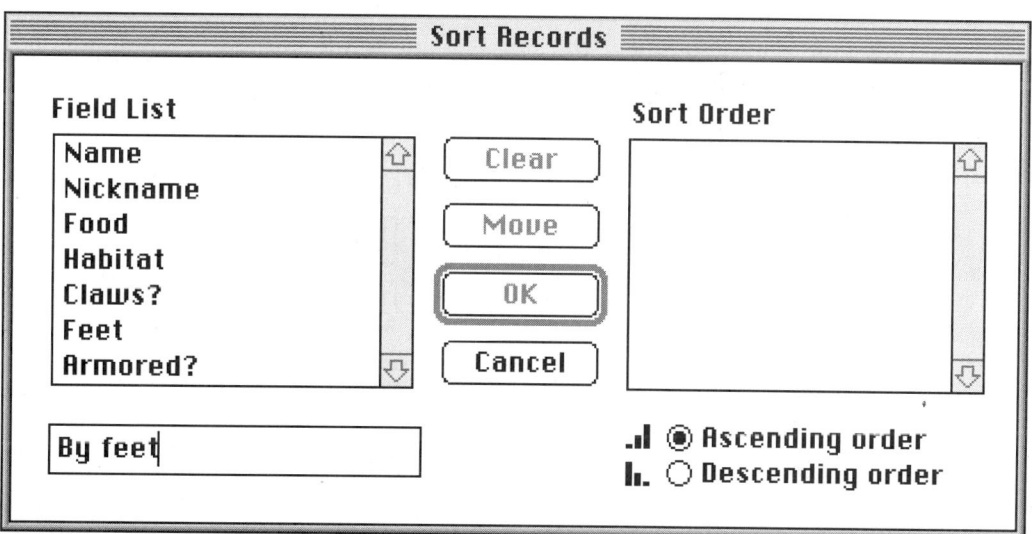; then pull over to New Search…. A dialog box will appear; enter a descriptive name for your search, such as Land & NOT armored, OK.

❏ When prompted for search criteria, enter land in the Habitat field and click the Armored? field until no appears.

❏ Click Store to store the results of this search. When you look at the screen, you will see the results of your previous search, not the one you just completed. To observe the results of the search you just stored, point to Search Popup and pull over to Land & NOT armored. The results of this search will now appear on the screen.

You have two stored searches; now you will prepare three **stored sorts.** Your sorts will be by fields Feet, Food, and Claws?

❏ Point to **Sort Popup**; then pull over to New Sort…. The Sort Records dialog box will appear (Figure 5.22). Enter the name of your first sort: By feet.

Figure 5.22
Sort Records dialog box

❏ In the `Field List`, click on field `Feet`; then click the `Move` button to move the field into `Sort Order`. You want to sort in ascending order, which is already selected, so click OK to store the sort.

Use the technique just described to prepare stored sorts by food and by claws; sort food ascending and claws descending. When you complete the two remaining sorts, you will have two layouts, two stored searches, and three stored sorts. You're ready to prepare a report. Your first report will be dinosaurs who lived on land and had armor (your stored search is `Land & armored`), will be sorted by field `Claws?` descending (your stored sort is `By claws`), and will use Layout 2. To prepare your **stored report,**

❏ Point to **Report Popup** 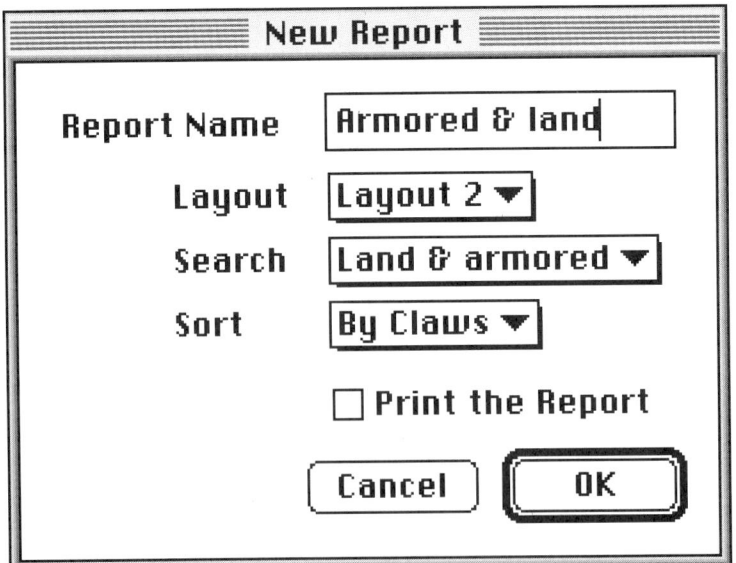 and pull over to `New Report...`. The `New Report` dialog box will appear (Figure 5.23).

❏ Enter a report name such as `Armored & land`.

❏ Hold the mouse button down on the rectangle to the right of `Layout` and pull down to `Layout 2`.

❏ Hold the mouse button down on the rectangle to the right of `Search` and pull down to `Land & armored`.

❏ Hold the mouse button down on the rectangle to the right of `Sort`, pull down to `By claws`, and click OK.

Figure 5.23
`New Report` dialog box

To see the results of your report, point to `Report Popup`  and pull over to `Armored & land`. Your new report will appear on the screen (Figure 5.24).

Figure 5.24
Results of your report `Armored & land`

Name	Habitat	Food	Armored?	Feet	Claws?
Stegosaurus	land	plants	yes ▼	○2 ◉4	☑
Ankylosaurus	land	plants	yes ▼	○2 ◉4	☐
Proceratops	land	plants	yes ▼	○2 ◉4	☐
Triceratops	land	plants	yes ▼	○2 ◉4	☐

In the Classroom

....

Planning a New Database

In a previous section, you learned to set up a new database about dinosaurs with data that we provided. Usually, however, when creating a new database, you must also collect the data and plan the appropriate field or categories.

The first step in the creation of a new database may be the most important one. Before creating the database, think about these questions: What is the nature of the information in the new database, and how do you want it organized? How will you want to search your database? If your students are planning a database, what fields do they want, or what do you want them to get from the database? One way of thinking through this phase of planning a database is to write down what kind of information you want from the database, the fields that would be necessary, the source of the data, and the order of the fields that might be most useful. Make sure to include enough information to make the database useful, but don't include a lot of surplus information.

Figure 5.25 indicates the tasks normally involved in starting a database from scratch. Who performs these tasks? For the first five steps (plans the database, designs the layout, collects data, enters data, checks data), the student, the teacher, or a third party (such as a software developer) could be involved. There are curriculum benefits to be derived from the students' involvement in each of these steps: students learn planning, organization, and research skills. Additional educational benefits come from student participation in the last four steps listed in Figure 5.25, which represent a cycle (forms search strategies, searches, sorts, draws conclusions, forms new search strategies, and so on). Students learn to look for relationships, pose and test hypotheses, and draw conclusions, all of which are important problem-solving skills. The teacher can also be involved in all of the remaining stages, depending upon the skill level of the participating students.

Figure 5.25
Flowchart for learning to use a database

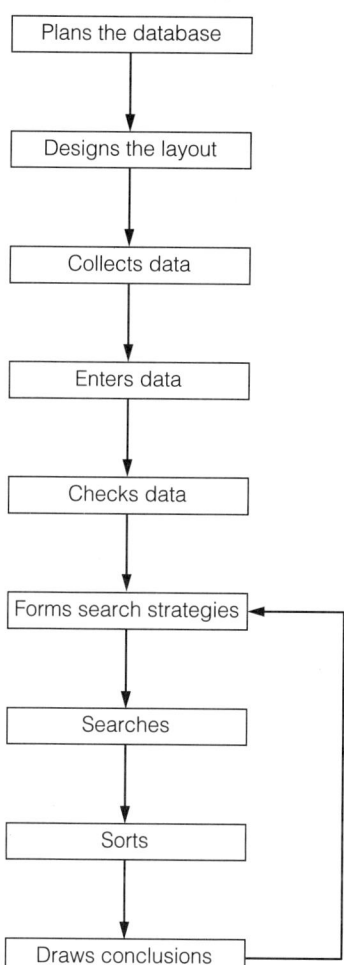

Suppose that you wanted your students to prepare a database on Native Americans of the eighteenth and nineteenth centuries, and you had information such as that in the following extract prepared by a group of young students (Pon, 1984, p. 28):

The Maidus' houses were made of tules.

They were round.

They looked like bowls.

They lived near or in the Buttes Mountains.

The city nearby is called Yuba City.

It is in Sutter County.

They lived near the Feather River.

They mostly ate acorns.

They ate deer and small animals.

They fished.

They ate seeds.

Men hunted and fished.

Women gathered acorns and cooked.

They danced and made musical instruments with reeds, especially at acorn harvest.

They told stories.

They had albino deer and acorn ceremonies.

They used mortars and pestles to grind acorns.

They hunted with bows and arrows and fished with harpoons.

They wore hides and rabbit skins in winter.

They used moccasins with high ankle covers for the mountains.

If you wanted to prepare a database based upon this information, you or your students might organize it into the following categories (Pon, 1984):

The Maidus' houses were made of tules. They were round. They looked like bowls.	TRIBE, DWELLING
They lived near or in the Buttes Mountains. The city nearby is called Yuba City. It is in Sutter County. They lived near the Feather River.	LOCATION
They mostly ate acorns. They ate deer and small animals. They fished. They ate seeds.	FOOD
Men hunted and fished. Women gathered acorns and cooked.	JOBS
They danced and made musical instruments with reeds, especially at acorn harvest. They told stories. They had albino deer and acorn ceremonies.	RECREATION

They used mortars and pestles to grind acorns.   TOOLS
They hunted with bows and arrows and fished
    with harpoons.

They wore hides and rabbit skins in winter.   CLOTHING
They used moccasins with high ankle covers
    for the mountains.

The database entry for the information on this one record could be as follows:

TRIBE: Maidu

DWELLING: Made of tules; round; looked like bowls

LOCATION: Buttes Mountains

FOOD: acorns, deer, small animals, fish, seeds

JOBS: women—gathered acorns, cooked; men—hunted, fished

RECREATION: music with reeds, danced, told stories

TOOLS: mortars and pestles to grind corn; bows and arrows; harpoons

CLOTHING: hides and rabbit skins; moccasins with high ankle covers

Searching and Sorting to Draw Conclusions

The students' questioning or inquiry techniques and searching and sorting skills are all important components in the effective instructional use of a database. The more tasks in Figure 5.25 that you can get your students involved in, the more they are going to learn. You will probably want to begin with lower-level questions such as "What animals in this database have four or more legs?" Then begin presenting the students with opportunities to respond to more complex questions. Working with database questions at higher levels will dispel the idea that databases are just rapid alphabetizers and list makers.

Let's practice searching with low-level and high-level questions. Use the file `Which1` to answer the following questions regarding atomic elements:

1. Low level: What is the symbol for carbon?

2. Low level: Which element (identified by atomic number) is missing from this list?

3. Higher level: Predict the melting point of element XX.

4. Higher level: How many electrons should this missing element (XX) have?

Using your `Dinosaurs` database and referring to Table 5.3, let's look at one way you might use this particular database with students. If they are novices in the use of analytical skills, then start out with simple questions such as "What did dinosaurs (in this database) who lived in water have in common?" In other words, begin asking questions that deal with only one field at a time (in this case, `Habitat`). Then work up to two or more categories in one question. Question 5 in Table 5.3 is actually a combination of the previous four questions. In our case, however, we have taken our students through the individual questions leading up to question 4.

Table 5.3
Questioning Strategy for `Dinosaurs` Database

Level of student inquiry skills	Teacher questions	Database field involved	Key word or phrase
Novice	1. What did dinosaurs who lived in water have in common?	Habitat	water
	2. What did dinosaurs who lived on land have in common?	Habitat	land
	3. What did dinosaurs who had claws have in common?	Claws?	yes
	4. What did dinosaurs who did not have claws have in common?	Claws?	no
	5. What did dinosaurs who lived on land and had claws differ from those who lived in water and did not have claws?	Habitat Claws? Habitat Claws?	land yes water no
Intermediate	6. What's the relationship between the habitat of dinosaurs and the presence of claws?		
Advanced	(Students could pose their own higher-level questions.)		

If your students have intermediate analytical skills, you may be able to begin with question 5 or 6. Note that question 6 is actually a rephrasing of question 5.

The following situation and questions could be one of the culminating activities for this database:

The evening news reported that scientists had located the remains of dinosaurs in an area that had been swamp land during the times that dinosaurs lived.

1. What would be a reasonable hypothesis, based upon the database, about the presence of claws on these dinosaurs? Their eating habits?

2. Suppose the next day you heard that these dinosaurs had claws. What else might you conclude about these dinosaurs? What other information would you want before you could be more certain of your answer?

Ideally, students who use databases will learn to identify patterns and trends and to apply, interpret, analyze, synthesize, and evaluate data more effectively and efficiently. How you approach the use of databases may affect the success and enthusiasm of your students.

Prior to using a database with the computer, you should provide your students with a concrete model of a database. This activity can be something as simple as having students write their name, gender, height, age, and favorite song on individual 3" x 5" index cards and then having them perform physical searches and sorts with the cards. The younger the student, the more important it is to provide hands-on experience with a physical database. Then have your students name or describe other databases, such as a telephone book, grade book, encyclopedia, and dictionary.

Students should begin with searching and sorting activities in an existing database. Begin with low-level questions and searching skills. Provide practice with searches requiring the use of one, two, and three search criteria; be sure to include questions requiring the use of AND and OR. As students become more proficient with retrieving factual information, provide them with other experiences using databases. Give them practice in formulating questions, breaking long questions into shorter questions, identifying questions that a particular database can and cannot answer, and distinguishing between irrelevant and relevant data for a given question. In addition, Parker (1986) suggested that students be actively engaged in (1) determining what information is needed to test a hypothesis, (2) reorganizing and synthesizing data to test ideas and find subtle relationships, and (3) drawing logical inferences and appropriate conclusions.

Searching activities will lead directly to sorting, to the drawing of conclusions, and to additional search strategies. There are numerous advantages to having students plan their own databases and fill them. If your students are going to do this, perhaps their first experience with planning a database could be with the entire class or in small groups, before trying to build a database alone. Gradually introduce students to forming search strategies and drawing valid conclusions based on their use of a particular database. Your students are now ready to perform the basic tasks in the preparation and use of a database.

Although it may be appropriate for you as the teacher to demonstrate skills involved in the use of a database, make certain that the students have as much hands-on experience with as many tasks as possible. Otherwise, they may get the idea that databases are for someone else to use.

Integrate the use of databases into your curriculum so that databases are not seen as content separate from the existing curriculum. In this way, students will be learning inquiry skills at the same time that they are learning social studies, science, or language arts.

If you expect students to use higher-level thinking skills, such as analyzing, synthesizing, and evaluating, then the database assignments you give them and the methods you use to evaluate their database skills should include activities that require higher-level thinking skills.

Using Databases in the Content Areas

Databases can be used in the classroom in a wide variety of content areas. As you consider the suggestions that follow, think about the advantages and disadvantages of using a database rather than more traditional sources of information. The computer should be more than an enrichment activity or a change of pace for the students, and the database should be more than a quick alphabetizer or list maker. For each activity, consider what goals can be achieved more effectively when the information is in database format. Can you think of higher-order questions that can be answered by searching or sorting in the database?

LANGUAGE ARTS Database book reports are popular with many teachers. The categories could include title, author, type of book (biography, historical novel, science fiction, mystery, and so forth), setting, main characters, and summary of the events in the book that the student liked best. Once a class has created a book report database, the students in the class can search it for books they might like to read, or they can even print out their own personalized summer reading list. In planning the database, the students may decide to include a field containing descriptive words they might like to use for searching in the completed database, such as *sports, animals, romance, foreign country, tearjerker,* and *suspenseful.* Other classes can add books to this database so that it continues to grow.

A synonym database (Synonyms) can help students write poetry. When students are writing poetry, they often try to think of a synonym that is more descriptive or that has a specific number of syllables. The fields could include synonyms of one syllable, two syllables, and three syllables. For example, synonyms for *eat* are *devour* and *gobble up.* Again, this type of database becomes more valuable as additional records are added to it.

Other uses of databases in the language arts include databases on dialects; diary (class or personal); famous quotations; funny stories; idioms; jokes; legal terms; misspelled words; notes for a research paper; novelists; parts of speech; personalized stories; poetry: author, title, theme, key words; poets; prefixes and suffixes (PreSuff); rules of grammar (Grammar); slang terms; and spelling rules with examples.

SOCIAL STUDIES Demographic information about countries (States) and cultures is a natural for databases, as illustrated in this chapter with African countries and Native American tribes. Facts about famous people, such as English monarchs, U.S. presidents, African American politicians, members of Congress (and their positions on important issues), and inventors and their inventions, can provide a rich learning environment for students at all grade levels and can easily be made into database files. One activity students enjoy with these files is to play a "Who am I?" game. The teacher lists a series of facts or characteristics, and the students search the database to identify the person or persons matching the description.

Additional ideas for databases in the social studies: comparison of cultures; contents of popular music or videos; demography, ethnicity, and income for a community; famous women; neuroses and psychoses; part-time jobs: pay, qualifications; personal characteristics and interests of classmates; school social group characteristics; treaties; TV ads; wars: causes and effects.

SCIENCE Databases about animal groups (Animals) (mammals, birds, insects, snakes); plant groups (flowers, grasses, trees, vegetables); and rocks and minerals are popular supplements to the science curriculum. A database of typical foods, listing their food groups, calories, and nutrients, can be used to make students more aware of eating a balanced diet. In chemistry, students can use a database of the results of chemical reactions to test their hypothesis about the identity of the compounds or elements involved.

Other suggestions for databases in the sciences: amphibians; animal behavior; binary numbers (Binary); chemical compounds; chemical elements (Which1, Which2, Which3, Periodic); chemical reactions; game fish; gems; geological formations; mathematics and science symbols; mathematical formulas; medical terms; metric prefixes; planets; poisonous plants; poisons and antidotes; statistical formulas; trees; vegetables; weather data.

OTHER Additional topics for databases include types of architecture with examples; artists and their works; classical music; famous works of art; great operas; musical instruments; and popular music.

Either students or the teacher can prepare databases based upon historical or constructed accounts of events, such as a murder mystery. All the data, related and unrelated, are placed in the database. Then students can work individually or in groups to solve the mystery based upon the information in the database.

Current events are good material for databases in science and social studies. In addition to providing a database of current events, this technique encourages students to read newspapers and news magazines in addition to viewing news and educational programs on television. A template (`Current`) is located in the `05db` folder in the `Tools` folder.

In the real world, large-scale databases are being used by physicians to make medical diagnoses. These databases include ailments and their symptoms, suggested treatments and their side effects, and ways to confirm diagnoses. Such databases are called **expert systems** because the data in them represent the collected wisdom of many experts in the field. Expert systems have been especially useful in medical schools to train medical students to make accurate diagnoses.

Databases—A Tool for the Teacher

The primary focus of databases in this book is instructional, but databases have applications that may not be related directly to instruction yet may still serve an educational or a personal use. Some of these uses are discussed in the following sections.

STUDENT RECORDS Every teacher maintains certain information about students that can be stored in a database. In addition to students' names, addresses, telephone numbers, and parents' names, a student database might include bus assignments, book numbers, locker assignments with combinations, and participation in special programs. A sample student records database (`Student`) is in the `05db` folder.

INVENTORIES Databases are especially useful for organizing and maintaining inventories. Teachers often need to keep track of books, records, tapes, software, art supplies, laboratory equipment, musical instruments, and so forth. An inventory of these items can be entered into a database and updated throughout the year.

FORM LETTERS **Mail merge** is a feature that allows the user to merge information from a database into a document prepared with the word processor. With

Figure 5.26
Letter to parent

September 6, 1997

<<Title>> <<P-FirstName>> <<P-LastName>>
<<Address>>
<<City>>, <<State>> <<Zip>>

Dear <<Title>> <<P-LastName>>,

We cordially invite you and your <<Relation>>
<<C-FirstName>> to a special party sponsored by
Ms. Moore's third grade classroom. The party will begin
at 6:00 p.m. on Saturday, October 23.

Sincerely,

James Carver

mail merge, you can use names and addresses in a database to create personalized form letters. Assume that you want to send out a letter to the parents or guardians of students in the third-grade classroom to invite them to the school for a special presentation one evening.

- ❑ Start a new word processing document. Put the current date on line 10, flush against the left margin (Figure 5.26).

- ❑ Move the insert cursor down four lines and choose `File/Mail Merge...`. Locate the file `Parents` and open it. This database contains parents' names, addresses, students' names, and the relationship (son or daughter). The `Mail Merge` dialog box will appear on the screen (Figure 5.27).

Figure 5.27
`Mail Merge` dialog box

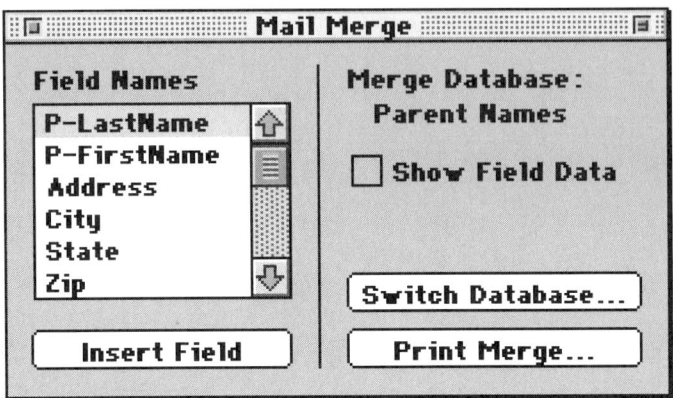

If you want the actual data to be shown on your word processing document rather than the place holders, click the `Show Field Data` *button on the* `Mail Merge` *dialog box.*

❏ Under `Field Names`, scroll down to `Title` and click the `Insert Field` button. This will insert the place holder for the person's title.

❏ Press the space bar once to place a space after the place holder `<<Title>>` in the word processing document.

❏ To insert the place holder for the parent's first name, double-click the field `P-FirstName` under `Field Names`. Press the space bar once to place a space after the place holder `<<P-FirstName>>`.

❏ To insert the place holder for the parent's last name, double-click the field `P-LastName` under `Field Names`. Press **M** <return> or **W** <enter> to go down to the next line.

❏ Use the procedure above to place the address place holder on the second line of the address and the city, state, and zip code on the third line of the address.

❏ Move down two lines and enter `Dear`, followed by a space.

❏ Merge in the place holders `Title` and `P-LastName`, followed by a comma.

❏ Go down to the next line and begin entering the text of the letter as shown in Figure 5.26. In the first sentence, you will need to merge in place holders for `Relation` and `C-FirstName` for the student's first name.

❏ Save your form letter.

❑ To print out a copy of your letter to each parent in the database, click
the `Print Merge...` button.

MAILING LABELS In this section you will prepare a new layout for the `Par-
ent Names` database so that you can print out mailing labels on commercially
prepared labels.

❑ Choose `Layout/New Layout...`.

❑ Choose `Labels` from the `New Layout` dialog box.

❑ Point to `custom` and pull down to `Avery 5160/5260/5660`.

❑ Click `OK`.

❑ The `Set Field Order` dialog box will appear (Figure 5.28).

*Avery 5160/5260/5660 is the
most common label size for
postal service mailers.*

Figure 5.28
`Set Field Order` dialog box

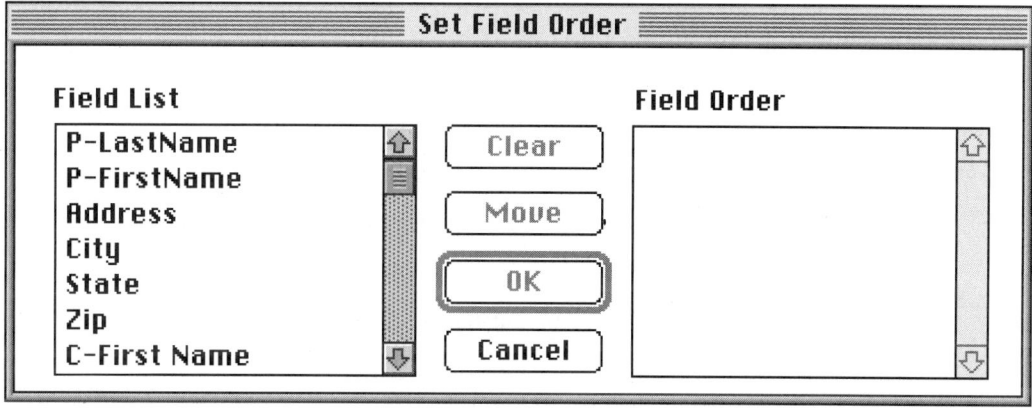

❑ Move the following fields in the indicated order from `Field List`
to `Field Order`: `P-FirstName, P-LastName,
Address, City, State, Zip`.

❑ Then click `OK`.

❑ Check to see that you are in `Page View`.

❑ Choose `Layout/Layout` and arrange your layout like the one in
Figure 5.29.

Figure 5.29
Layout/Layout view of the new layout

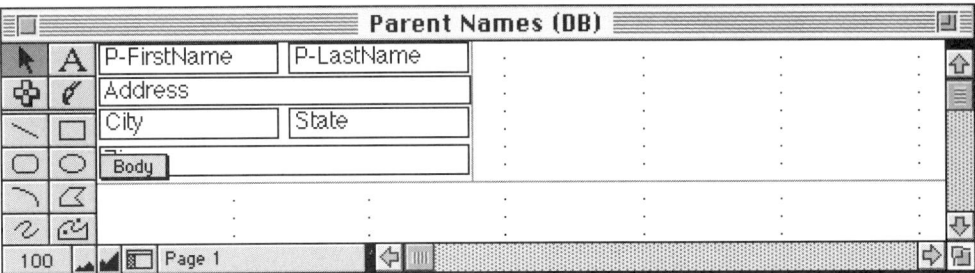

You can also use the Assistant to prepare labels.

Keep the following points in mind as you arrange your layout to ensure that the last name is placed immediately to the right of the first name and the name of the state is placed immediately to the right of the city when you print.

❑ Fields cannot touch each other.

❑ Fields that you want to close up must be exactly the same size; use the `Info` dialog box to resize fields.

❑ Align your fields with `Arrange/Align Objects`.

When you have completed your layout and are in label layout in Browse,

❑ Point to `Layout/Edit Layouts…`.

❑ Choose the label layout you just prepared and click `Modify`.

❑ In the `Layout Info` dialog box under `Slide Objects`, click `Slide objects left` to select it (if it is not already selected).

Now try printing out a copy of your labels.

💾 **LESSON PLANS** A convenient way to organize lesson plans is to keep them in a database. The fields might include objectives, learning activities, materials needed, time required, prerequisite skills, assignments, references, and date last changed. This technique is especially useful for special classroom activities that you would like to be able to do on just a few minutes' notice. A sample lesson plan database (`Planner`) is included in the `05db` folder.

💾 **OTHER INSTRUCTIONAL ACTIVITIES** The teacher can also use a database to introduce a topic or unit. For instance, the database named `Binary` in the `05db` folder could be used to introduce a unit on binary numbers. Or the same procedure can also be used to give a pretest or preassessment, to review or summarize a unit of instruction, or to present a quiz.

A database can be used to present examples of a rule or concept, such as with the `Grammar` template. The template can be modified so that the progress of each student can be monitored for each rule or concept.

Questions and Answers

Q1: **How can I edit the data in a field?**

A: You edit the data in a field the same way you do in a word processing document.

Q2: **How do I change the name of a field?**

A: With the database open, go to `Layout/Define Fields…` and click the name of the field you want to change. Type in the new name; click the `Modify` button; then click `Done`.

Q3: **How can I quickly find out the number of records in a database?**

A: With the Tools menu showing, look just below the Record Book.

Q4: **How can I duplicate a record?**

A: Click on the record you want to duplicate; then choose `Edit/ Duplicate Record`. The duplicate record will now appear as the last record in the database.

Q5: **What's the difference between a text field and a name field?**

A: A text field can contain up to 510 characters (minus 20 characters for each style change) consisting of letters, numbers, or symbols. A name field is meant for a full name. When a name field is sorted, it is sorted by the last word in the field.

Q6: **What is a value list field?**

A: A value list field presents items from a scrolling list with preset choices, or the user can enter other values.

Q7: **What is a Record Info field?**

A: A Record Info field can be used to record the time and date the record was created or modified, or the name of the creator or modifier.

Who? | Andrea |

Andrea	⬆
Sarah	
Chris	⬇

Value list field with three values.

Q8: **Can I remove fields from an existing database?**

A: You can remove fields from a particular layout (but not the database) by pointing to `Layout/Layout,` selecting the field and field name you want to remove, and then choosing `Cut` or `Delete`. If you want to remove a field from the entire database, go to `Layout/Define Fields` and then click on the field you want to remove. Then click `Delete,` answer the question, and click `Done`.

Q9: **Can I insert new fields into an existing database?**

A: Yes. Point to `Layout/Define Fields`, enter the name and type of your field, and then click `Create` and `Done`. The new field will initially show only on the layout that was on the screen when you entered the new field. You can then edit the field from `Layout/ Layout`.

Activities

1. Use the `States` database to answer the following questions:

   a. Can the following questions be answered with this database?

     (1) Which state has the largest population?

     (2) Which states have the highest per capita income?

     (3) Which state is the best place to live?

     (4) Would you gain or lose time in flying from Lincoln, Nebraska, to Atlanta, Georgia?

     (5) Which states were admitted to the Union after 1900?

     (6) What is the relationship between the number of congressional representatives a state has and the state's population?

   b. Identify each question above as either a low-level or a high-level question.

2. All the information in the `Africa` database can be found in a world atlas. Similarly, the information in the `PreSuff` database can be found in a dictionary or a book on etymology. Discuss the advantages and disadvantages of using a computerized database rather than an atlas or a dictionary.

3. Discuss the pros and cons of using a computerized database for the following information as compared with using the traditional format given in parentheses. Consider ease of use and educational value as well as flexibility in accessing the information.

   a. Famous quotations (book of famous quotations).

   b. Equivalent phrases in different foreign languages (several foreign-language phrase books).

   c. Periodic table of elements (printed chart).

   d. Formulas for volume and area (book of mathematical formulas).

   e. Poisons and antidotes (printed chart or first-aid book).

   f. Famous English novelists (English literature textbook).

   g. Values of trigonometric functions (calculator).

   h. Idioms and their meanings (dictionary of idioms).

   i. Wars and their causes and effects (history textbook).

4. Use your `Dinosaurs` database that you created to answer these "Who am I?" questions:

   a. I ate plants, lived on land, and had claws. Who am I?

   b. I lived in the swamps and water and had claws. Who am I?

   c. I ate plants, lived on land, and was not armored. Who am I?

5. One of the criticisms of electronic databases is that they mislead students because not all the information on a topic is in the database. Perform the same searches on your `Dinosaurs` database and the `Dino 80` database; all the dinosaurs in the database you prepared are also in the other database. What do you conclude from this comparison? If your conclusions were different, would this mean that databases are misleading? Does this more accurately represent the real world and the changing nature of a discipline? What are your reactions?

6. The same basic information can be presented in a variety of ways. Compare the following four databases: `Which1`, `Which2`, `Which3`, `Periodic`. What purpose do you think each of these databases serves? How could each one be improved? Justify your responses.

7. Suppose your students are going on a field trip to an art museum to view Impressionist paintings. While they are at the museum, each student will take notes about one of the paintings and its artist. They will also record their personal impressions of the painting. When they return to school, they will enter this information into a class database. Design the template for the database and print out a copy. (The students will take a printout of a blank template with them to the museum for making notes.)

8. Open the file `Africa` and make the following changes:

   a. Go to layout `Multiple Records`. Prepare a new layout of type `Duplicate`. Then go to `Layout/Layout` and delete the following fields from your new layout: `Capital`, `Area`, `Population`, `Languages`, `Religion`.

      In addition, delete the graphic of Africa in the header and replace it with a different graphic. You can either paste the graphic into the header or use `File/Insert`. You must be in `Layout/Layout` to place graphics into the document.

   b. Prepare a new layout of type `Blank`. Then go to `Layout/Layout` and `Layout/Insert Field...` to insert the following fields into your new layout: `Country`, `Life Exp`, `Lit-`

eracy, and `GNP`. When you are satisfied with your new layout, save the database; the new layout will then be saved.

c. Go to layout `Area-Pop-Life-Liter` and then to `Layout/ Layout` to change the format of the following fields to `Commas` with `Options/Field Format…`: `Area, Population`.

d. Prepare two new stored sorts and two new stored searches. Then prepare three new reports. When you are finished, save a copy of the database.

9. Open any existing database and choose `Layout/List`. All the fields of the database will be displayed in column format. Move the mouse cursor over the field names, and the appearance of the cursor will change. If the cursor looks like this ◄▢►, then you can drag it to change the order of the fields. If the cursor looks like this ◄▬►, then you can change the width of the field. What are the advantages of the `List` layout?

10. If you have access to the ClarisWorks education stationery files listed below, explore each one of them to stimulate ideas:

Contact Database

Family and Friends List

Making a Presentation

Recipes

Student Database

Summary

We live in a data-rich world. Any tool that will help us manage this information can make our lives more productive. The use of databases is one way to assist us and our students in the management of information.

Databases are a tool for learning as well as a tool for managing information. Students can use databases to look for relationships, pose and test hypotheses, and draw conclusions. They can use databases for organizing all kinds of data. As they explore the Internet, they may need to redefine their idea of a database. Teachers should plan database activities that are relevant to their students' curriculum and that require students to use higher-order thinking skills.

Key Terms

categories 122

database 120

database application 124

expert systems 156

field 122

file 0

Layout Popup 144

mail merge 156

record 122

report 143

Report Popup 146

search 126

Search Popup 144

sort 125

Sort Popup 145

stored report 146

stored search 145

stored sort 145

References

Hartson, T. (1993). Kid-appeal science projects. *Computers in Education, 20*(6), 33–36.

Hunter, B. (1985). Problem solving with databases. *The Computing Teacher, 12*(8), 20–27.

Lai, K. (1991). Integrating database activities into a primary school curriculum: Instructional procedures and outcomes. *Computers in the Schools, 8*(4), 55–63.

Messing, J., & McLachlan, R. (1994). *History, hypermedia, and the birth of a nation.* (ERIC Document No. ED 388275)

Parker, J. (1986). Tools for thought. *The Computing Teacher, 14*(2), 21–23.

Pon, K. (1984). Databasing in the elementary (and secondary) classroom. *The Computing Teacher, 12*(3), 28–30.

Werking, R. H. (1991). How teachers teach, how students learn: "Doing" history and opening windows. *Library Hi Tech, 9*(3), 83–86, 120.

6

Problem Solving with Spreadsheets

O B J E C T I V E S

Edit existing spreadsheets.

Design a new spreadsheet.

Analyze, interpret, and predict with spreadsheet data.

Prepare graphs with spreadsheet data.

Integrate spreadsheets and graphs into the curriculum.

IN THIS CHAPTER WE are going to work with an application whose primary purpose is to calculate and make predictions on the basis of numerical data. This application is called a **spreadsheet.** At its simplest, a spreadsheet is a grid with letters across the top naming the **columns** and numerals on the left side representing **rows** (Figure 6.1). Traditionally, spreadsheets have been used for preparing budgets and for financial forecasting. However, you can also use a spreadsheet to keep a grade book or to prepare charts, tables, and schedules. The more you learn about spreadsheets, the more ideas you will generate on how to use them. Students can use a spreadsheet to calculate the cost of keeping a pet, to record and analyze data on a science experiment, to observe the impact of a change in one variable on another variable, or to compare statistics.

The original spreadsheet was the accounting ledger. Then, around 1979, someone came up with the idea of an electronic spreadsheet, and VisiCalc (**Visi**ble **Calc**ulator) was born. VisiCalc was the first popular electronic spreadsheet for desktop computers. Since then, other business stand-alone spreadsheets have replaced VisiCalc; these include Lotus, Excel, and Quattro Pro.

Figure 6.1
View of the Concessn Spreadsheet

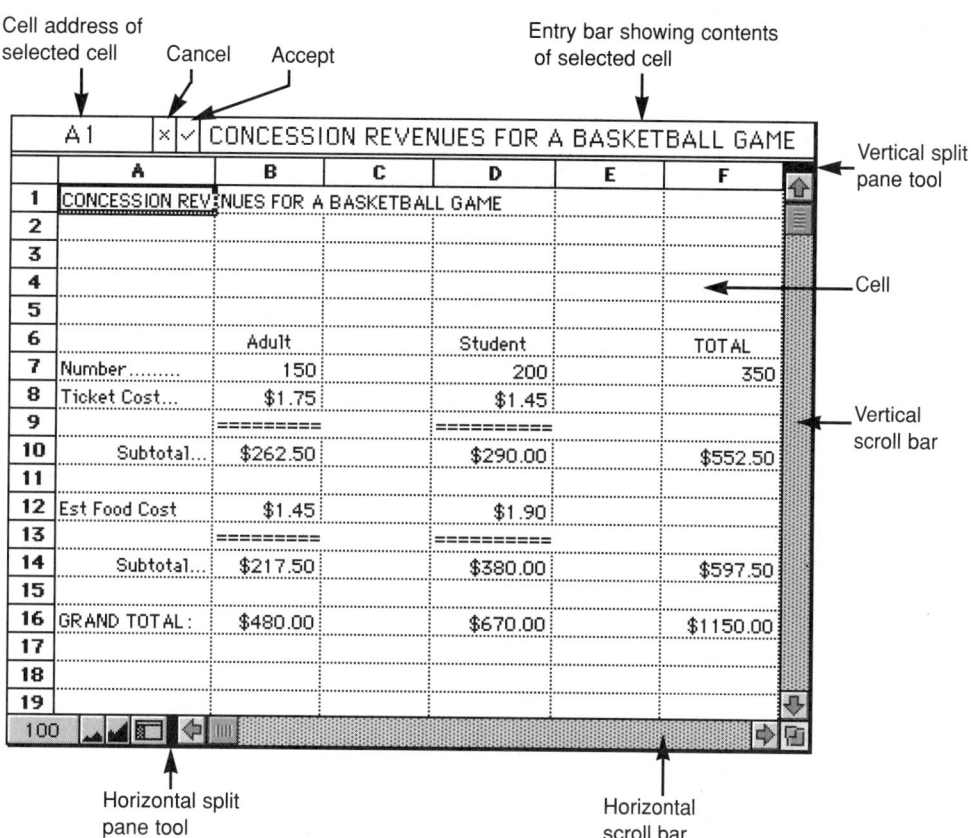

Cell address of selected cell

Cancel

Accept

Entry bar showing contents of selected cell

Vertical split pane tool

Cell

Vertical scroll bar

Horizontal split pane tool

Horizontal scroll bar

	A	B	C	D	E	F
A1	✕ ✓	CONCESSION REVENUES FOR A BASKETBALL GAME				
1	CONCESSION REVENUES FOR A BASKETBALL GAME					
2						
3						
4						
5						
6		Adult		Student		TOTAL
7	Number........	150		200		350
8	Ticket Cost...	$1.75		$1.45		
9		=========		=========		
10	Subtotal...	$262.50		$290.00		$552.50
11						
12	Est Food Cost	$1.45		$1.90		
13		=========		=========		
14	Subtotal...	$217.50		$380.00		$597.50
15						
16	GRAND TOTAL :	$480.00		$670.00		$1150.00
17						
18						
19						

100

Getting Started

By looking at an example of a spreadsheet, we can find out what a spreadsheet is and what it can do. Open the spreadsheet Concessn.

❑ Select File/Open....

❑ Find the 06ss folder and open the file Concessn.

When the file is open, the name of the document (in this case, Untitled, because it was saved as a stationery file) will be displayed at the top of the document window and the current location of the cursor (cell A1) will be displayed in the **entry bar** at the top of the document window (Figure 6.1). This spreadsheet shows the estimated revenues from expected ticket sales and concessions at a women's basketball game.

The intersection at which a column and a row meet is referred to as a **cell.** The address or name of the cell is the name of the column and row where they intersect; cell B7 is where column B and row 7 meet. A cell can contain text, a numeral, or a formula; formulas can create text, numbers, dates, or time results.

....

Finding Your Way Around

Let's go to cell AB500 to get an idea of the potential size of a spreadsheet. The fastest way to get there is to choose

❑ Options/Go To Cell.... Then release the mouse button.

❑ Type the cell name AB500 and click OK.

Use the same technique to return to cell A1. At any given time, you are looking only at a small section of the total spreadsheet. That part of the spreadsheet that contains data is sometimes referred to as a **worksheet.** You can move to other parts of the spreadsheet or worksheet by using the Go To option, or you can click or drag on the scroll bars at the right and bottom of the document window. You can move from cell to cell with the mouse, the arrow keys, the <enter> key, the <tab> key, and **M** the <return> key. Try each of these techniques and compare them.

Recalculating

Place the cursor in cell B7 of the Concessn worksheet by clicking cell B7. Notice that 150 now appears in the entry bar. Let's assume that instead of 150 adults attending the game, 250 attend. Enter 250 into cell B7; notice that what you have just entered (250) does not yet show in cell B7, but it does show in the entry bar at the top of the document window (Figure 6.2). Click the accept button ✓ (at the left of the entry bar), and the change will show in cell B7 (Figure 6.2). Which cells changed? You may want to reenter 150 and 250 several times into cell B7 so that you can actually observe the changes. (Compare Figures 6.1 and 6.2.) You should have found seven additional cells changed (F7, B10, F10, B14, F14, B16, and F16). The values in these seven cells all depend in some way on the value in cell B7. This activity should give you some idea of the power of a spreadsheet for recalculating values. Make changes in other cells and observe the results.

The <tab> key will select the next cell to the right, and **M** the <return> key will select the next cell down. The arrow keys and the <enter> key can be changed in Edit/Preferences.../Spreadsheet to work as follows:

<enter> key
❏ Stay in Current Cell
❏ Move Down One Cell
❏ Move Right One Cell

arrow keys
❏ Selects Another Cell
❏ Move Insertion Point in Entry Bar

Figure 6.2
When the number in cell B7 is changed to 250, all the cells related to B7 are automatically changed when you click the accept button

B7	×✓	250			
	A	**B**	**C**	**D**	**E**	**F**
1	CONCESSION REVENUES FOR A BASKETBALL GAME					
2						
3						
4						
5						
6		Adult		Student		TOTAL
7	Number.......	250		200		450
8	Ticket Cost...	$1.75		$1.45		
9		========		=========		
10	Subtotal...	$437.50		$290.00		$727.50
11						
12	Est Food Cost	$1.45		$1.90		
13		========		=========		
14	Subtotal...	$362.50		$380.00		$742.50
15						
16	GRAND TOTAL:	$800.00		$670.00		$1470.00
17						
18						
19						

100

Now open the file Fastfood (Figure 6.3). This document shows the cost of various items at three different fast-food restaurants. Click cell B2. In place of $1.85, enter the numeral 2 (without the $ symbol) and click the accept button. What happened? At least two things: the 2 you entered is now $2.00 in cell B2, and the total changed from $3.40 to $3.55 in cell B7 (Figure 6.4). The spreadsheet recalculated the total when you entered a different price for the hamburger at Matt's. How was the spreadsheet able to do that? Place the cursor in cell B7. Now look in the entry bar near the top of the document, and you will see =SUM(B2..B5). SUM is a **function** whose purpose is to calculate the total or sum of something; in this case, the something is the contents of cells B2 through B5, the cost of a meal at Matt's. The .. is read as "through"; the **range** B2 through B5 is the **argument** or **parameter list** for this particular calculation.

Figure 6.3
The Fastfood worksheet showing prices of four items at three restaurants

B2	x	✓	1.85		
	A	**B**	**C**	**D**	**E**
1	Menu	Matt's	Mary's	Chris's	MyPlace
2	Hamburger	$1.85	$1.65	$1.30	
3	Fr fries	$0.45	$0.40	$0.55	
4	Shake	$0.75	$0.80	$0.75	
5	Cookie	$0.35	$0.29	$0.65	
6		========	========	========	========
7	Total:	$3.40	$3.14	$3.25	
8					
9					

Figure 6.4
When you enter 2 into cell B2 and accept it, the total in cell B7 changes

B7	x	✓	=SUM(B2..B5)		
	A	**B**	**C**	**D**	**E**
2	Hamburger	$2.00	$1.65	$1.30	
3	Fr fries	$0.45	$0.40	$0.55	
4	Shake	$0.75	$0.80	$0.75	
5	Cookie	$0.35	$0.29	$0.65	
6		========	========	========	========
7	Total:	$3.55	$3.14	$3.25	
8					
9					
10					

Types of Spreadsheet Data

Cells can be blank, or they can contain any of the following:

1. Text, which is used for descriptive information that does not require calculation.

2. Values, which can be

❏ Numbers.

❏ Formulas. For instance, =B2 + B3 would be a formula to calculate the cost of a hamburger and fries at Matt's. What is the purpose of the = symbol? It indicates that what follows it is to be treated as a value and not to be treated as text. If you entered the letter B first, it would be treated as text, so by beginning with the = symbol, the entry is treated as a value unless the numeral is enclosed in quotes. Therefore, if you wanted to treat the numeral 5 as text, you would enter ="5" into the cell.

❏ Functions, which are built-in formulas. A function will have the following format: the symbol = followed by the name of the function and any parameters or arguments. For example, in cell B7 of the Fastfood worksheet, the =SUM(B2..B5) function sums cells B2 through cell B5; B2..B5 is the argument or parameter list.

The following operators (Table 6.1) can be used in combination with numbers, formulas, and functions.

Table 6.1
Operators and Order of Precedence in ClarisWorks

Operator	Name	Type	Level of Precedence
%	division	—	7
^	exponentiation	numeric	6
−, +	minus, plus	sign	5
*, /	multiplication, division	numeric	4
+, −	addition, subtraction	numeric	3
&	concatenation	text	2
=, >, >=, <, <=, <>	equal to, greater than, greater than or equal to, less than, less than or equal to, is not equal to	relational	1

Formatting Cell Contents

You can format (change the appearance of) the contents of a single cell, row, column, or **block** of cells.

❑ Place the cursor in cell E2 of the Fastfood worksheet.

❑ Enter 1 for $1; click the accept button. How does the appearance of the entry compare to cells B2, C2, and D2? These three cells are formatted for dollar entries, but E2 is not. In a moment, we will change the format of E2.

❑ For now, enter .33 in cell E3, .55 in cell E4, and .4 into E5. (Notice that you can accept what you enter with the accept button or you can accept what you enter *and* move down one cell with the Ⓜ <return> key, the Ⓦ <enter> key, or an arrow key.)

What's the total bill for the meal at MyPlace? Your worksheet cannot calculate the total until you give it instructions.

❑ Enter the SUM function into cell E7 by placing the cursor on cell E7; then choose

You can use the <enter> key to move down to the next cell only if it has been set to move down one cell in Edit/Preferences....

Figure 6.5

To paste a function, choose `Edit/Paste Function...`

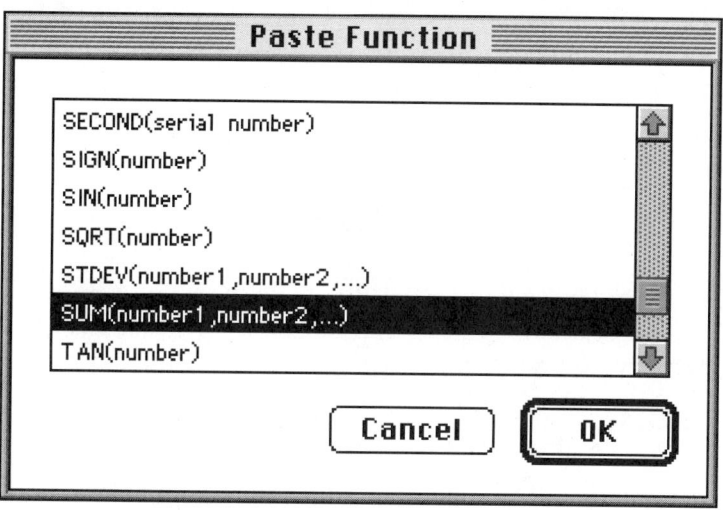

❏ `Edit/Paste Function...` and release the mouse button (Figure 6.5).

❏ Scroll down the list of functions until you see `SUM(number1,number2,...)` and click the name once to highlight it.

❏ Click `OK`. (The parameter list inside the parentheses is a prompt to the user as to what should be placed there. In the next step, you will replace the information in the parameter list with the range that you want there.)

❏ Highlight the parameter list (everything inside the parentheses but *not* the parentheses); then point to cell E2, depress the mouse button, drag to cell E5, and release the mouse button.

❏ Click the accept button, and the appropriate cost will be shown in cell E7.

Now let's format our new prices for `MyPlace` so that they have the dollar signs and two decimal places similar to the other food places. We are going to be selecting choices from menus. Compare this procedure with going to a supermarket; depending upon what you want, you go to a certain section of the supermarket. It's the same way with formatting the contents of a cell, a row, a column, or a section of a spreadsheet. Look at Table 6.2 for the choices you have in formatting a worksheet. The table will be more meaningful if we actually change the format of a section of a worksheet.

Functions don't have to be selected from the alphabetical function list under `Edit/ Paste Function...`. You can type in the name of the function; however, you must begin with the = symbol, and you must be exact in typing in the function name and parameters. In the case of the SUM function, you could also have highlighted the range E3 through E7 (one cell beyond the range), then on the Shortcuts palette clicked the button ∑ .

Table 6.2
Formatting Choices for a ClarisWorks Spreadsheet

Number	Format/ Number:	General	Currency	Percent	Scientific	Fixed	Commas	Negatives in ()	Precision
Date	Format/ Number:	9/6/97	Sep 6, 1997		September 6, 1997	Tue, Sep 6, 1997		Tuesday, September 6, 1997	
Time	Format:	5:30 PM		5:30:20 PM	17:30	17:30:20			
Text	Format:	Font	Size	Style	Text Color	Alignment			
Protection	Options/Protect Cells								
Width/ Height	Format/Column Width Format/Row Height								
Borders	Format/ Border:	Outline	Right	Top	Left	Bottom			

❏ We are interested in formatting the block of cells from E2 through E7, so point to cell E2, depress the mouse button, and drag through cell E7 (Figure 6.6). To format this block of cells, choose `Format/Number.../Currency/OK`.

❏ Now let's reposition the title in cell E1 to the right side of the cell; click cell E1 and choose `Format/Alignment/Right` so the label is flush against the right margin.

Figure 6.6
The range E2..E7 has been selected and can now be formatted

E2	×	✓	1

	A	**B**	**C**	**D**	**E**
1	Menu	Matt's	Mary's	Chris's	MyPlace
2	Hamburger	$2.00	$1.65	$1.30	1
3	Fr fries	$0.45	$0.40	$0.55	0.33
4	Shake	$0.75	$0.80	$0.75	0.55
5	Cookie	$0.35	$0.29	$0.65	0.4
6		=========	=========	=========	========
7	Total:	$3.55	$3.14	$3.25	2.28
8					
9					

100

Saving and Printing a Spreadsheet

To save your spreadsheet on your own data disk,

- ❏ Insert your data disk.

- ❏ Choose `File/Save As...` and release the mouse button. Locate your data disk.

- ❏ Enter the name you want to give the file and click the `Save` button.

To print your document, first be sure that you are at a computer connected to a printer that is on. There are basically two approaches you can take to printing your spreadsheet. In the simplest approach, choose `File/Print...`
Ⓜ `Print` or Ⓦ `OK` and release the mouse button. That's it . . . almost!

This approach may be the simplest, but if there are data in distant cells, you may end up printing several pages of blank worksheet. Therefore, a more cautious approach would be to

- ❏ Highlight the range you want to print.

- ❏ Choose `Options/Set Print Range...` (Figure 6.7).

- ❏ You can set the range so the printer will print all cells with data or print the cell range indicated (if you highlighted text). You can also manually enter a different range.

If you are prompted to print the column and row headers and the cell grid, you can either ignore the prompts or respond to them.

Figure 6.7
`Print Range` dialog box to select the print range in a spreadsheet

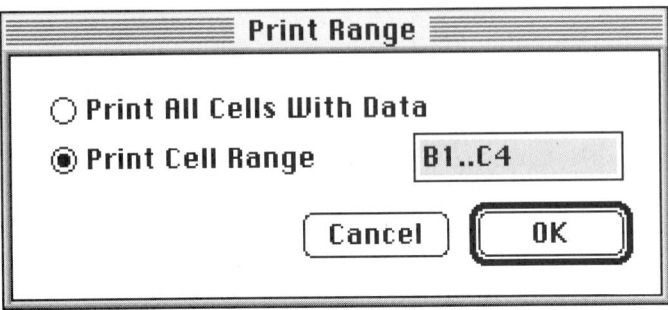

Entering Data into a Template

💾 Open the spreadsheet file `Grades`. This document is a template of a very simple grade book. What appears on your screen is shown in Figure 6.8. Don't be concerned about the #NUM! messages on the template; they will disappear when you enter your grades. Enter the names and grades from Table 6.3 into the template, beginning with row 2 of the worksheet.

Figure 6.8
Empty grade book using the file `Grades`

A2	x ✓							
A	**B**	**C**	**D**	**E**	**F**	**G**	**H**	
1 Name	Quiz1	Quiz2	Quiz3	Quiz4	Quiz5	Quiz6	Average	
2							#NUM!	
3							#NUM!	
4							#NUM!	
5							#NUM!	
6							#NUM!	
7							#NUM!	
8							#NUM!	
9							#NUM!	
10							#NUM!	
11							#NUM!	
12							#NUM!	
13							#NUM!	
14							#NUM!	
15							#NUM!	
16							#NUM!	
17 AVERAGE:	#NUM!	#NUM!	#NUM!	#NUM!	#NUM!	#NUM!		
18								
19								
100								

Table 6.3

Grades to Enter into a Grades Spreadsheet

Name	Quiz1	Quiz2	Quiz3	Quiz4
Andrea	94	88	89	97
Sarah	95	94	89	92
Chris	97	80	82	83
Matt	80	86	91	89
Emilie	93	84	90	90
Erin	92	85	91	92
Jason	91	86	93	91.
Ashley	90	83	94	89
Clinton	98	81	89	92
Lisa	89	86	89	94
Sherry	92	83	88	90
Jamie	89	92	85	88

After you have entered the data from Table 6.3 into your worksheet, see if you can answer the following questions:

1. What's the class average for quiz 1?

2. What does Chris need to make on quiz 5 to have an 88 average?

3. What's the lowest that Matt can make on quiz 5 and still have an 85 average?

4. You made an error in recording quiz 2 for Ashley; she actually made an 87. What effect does that have on her average? On the class average for quiz 2? (See Figure 6.9.)

Save this document (File/Save) with the name MyGrades on your data disk for a later activity with graphing.

Figure 6.9
Completed grade book

	A1	× ✓	Name					
	A	**B**	**C**	**D**	**E**	**F**	**G**	**H**
1	Name	Quiz1	Quiz2	Quiz3	Quiz4	Quiz5	Quiz6	Average
2	Andrea	94	88	89	97			92.00%
3	Sarah	95	94	89	92			92.50%
4	Chris	97	80	82	83			85.50%
5	Matt	80	86	91	89			86.50%
6	Emilie	93	84	90	90			89.25%
7	Erin	92	85	91	92			90.00%
8	Jason	91	86	93	91			90.25%
9	Ashley	90	83	94	89			89.00%
10	Clinton	98	81	89	92			90.00%
11	Lisa	89	86	89	94			89.50%
12	Sherry	92	83	88	90			88.25%
13	Jamie	89	92	85	88			88.50%
14								#NUM!
15								#NUM!
16								#NUM!
17	AVERAGE:	91.67	85.67	89.17	90.58	#NUM!	#NUM!	
18								
19								

| 100 |

Sorting

Suppose we want to print out the average grade of each student in your
MyGrades document in order from the highest to the lowest average. We will
be arranging the worksheet data according to the information in column H. The
block of cells we want to work with ranges from cell A2 through H13.

❑ Select the range A2 through H13.

❑ Choose Calculate/Sort... and enter H2 as the first order key
(Figure 6.10).

❑ To the right of the first order key, click the circle to the left of this icon
○ **l.** so that it looks like ◉ **l.** .

❑ Click OK.

*An alternate way to sort is to
highlight the same range and,
on the Shortcuts palette, click
the button.*

Figure 6.10
Sorting by the data in column H

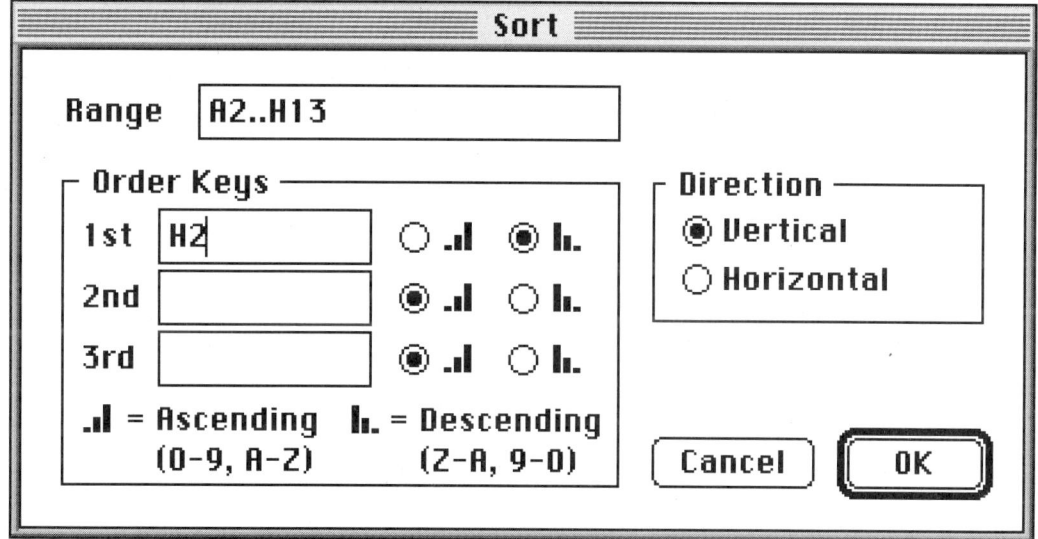

Your grades are now sorted by student average. What student has the highest
average? What student has the lowest average? How could you sort this worksheet alphabetically by name? When you are planning your own spreadsheet,
you should enter last name first or use a separate column for last names. Then
you will be able to sort alphabetically by last name.

Starting a New Spreadsheet

We are going to prepare a budget for a school club. To start a new spreadsheet, choose `File/New.../Spreadsheet/OK`. Figure 6.11 shows how the final worksheet will appear after you have entered the data. Figure 6.12 shows the formulas and functions as you will enter them. Before entering the data, study Figure 6.13. Placing the information on a paper worksheet is a good way to start planning a spreadsheet. You can enter a row at a time or a column at a time; that's your choice. We suggest that you enter the contents of column A first. Click cell A2 and begin typing the information into the cells of column A.

Figure 6.11
When you have entered the data for September, your `Club` spreadsheet should look like this figure

		September
Income:		
	Dues	150
	Other	200
	Prev Bal	0
Total Income		350
Expenses:		
	Awards	0
	Fld trip	137
	Drinks	50
	Snacks	72
	Other	0
Total Expenses		259
Balance		91

Figure 6.12
Your completed `Club` spreadsheet with the formulas showing (`Options/Display…/Formulas`)

```
Income:
        Dues                    150
        Other                   200
        Prev Bal     =B18

Total Income         =SUM(C3..C5)

Expenses:
        Awards                    0
        Fld trip                137
        Drinks                   50
        Snacks                   72
        Other                     0

Total Expenses       =SUM(C10..C14)

Balance              =C7-C16
```

Figure 6.13
Worksheet of a club's budget

	A	B	C	D	E	F
1			September			
2	Income:					
3		Dues	150			
4		Other	200			
5		Prev Bal	=B18			
6						
7	Total Income		=SUM(C3..C5)			
8						
9	Expenses:					
10		Awards	0			
11		Fld trip	137			
12		Drinks	50			
13		Snacks	72			
14		Other	0			
15						
16	Total Expenses		=SUM(C10..C14)			
17						
18	Balance		=C7-C16			
19						
20						
21						

With four exceptions, all the entries in Figure 6.13 are label entries. The four exceptions are cells C5, C7, C16, and C18. Can you tell from the function name or the formula what they do? The formula in cell C5 carries forward the balance from cell B18 (which in this case is blank); C7 sums the contents of cells C3 through C5; cell C16 sums the contents of cells C10 through C14; cell C18 subtracts the expenses (cell C16) from the income (cell C7). Now complete the task of entering all of the information from Figure 6.13 except for the expenses for the month of September. You will enter that amount later.

Copying Formulas and Functions

Usually, you would want to keep a budget for each month. We can do this very easily by copying the formulas in a column and pasting them into other columns.

COPYING FROM ONE COLUMN TO A SECOND COLUMN Suppose that you want to include the month of October in this budget. You will need to copy the contents of cells C5, C7, C16, and C18. You could perform this by copying and pasting each cell individually. A more efficient technique is to copy the range from C5 (the first cell in column C with a formula/function) through C18. To do this,

❑ Depress the mouse button on cell C5 and drag to C18.

❑ Choose `Edit/Copy` to copy the data.

❑ Click on cell D5; then choose `Edit/Paste` to paste the data into column D.

Type `October` in cell D1 at the top of the new column.

COPYING FROM ONE COLUMN TO SEVERAL COLUMNS Suppose at this point that you decide that you need to have a budget though June. You now need to copy the contents of column D (cells D5 through D18) so the information can be pasted to columns E through L.

❑ Depress the mouse button on cell D5 and drag to D18 to highlight the range to be copied; then drag to your right until columns D through L are highlighted.

❑ Choose `Calculate/Fill Right`.

You have now entered the labels, formulas, and functions. Now you need to enter the amounts for income and expenses for September. So enter the numerals for cells C3, C4, C11, C12, and C13 as shown in Figure 6.13. In addition, enter the following data for October:

Dues: 20

Other: 70

Awards: 50

Fld Trips: 170

Drinks: 40

Snacks: 95

Other: 10

Do you remember how to format cells? If not, refer back to the section titled "Formatting Cell Contents." You may need to make the columns wider, in addition to making the dollar format change. You should make those changes now. Were there any surprises? **M** What do the parentheses in D18 mean?

One way to widen a column is to place the cursor in the column whose width you want to change. Then choose `Format/Column Width…` *. Enter the width you want (72 is the default width) and click* `OK`*.*

Editing

We all make mistakes or change our minds. Fortunately, there is a way to edit cell contents in a spreadsheet. One way is to highlight the area we want to change, then either cut or clear the data and reenter it. Another way is to click the cell you want to edit; the contents will appear in the entry bar. Then you can use standard editing techniques to make the changes you need to make in the entry bar.

You can also insert (`Calculate/Insert Cells...`) or remove (`Calculate/Delete Cells...`) columns and rows. If you want to insert columns, remember that the new column will be inserted to the left of the column where the cursor is located. With new rows, the new row will be inserted above the row where the cursor is located. When you cut or clear cells, rows, or columns, the empty cells will still be there; they are not deleted, just the data in them.

Questions and Answers

Q1:   How can I examine the formulas and functions I have entered into a spreadsheet?

A: There are two ways to view formulas and functions. You already know one way: when you click on a cell, the contents of the cell are shown in the entry bar at the top of the document window. In the case of formulas and functions, the formula or function is shown in the entry bar and the results of the formula or function are shown in the cell. The second way is to choose `Options/Display.../Formula/OK`. This method shows all the formulas and functions in the worksheet in the cells. Use the same technique (`Options/Display.../Formula/ OK`) to switch back to the results (rather than the formulas) showing in the cells.

Q2:   Is it possible to keep titles on the screen as you move around in the worksheet?

A: To keep titles (that are in columns) on the screen, choose the Vertical Split Pane tool just above the scroll bar on the right (Figure 6.1). When the cursor appears as a double-headed arrow, point and drag down to a point just below the title names on the worksheet. To keep titles on the left side of a document, use the same basic technique with the Horizontal Split Pane tool at the bottom left of the document window. If you save your document with the new panes you have just arranged on your worksheet, the next time you open the document, the panes will still be there (Figure 6.14).

Figure 6.14
Split panes in a document window

		1	× ✓				
n / d Fraction	TENTHS ======	HUNDREDTHS ===========	THOUSANDTHS ===========	10,000ths ============	100,000ths ============
1 / 2	0.5	0.50	0.500	0.5000	0.50000
2 / 4	0.5	0.50	0.500	0.5000	0.50000
1 / 6	0.2	0.17	0.167	0.1667	0.16667
3 / 8	0.4	0.38	0.375	0.3750	0.37500
1 / 9	0.1	0.11	0.111	0.1111	0.11111
9 / 1	9.0	9.00	9.000	9.0000	9.00000
/	#DIV/0!	#DIV/0!	#DIV/0!	#DIV/0!	#DIV/0!
/	#DIV/0!	#DIV/0!	#DIV/0!	#DIV/0!	#DIV/0!
/	#DIV/0!	#DIV/0!	#DIV/0!	#DIV/0!	#DIV/0!
/	#DIV/0!	#DIV/0!	#DIV/0!	#DIV/0!	#DIV/0!
/	#DIV/0!	#DIV/0!	#DIV/0!	#DIV/0!	#DIV/0!
/	#DIV/0!	#DIV/0!	#DIV/0!	#DIV/0!	#DIV/0!
/	#DIV/0!	#DIV/0!	#DIV/0!	#DIV/0!	#DIV/0!
/	#DIV/0!	#DIV/0!	#DIV/0!	#DIV/0!	#DIV/0!
/	#DIV/0!	#DIV/0!	#DIV/0!	#DIV/0!	#DIV/0!

100

Q3: **Can you have two distant parts of a worksheet on the screen at the same time?**

A: By using the technique described in the previous answer, you can have distant parts of the worksheet on the screen at the same time. To scroll around in a particular window, simply use the scroll bars in that particular window. Another way is to use either **M** View or **W** Window/New View and then resize and position the new window.

Q4: **What other built-in functions are there in ClarisWorks?**

A: ClarisWorks has functions that fall into eight categories (Appendix F): business and financial, date and time, information, logical, numeric, statistical, text, and trigonometric.

Q5: **Sometimes I need a different column width. How do you change the width of the columns?**

A: There are two ways to change the column width. You have already widened a column with `Format/Column Width…`. Another way is to place the mouse pointer on the right margin of the column whose width you want to change. When the cursor changes to a vertical line with arrows on either side, then point and drag to the left to narrow the column or drag to the right to widen the column.

Q6: **Can I make the rows taller?**

A: You can change the height of the rows by using the same basic technique described previously for resizing columns.

Q7: **Can I place data from a word processing document into a spreadsheet?**

A: Yes, you can; assume that you have three columns of data that have been separated by using the <tab> key:

Jerria   Knox City   1940

Gloria   Sunset   1932

One way to place the data into a spreadsheet is to copy the data and then paste (or drag/drop) it into your spreadsheet. Another way is to save your word processing data as a text file. When you save it, choose the ClarisWorks button (Figure 6.15A or B) and pull down the menu list until you see the word `Text`. Replace `Untitled` with the name you want to use and then save the file. To open the file in spreadsheet format, use `File/Open…`. When the dialog box appears (Figure 6.16A or B), from `Document Type` choose `Spreadsheet`. When you see the name of the text file, open it. The data will appear in spreadsheet format.

If you want to use the data from your text file in an existing spreadsheet, click on the cell where you want to insert the data and choose `File/Insert…`. When the name of the text file appears, click the Insert button.

Ⓜ **Figure 6.15A**
Point to the ClarisWorks button and pull down to Text

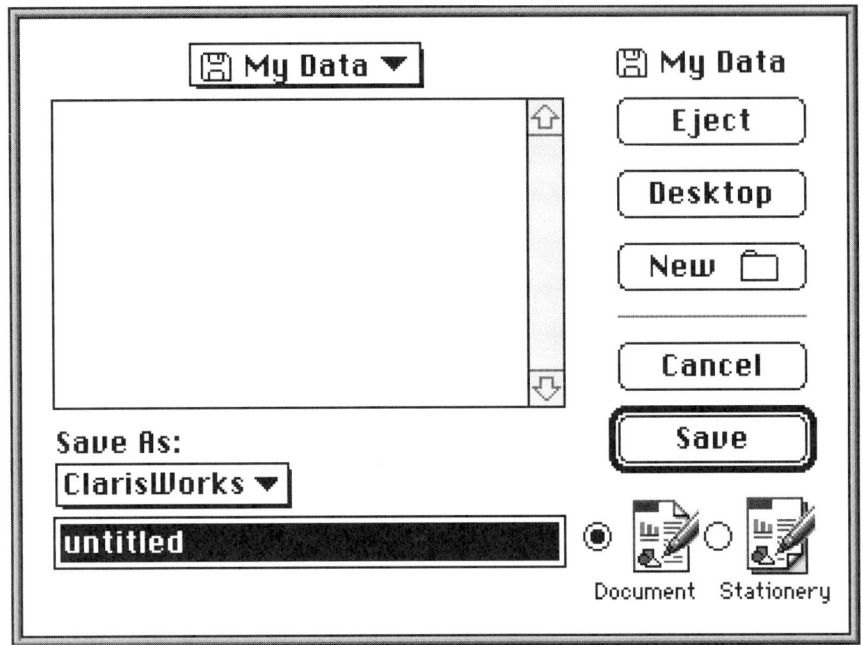

Ⓦ **Figure 6.15B**
Pull down to Text File, DOS (*.txt)

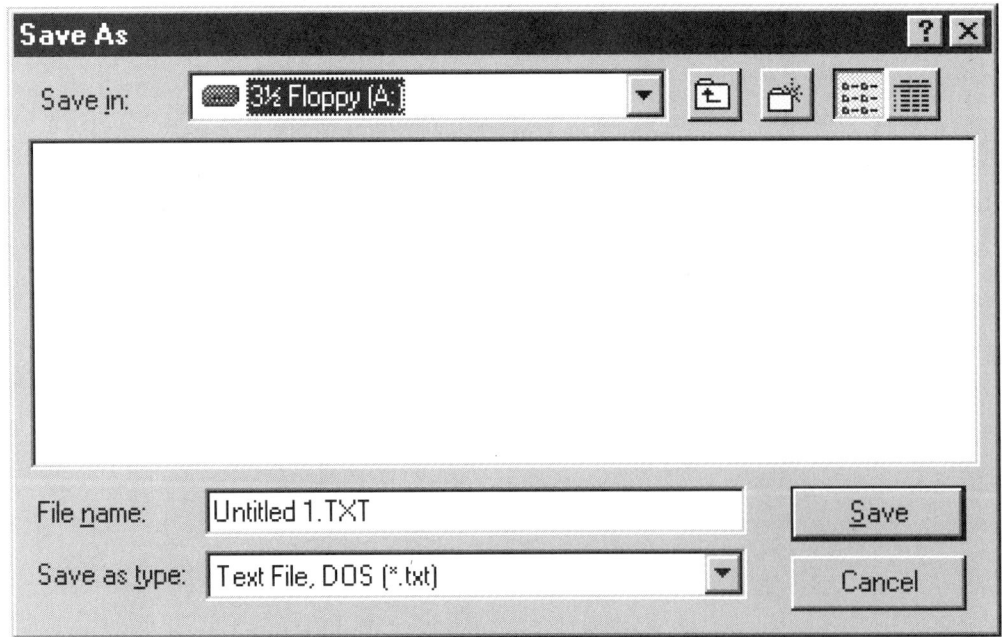

M **Figure 6.16A**
Point to the Document Type button and choose Spreadsheet

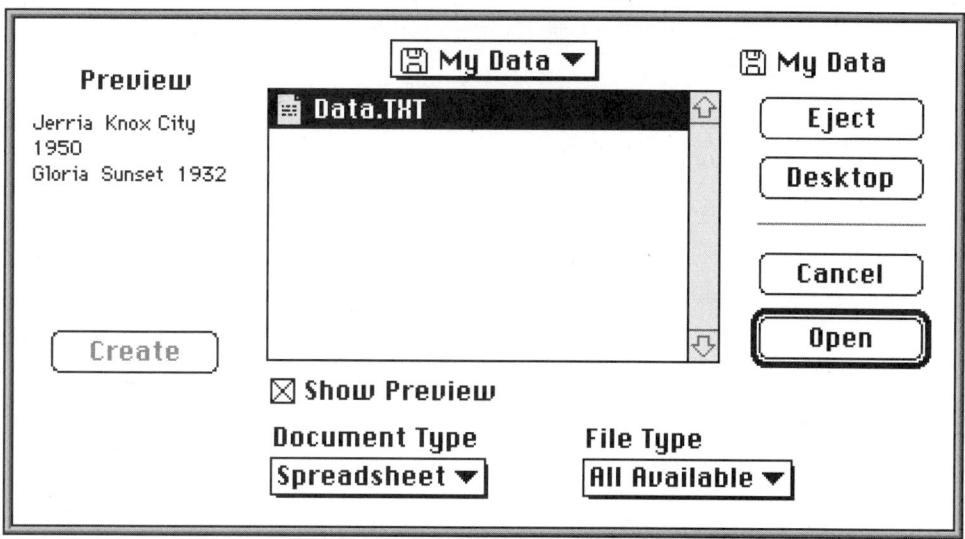

W **Figure 6.16B**
Point to the Document Type and choose Spreadsheet

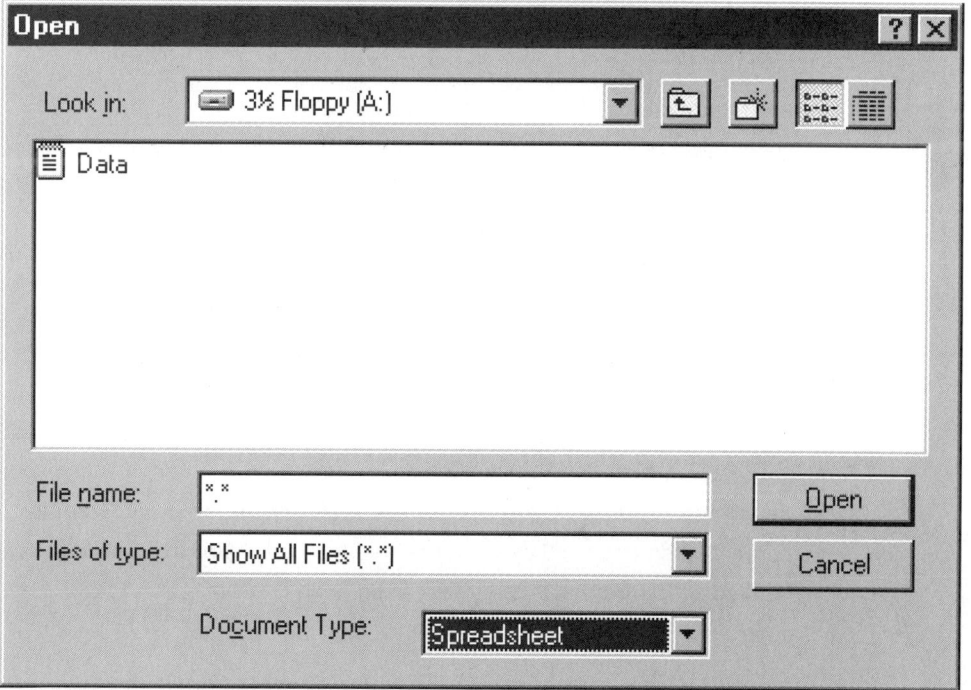

Q8: **Can I get spreadsheet data into a word processing document?**

A: You could copy the spreadsheet data and then paste them directly into the word processing document. However, you may have formatting problems with the data. A more satisfactory technique is to

❏ **M** Click `View/Show Tools…` or **W** `Window/Show Tools…` to place the Tools menu on the screen in the word processing document.

❏ Then click the spreadsheet tool ✚.

❏ Choose a place in the word processing document where you want to place a spreadsheet frame.

❏ With the mouse button down, drag diagonally to place a spreadsheet frame on the document. Now you can either copy/paste the data from the original spreadsheet or insert from the spreadsheet file.

Q9: **I have spreadsheets from Excel. Do I have to reenter the data to use them in ClarisWorks?**

A: You should be able to open an Excel spreadsheet. Go to `File/Open…`; then, under `Document Type`, pull down to `Spreadsheet`.

Q10: **I don't like dealing with all the extra rows and columns in my spreadsheet. Can I adjust the actual size of the spreadsheet?**

A: You can adjust the spreadsheet size with `Format/Document…`; in the dialog box that appears, you can change the number of columns across and rows down. In a spreadsheet frame, the default number of rows is 50 and columns is 10. If you want to change the number of rows and columns in a spreadsheet frame, select the frame (or click somewhere inside the frame), choose **M** `View` or **W** `Window/ Open Frame`, and then choose `Format/Document…` and make the appropriate changes.

Q11: **How can I protect certain parts of my worksheet?**

A: To protect an area of your worksheet, highlight the area you want to protect; then choose `Options/Lock Cells`. If you need to edit locked cells, you must first unlock them (with `Options/Unlock Cells`).

Q12: **Can I drag and drop data in a spreadsheet as I can with text and graphics?**

A: Yes, you can highlight and then drag and drop parts of a spreadsheet. Be careful, though, because you can really create havoc with your formulas if you are careless. Practice with a spreadsheet that has a backup copy.

Q13: **Can I use color in a spreadsheet?**

A: Yes. Highlight the area in your spreadsheet you want to color; then choose the fill color and patterns that you want. You can also insert graphics into your spreadsheet.

Q14: **Can I link spreadsheets as I can link text frames?**

A: Yes, you can link spreadsheet frames but not spreadsheet documents. To make a frame linkable, select the frame and choose `Options/ Frame Links`. Then you use the same procedure as you would with a text frame to link the spreadsheet frames. You cannot link a spreadsheet frame to a text frame.

Q15: **Sometimes I change a number in a spreadsheet that should make a difference in a formula and nothing happens. What's wrong?**

A: Someone has probably turned off the `Auto Calc` feature (under `Calculate`). If this is the case, you can recalculate by choosing `Calculate/Calculate Now,` or you can turn on the `Auto Calc` feature (under `Calculate`).

In the Classroom

Spreadsheets can be used to supplement instruction in a variety of content areas. However, one question you will have to answer is whether the task can be accomplished more effectively or efficiently with a spreadsheet, a database, or some other format. The use of a spreadsheet should be considered more than just a quick way to prepare a budget or a grade book. It should be an integral part of the learning activities in a content area. Can you think of ways that a spreadsheet could enhance learning in your classroom? Compare some of your ideas for using a spreadsheet with the following suggestions:

❑ Calculate the expense of keeping a pet.

❑ Calculate how much water and money are wasted by a dripping faucet.

❑ Calculate the time to travel to various cities by various means of transportation.

❑ Compare various characteristics of American cities, such as average temperature and population.

❑ Compare the climates of several countries.

❑ Assess the quality of life in various cities or countries by working with such characteristics as annual snowfall, population, crime rate, and income.

❑ Survey and determine the average of selected characteristics of a school class, neighborhood, or family.

❑ Survey local part-time job opportunities and determine average salaries.

❑ Develop a budget for the first Thanksgiving.

❑ Compare prices of selected food items in several stores.

❑ Convert Fahrenheit to Celsius temperatures.

❑ Explore relationships in the chemical periodic chart.

❑ Compare characteristics of the major groups of vertebrates or invertebrates.

Science

Since spreadsheets can calculate, they are especially useful when studying any science topic involving numerical calculations. The file `Planet` (Figure 6.17) calculates the length of time necessary to travel in a spaceship from Earth to another planet, and the age of the student when he or she arrives at the destination. A student enters his or her age and then clicks the accept button ✓ . This activity is a good way of beginning or culminating a unit on space or teaching the concept of very large numbers in mathematics. As an extension to this activity, students could insert another column that computes their age when they return to Earth. They could replace the planets with stars by finding information in the library or on the Internet about the names and distances from Earth of various stars in our galaxy. If they have studied units of measurement in mathematics, they could compute the time of arrival in days and change the miles to kilometers. This activity could also serve as the stimulus for a class discussion about issues related to interplanetary travel. If it takes more than five years to travel to Pluto and back, what would you do with all that time? What provisions should be made for exercise and relaxation? Would you feel cramped in a small space for such a long time? For language arts, students could write a creative story about their experience on such a trip. They could enhance their report by placing the story into page layout format with graphics they find on the Internet.

Figure 6.17
Contents of the file `Planet`

A5	x ✓	0				
YOUR AGE	PLANET	DISTANCE FROM EARTH (miles)	SPACESHIP SPEED (mph)	TIME OF ARRIVAL (months)	TIME OF ARRIVAL (years)	AGE AT ARRIVAL (years)
====	============	==============	==========	===========	==========	=========
0.0	Venus	16,000,000	150,000	0.15	0.01	0.01
0.0	Mars	49,000,000	150,000	0.45	0.04	0.04
0.0	Mercury	57,000,000	150,000	0.52	0.04	0.04
0.0	Jupiter	390,000,000	150,000	3.56	0.30	0.30
0.0	Saturn	793,000,000	150,000	7.24	0.60	0.60
0.0	Uranus	1,690,000,000	150,000	15.43	1.29	1.29
0.0	Neptune	2,701,000,000	150,000	24.67	2.06	2.06
0.0	Pluto	3,577,000,000	150,000	32.67	2.72	2.72

Type in your age and press the <return> or <enter> key.

| 100 | | | |

The files `Seesaw` and `Machines` help students to understand the relationship among fulcrum, effort arm, and resistance arm. With `Seesaw`, they discover the relationship between distance and weight for two people sitting at opposite ends of a seesaw. With `Machines`, they calculate the mechanical advantage of a variety of common tools such as scissors, tin snips, and hedge clippers.

· ·

Mathematics

The file `Mystery` illustrates how students can use a spreadsheet to reinforce their recognition of number patterns. The spreadsheet contains numbers in column A. The first student performs some operation with the numbers from column A, and the second student tries to determine the number pattern. For instance, the first student might enter the following formula in column B: `=A2*2+1` and then use `Calculate/Fill Down…` to fill in column B using the formula entered. The other student tries to discover the relationship between the two columns of numbers without looking at the formula. As a variation, a student could be asked to give a number *not* currently found in column A and the corresponding number for column B.

Since spreadsheets can perform complex calculations quickly, they are an excellent tool for solving mathematical problems using a guess-and-test strategy to look for patterns. The following problem is an example (Figure 6.18):

> Squares with side X are cut from a rectangular sheet of metal with sides A and B. An open box (a box without a top) is made from the resulting sheet. Our task is to find the length of X that will give the maximum volume for the box.

Figure 6.18
The box problem: What size squares should be cut from each corner of a sheet of metal in order to make an open box that has the maximum volume?

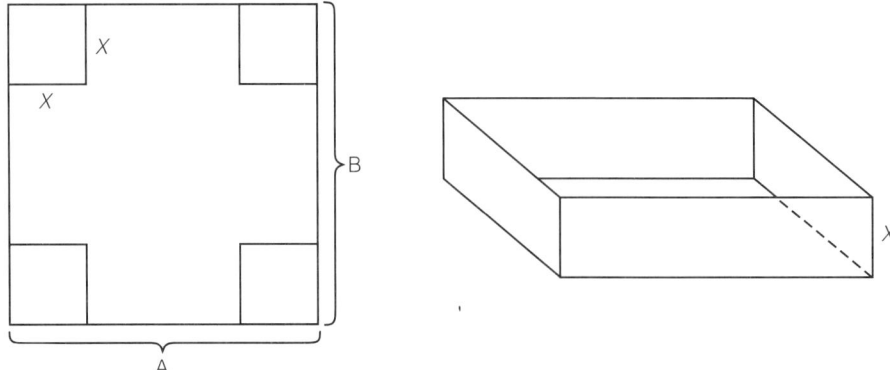

💾 Open the file Box. Assuming that sides *A* and *B* are both 20 units, try different values for *X* (the side of the cutout square) until you find the maximum volume of the box. (To keep a record of your results, write down in a table the values for *A*, *B*, and *X* that you find.) You probably tried only integer values for *X*, so now try to find what value of *X*, to the nearest tenth, will maximize the volume of the box. Repeat these steps, assuming that sides *A* and *B* are both 30 instead of 20. Does the same value of *X* (the inside of the cutout square) still produce the largest volume? Now change the values for *A* and *B* to 40 instead of 30. How did the value of *X* change? Try to be specific; for example, "When sides *A* and *B* are both increased by 10, the side of the cutout square is increased by. . . ." Continue experimenting until you can make a statement about how, given the lengths *A* and *B*, you can find the length of the side of the cutout that produces the largest box.

💾 A guess-and-test strategy can also be used to solve word problems in algebra. The file Mixture (Figure 6.19) illustrates this point (Arganbright, 1984). A student enters different numbers in cell B8 as trial values for the percentage of Coffee 1, then observes the effect on the cost of the blend in cell E12. Students could also use the problem's algebraic solution to design the spreadsheet themselves so that they can study the relationship between the cost of the two coffees and the proportions in the final blend.

Figure 6.19
Contents of the file Mixture

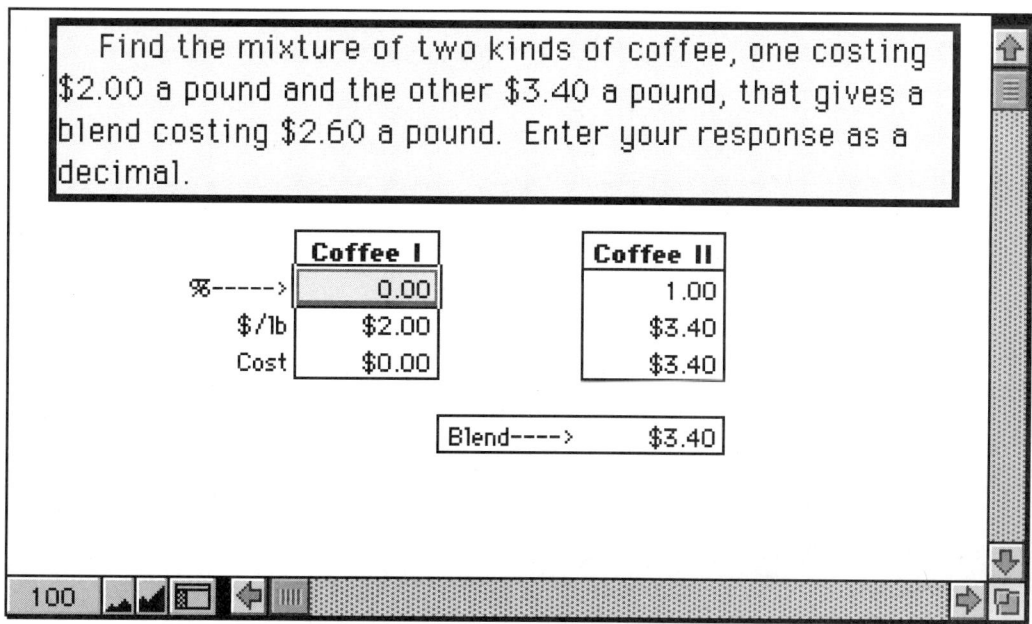

Spreadsheets can also be used in mathematics to study such problems as how much water and money are wasted by a dripping faucet, to calculate slope, to determine the time necessary to travel to various locations, and to convert non-metric units of measurement to metric units.

Social Studies

Spreadsheets are useful and appropriate when studying social studies—for example, a comparison of various characteristics of major cities: annual rainfall, population, crime rates, and the like; an assessment of the quality of life in two or more localities by comparing items such as annual income, manufacturing, and cost of housing; and a determination of average local salaries and job opportunities for part-time employment.

The file `States` is a spreadsheet that students can use to look for relationships among states' characteristics, such as population, area, number of electoral votes, and date of statehood. If you wanted students to compare the ten least populous states with the ten most populous states, the worksheet could be arranged to exclude the other states in this analysis. Either the teacher or the students can do the arranging, depending upon the objectives of the teacher and the skill level of the students. How do these two groups of states differ? In what way are they the same? What categories are directly related to the number of congressional representatives? If you ran for president, which states might you concentrate your efforts on? Why?

The spreadsheet `States` resembles in many ways the database `States`. What are the advantages of using a spreadsheet for this type of data?

Other

Originally, spreadsheets were used for financial planning and budgeting. You can use spreadsheets to prepare balance sheets, budgets, and other financial statements in order to calculate the rise and fall of stocks on the stock market, and to prepare financial projections in business and economics classes.

If you want to analyze numerical data, an electronic spreadsheet is usually the most effective tool to use. Students do not have to understand everything about spreadsheets before they begin to use them in the classroom. For instance, using the file `Planet` requires no particular spreadsheet skills on the part of the students. They simply enter their age and click the accept button ✓ , and the spreadsheet displays how long it would take them to travel by spaceship from

Earth to each of the other planets and how old they would be when they arrived (Figure 6.17).

Students should use filled spreadsheets or templates before learning how to create their own. For example, in the beginning of this chapter you modified the `Fastfood` spreadsheet by adding the formulas and prices for a new restaurant. Then, once you understood how spreadsheets could be used, you started the `Club` spreadsheet.

If you want students to be able to prepare or modify spreadsheets, one of the best ways to get them started is to give them a blank paper worksheet. In the `06ss` folder is the spreadsheet `Wrksheet` containing a blank worksheet form that you can print for your students to use. The document was prepared to be printed sideways, so you need to choose the appropriate option from `File/Page Setup...`.

Before you attempt to integrate the use of spreadsheets to teach other subject matter, you should be certain that the students have the necessary skills for the particular task to be performed with the spreadsheet. For instance, if the task involves the use of the operators >, +, −, /, then the students need to have some practice with them before using them within the context of another lesson. One way students can practice writing spreadsheet formulas is with an activity such as the one in the spreadsheet `Practice`. By learning new spreadsheet skills first, students can avoid the confusion of learning two different things (use of the spreadsheet and the subject-matter content) at the same time.

Graphing

Open the file `Weather`. We are going to prepare a bar graph for the high, low, and average temperatures for March 1 and March 2, so we are interested in the block of cells represented by A1 through C3 of this spreadsheet.

❑ Highlight the block A1 through C3 (Figure 6.20).

❑ Choose `Options/Make Chart...`, and the `Chart Options` dialog box will appear on the screen (Figure 6.21).

❑ Since `Bar` is already selected, click `OK`.

❑ Your new bar graph will be displayed on the screen (Figure 6.22).

Figure 6.20
The block A1 through C3 has been highlighted

A1	×✓	Date					
	A	**B**	**C**	**D**	**E**	**F**	**G**
1	Date	Hi	Lo	Avg	Normal		
2	Mar 1	44	35	40	30		
3	Mar 2	51	31	41	31		
4	Mar 3	45	28	37	31		
5	Mar 4	49	27	38	31		
6	Mar 5	50	38	44	32		
7	Mar 6	67	30	48	32		
8	Mar 7	73	46	60	32		
9	Mar 8	72	36	57	33		
10	Mar 9	36	25	31	33		
11	Mar 10	29	22	26	34		
12	Mar 11	35	22	28	34		
13	Mar 12	45	22	34	34		
14	Mar 13	37	31	34	35		
15	Mar 14	41	33	37	35		
16	Mar 15	38	32	35	35		
17	Mar 16	44	31	38	36		
18	Mar 17	46	31	39	36		

100

Figure 6.21
Gallery section of the Chart Options dialog box

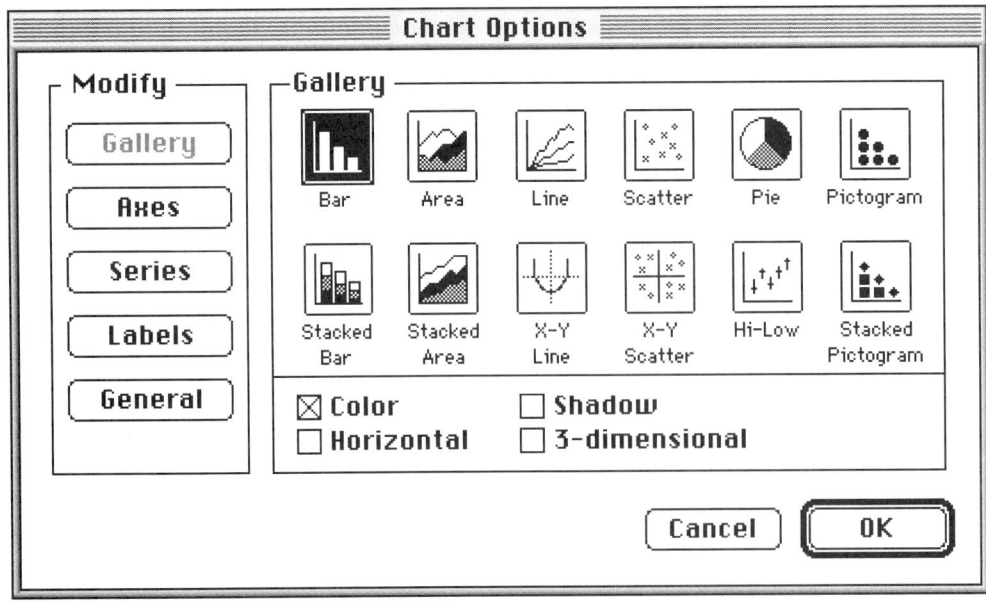

Figure 6.22
Graph representing the data you selected

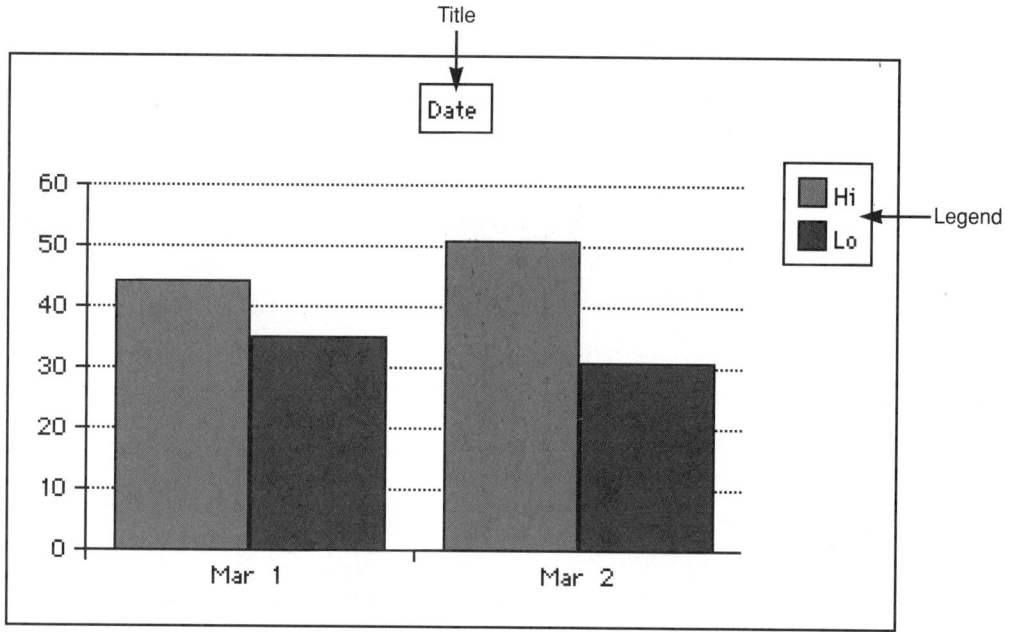

Compare your graph with Figure 6.22 and with the data in the range A1..C3 of the spreadsheet.

With the graph showing on the screen, let's explore some of the things we can do with your graph. Click inside the legend (Figure 6.22) but not on a legend item. Now experiment with Fill Color, Pattern, and Gradient; also try Pen Color, Pattern, and Width.

Now select one of the items inside the legend (either Hi or Lo) by clicking the square just to the left of the name of the item. Now explore the same tools on the Tools panel as you did when you selected the legend, but this time observe the changes in the graph itself. Now select the title and explore the same characteristics with the title.

When you have finished experimenting with the title and the legend, double-click on the graph in an area outside of the title and the legend. The Gallery section of the Chart Options dialog box should appear on the screen (Figure 6.21).

If your graph is not similar to that in Figure 6.22, try selecting the appropriate block of the spreadsheet again and then choose Options/Make Chart... OK.

When you click the legend, it appears like this.

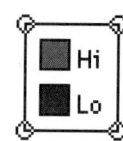

Let's change our bar graph to a line graph by

❏ Clicking Line 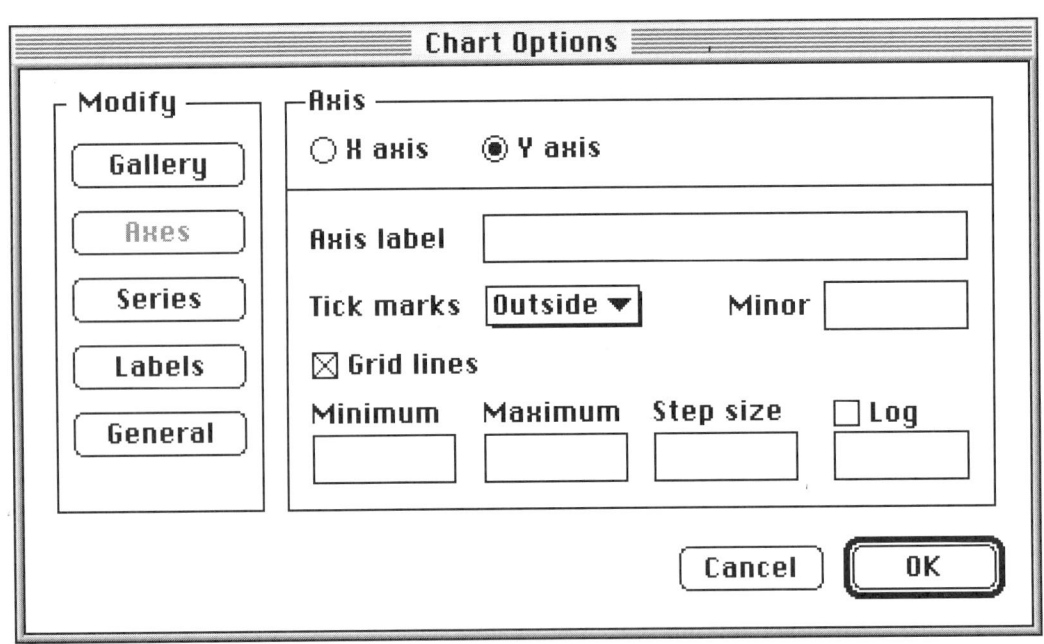.

❏ Click OK to observe the appearance of our graph.

❏ Return to the Chart Options dialog box by double-clicking the graph. Now try Scatter ⊡, Pictogram ⊞, and Hi-Low ⊡ graphs. Which of these types do you prefer to show the differences between days on the high-low temperatures?

Return to the Chart Options dialog box. Experiment with the following options located at the bottom of the dialog box (Figure 6.21): Color, Shadow, Horizontal, 3-dimensional.

Now we are going to explore the axes of the graph.

❏ Return to the Chart Options dialog box.

❏ Click the Axes button at the left (Figure 6.23).

An alternate way to get to the axes from the graph is to double-click either the X or Y axis.

Figure 6.23
Axes section of the Chart Options dialog box

Chart Options

Modify
- Gallery
- Axes
- Series
- Labels
- General

Axis
○ X axis   ◉ Y axis

Axis label [＿＿＿＿＿＿＿]

Tick marks [Outside ▼]   Minor [＿＿＿]

☒ Grid lines

Minimum [＿＿]   Maximum [＿＿]   Step size [＿＿]   ☐ Log [＿＿]

[Cancel] [OK]

❏ Explore the following: name the X and Y axes, change the position of the tick marks, turn grid lines on and off, enter values for minimum and maximum, enter a step size. For the Y axis, alternate between 1 and 5 for minor. What happens to the graph?

Now let's explore the Series section of Chart Options (Figure 6.24). In this section, you can edit one or all of the items in the legend. You can select from among five displays, and you can select placement of data labels from among nine positions. If you display data as a line graph, you can select from among various colors and twelve symbols.

Figure 6.24
Series section of the Chart Options dialog box

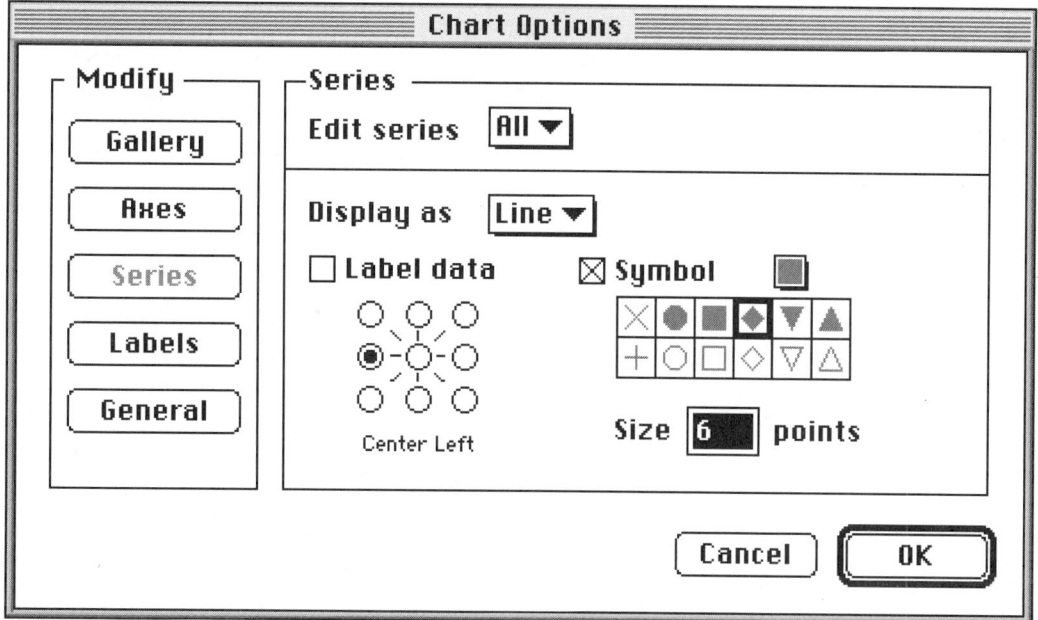

Explore the Labels section (Figure 6.25). In this section, you can replace or edit the title, display it as vertical or horizontal, and select shadow, in addition to placing the title on the graph. For the legend, you can choose horizontal, choose shadow, and choose to use a symbol.

Figure 6.25
Labels section of the Chart Options dialog box

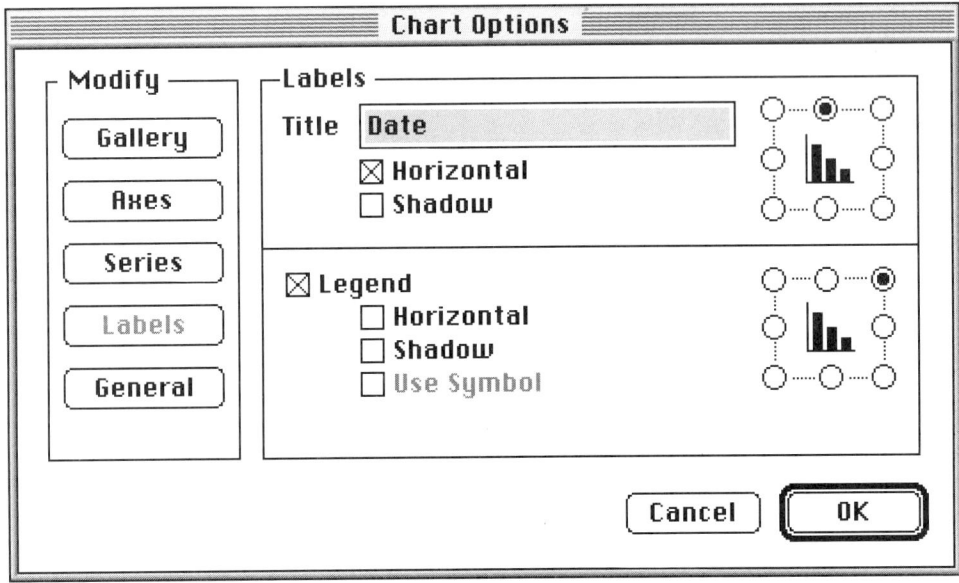

In the General section (Figure 6.26), you can edit your graph range, select series in rows or columns, and choose to use numbers as labels. Experiment and observe the results on your graph.

Figure 6.26
General section of the Chart Options dialog box

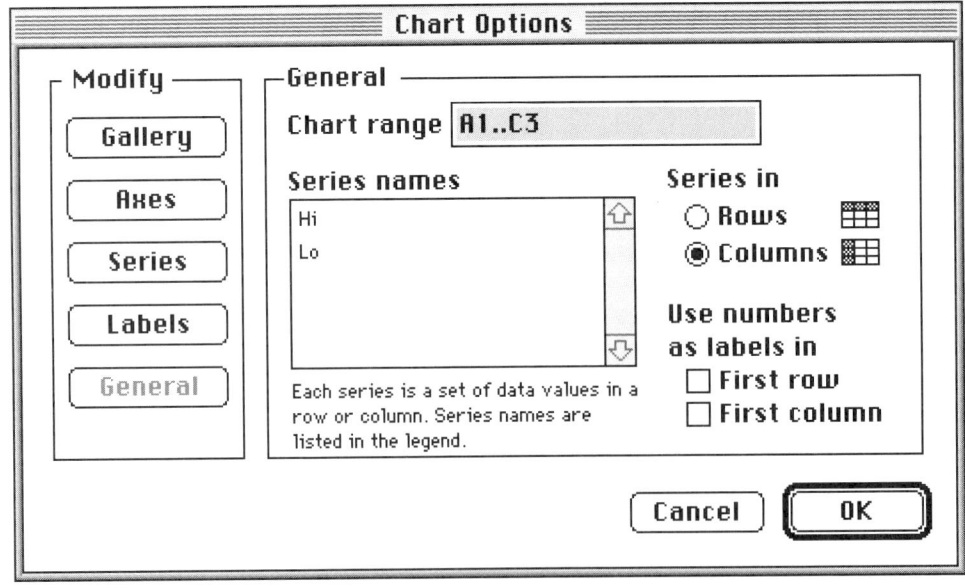

Data Sources

When working with spreadsheets, students can collect data or information themselves, they can enter the data supplied by someone else, or they can analyze an entire worksheet prepared by someone else. Whether you, your students, or a third party collects or enters the data in a spreadsheet, you need to ask the following questions about the data: Are the data accurate? Are they up-to-date? Has appropriate credit been given to the source of the information? Was the spreadsheet checked for accuracy after the data were entered?

If you are faced with the question of finding data for the social sciences, remember that the following sources are particularly rich in information: *Historical Statistics of the U.S., Statistical Abstracts of the U.S., U.S. Census,* and *World Almanac.*

Spreadsheets as a Tool for the Teacher

Spreadsheets are very useful in the curriculum, but they also can be used as management tools for teachers. They simplify such tasks as preparing a budget for a field trip, keeping records of classroom lunch money, preparing classroom handouts or visuals, making estimates of expenses and income, balancing budgets, keeping inventories, managing sports or recreational activities, preparing a grade book, constructing tables or charts, and organizing information for reports.

Activities

1. Use the file `Concessn` to answer the following questions.

   a. To reach a financial goal of $1200, what would have to be charged for an adult ticket (assuming everything else remains the same)?

   b. If student ticket prices were changed to $1.75, what would the expected total income be?

   c. What would the expected income be from food purchased by students if only 160 students attended?

2. Use the file `Fastfood`.
   Insert a new row between `Fr Fries` and `Shake`, and call it `Onion Rng`. The following prices are being charged: Matt's = $.50; Mary's = $.45; Chris's = $.47. What's the most that MyPlace could charge for this meal and still be the least expensive place to eat of these four places?

3. Use the file `States`.

   a. For each state, one electoral vote represents how many people? Are electoral votes truly proportional to the population? Which five states gain the most advantage in electoral votes? Which states have the least advantage?

   b. Insert a new column for density (population divided by area). Is there a relationship between the date a state entered the Union and its population density? What explanation can you offer for this? Which states are exceptions?

4. Plan a spreadsheet for keeping an inventory of objects related to your classroom. Include individual costs and total costs of the inventory.

5. What spreadsheet skills would your students need to participate in the following activities?

   a. Collecting data on root words.

   b. Entering the formula for determining average monthly rainfall, given the rainfall amounts for each of the twelve months.

   c. Starting a new spreadsheet.

   d. Estimating the number of students who would need to attend a school activity (file `Concessn`) to generate $2000 (cell F16) if 125 adults attended.

6. Would you use a database or a spreadsheet for the following activities? Why?

 a. Estimating the expenses and income involved in producing a school yearbook.

 b. Keeping a record of the names and addresses of teachers in a professional organization.

 c. Determining the relationship between the density of a chemical element and its electron configuration.

 d. Keeping a record of the types and locations of wild flowers found in your city.

 e. Collecting data on the types, origin, and meaning of slang terms used by students.

7. Open the file you saved under the name of MyGrades. Prepare a series of graphs that best represent the range of scores.

8. If you have access to the following ClarisWorks education stationery files, explore them for ideas to use:

 ESL Project

 Event Budget

 Event Schedule

 Gradebook

 Home Budget

 In Case of Emergency

 Writing Styles Matrix

Summary

Spreadsheets can be useful for a wide range of instructional activities. Traditional uses include budgeting and keeping inventories; other uses include the manipulation of data in a variety of content areas. With spreadsheets, you can use a "what-if" technique by changing values in selected cells to determine the effect on other cells.

Key Terms

argument 172	parameter list 172
block 174	range 172
cell 170	row 168
column 168	spreadsheet 168
entry bar 170	values 173
function 172	worksheet 170

References

Abramovich, S., & Levin, I. (1993). Microcomputer-based discovering and testing of combinatorial identities. *Journal of Computers in Mathematics and Science Teaching, 12,* 331–353.

Arganbright, D. (1984). Mathematical applications of an electronic spreadsheet. In V. Hansen & M. Zweng (Eds.), *Computers in mathematics education (1984 yearbook).* Reston, VA: National Council of Teachers of Mathematics.

Bombaugh, R. (1993). A body of data. *Science Scope, 17,* 54–57.

Carter, C. R. (1992). Implementing the curriculum and evaluation standards: Using technology in graphing. *Mathematics Teacher, 85,* 118–121.

Cashian, P. (1990). Spreadsheet investigations in economics teaching. *Economics, 26*(2), 73–84.

Chesebrough, D. (1991). Using computers: Chances are. . . . *Learning, 19*(9), 56.

————. (1993). Using computers: Candy calculations. *Learning, 21*(7), 40.

Choat, D. (1991). See the U.S.A! Teaching with technology—Curriculum connection. *Instructor, 101*(2), 75–77.

Crisci, G. (1992). Play the market—Curriculum connection. *Instructor, 101*(5), 68–69.

Drago, P. (1993). Teaching with spreadsheets: An example from heat transfer. *Physics Teacher, 31,* 316–317.

Kellogg, D. (1993). Spreadsheet circuitry. *Science Teacher, 60*(8), 21–23.

Masalski, W. J. (1990). *How to use the spreadsheet as a tool in the secondary school mathematics classroom.* (ERIC Document No. ED 328427)

McCallister, C. (1991). *Phi, Rho, P. M., Biserial and Point-Biserial "r": A review of linkages.* (ERIC Document No. ED 336394)

Misovich, M., & Biasca, K. (1991). The power of spreadsheets. *Chemical Engineering Education, 25,* 46–49, 52.

Neuwirth, E. (1996). Spreadsheets: Helpful for understanding mathematical structures. *Mathematics Teacher, 89,* 252–254.

Pinter-Lucke, C. (1992). Rootfinding with a spreadsheet in pre-calculus. *Journal of Computers in Mathematics and Science Teaching, 11,* 85–93.

Ramondetta, J. (1992). Using computers. Learning from lunchroom trash. *Learning, 20*(8), 59.

Rudnicki, R. (1990). Using spreadsheets in population geography classes. *Journal of Geography, 89*(3), 118–122.

Sgroi, R. J. (1992). Systematizing trial and error using spreadsheets. *Arithmetic Teacher, 39*(7), 8–12.

Timmons, T. (1991). A numerical and graphical approach to Taylor Polynomials using an electronic spreadsheet. *PRIMUS, 1,* 95–102.

Wilson, M. R., & Krapel, C. M. (1995). Power on! Exploring mean, median, and mode with a spreadsheet. *Mathematics Teaching in the Middle School, 1,* 490–495.

7

Hypermedia
Working with HyperStudio

O B J E C T I V E S

Construct and edit instructional hypermedia stacks.

Construct instructional activities with HyperStudio.

Integrate hypermedia activities into the curriculum.

What Is Hypermedia?

In the 1960s, Ted Nelson coined the term **hypertext** to refer to an environment in which we can electronically browse among large chunks of text, following tangents reflecting our interests and jumping from one chunk to another, bypassing information that does not interest us (Turner & Land, 1994). The term **hypermedia** is frequently used to extend that concept to include additional forms of media such as graphics, music, animation, and digitized audio and video. HyperCard was the first hypermedia application to gain widespread attention on a desktop computer when Apple Computer began shipping it with every Macintosh in 1987. Since then, there has been a variety of hypermedia applications on a range of computer platforms. One of those products is HyperStudio, which is available for both the MacOS and Windows operating systems. HyperStudio is easy enough to use so that both teachers and students can learn to use it.

The Potential of Hypermedia

Marchionini (1977) identified three features of hypermedia with great potential for instruction. One of these features is that a hypermedia system allows vast chunks of information in a variety of media to be stored compactly and accessed easily and quickly. Another feature is that hypermedia presents an enabling rather than a directive environment. Learners can have a high degree of control by choosing to follow suggested paths through information or to blaze new paths through the information consistent with their objectives and abilities. A third feature of hypermedia is that it has the potential to alter the roles of teaching and learning by enabling students to develop unique interpretations and insights that they can share with teachers and other students (Turner & Land, 1994).

Basic Units in HyperStudio

HyperStudio files are called **stacks.** You can think of a stack as a collection of cards or screens in which the individual cards can theoretically be viewed in any order. The basic building block in HyperStudio is the **card,** which is what you see when you are looking at the computer screen with a stack open. A card can contain text, graphics, or other objects. Text is presented in a **field,** which in HyperStudio is referred to as a text object. A field can be restricted to a single card, or it can be grouped so that the field can be shared with other cards. Another type of object in HyperStudio is the **button.** A button is a hot spot on a card and can be activated with a mouse click. Cards can be linked to other cards by means of a button. A graphic can also be treated as an object in HyperStudio, which means that it can perform some of the same operations as a button.

To begin, you need to go to `Preferences` *under* `Edit`. *If* `Show card number with stack name` *under* `Stack preferences` *is not selected with an X or a* ✔ *, click it until it is selected; then the card number will appear with the name of the stack on your screen. In addition, under* `Program preferences,` *click* `I'm an experienced HyperStudio user,` *even if you aren't! If you don't, some of the items we refer to in our instructions will not appear on your screen!*

🅜 *When you are prompted about using the same size card and number of colors, answer* `Yes` *unless you want to make changes.*

🅦 *When you are prompted about using the same size card, answer* `Yes` *unless you want to make changes.*

Starting a New Stack

Your first stack is going to be a short stack with eight cards on common symbols and information found on a weather map (Figure 7.1). The first card of the stack will show a weather map.

❑ Start the application HyperStudio.

❑ Point to `File/New Stack` to start your new stack. A blank card will appear on the screen.

❑ To add clip art (the weather map) to the page, choose `File/Add Clip Art...`. Find the graphic file `US_Map` and open it.

❑ Choose one of the following: 🅜 double-click the Lasso tool to select the graphic or 🅦 use the Lasso or the Selection tool to select the graphic. Then click `OK`.

If you hold the mouse button down, you can adjust the position of the graphic on the card.

You're now ready to add a transparent button to cover the card so that the user can click anywhere on the screen to go to the next card.

❑ Choose `Objects/Add a Button...`. The `Button Appearance` dialog box (Figure 7.2) will appear on the screen.

Figure 7.1
Storyboard for a stack on weather symbols

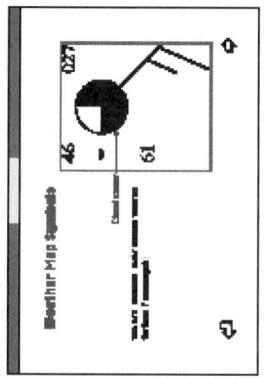

Cards: THREE through EIGHT -
grouped with Card TWO
•Graphic Object - Weather
  Symbols
•Fields - Title: Weather Map
  Symbols
•Buttons (Show through from
  Card Two)
  •Go to next card
  •Return to
•Buttons (Show only on the
  card; not group)
  •Cloud Cover, Dew Point,
   Pressure, Temperature,
   Weather, Wind Bard
     ❑ Transparent
     ❑ Show name
     ❑ No click

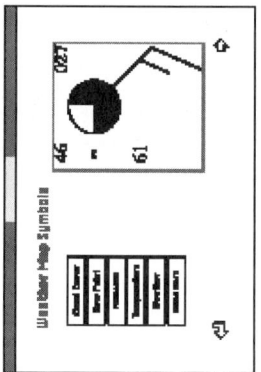

Card: TWO
•Graphic Object - Weather
  Symbols
•Fields - Title: Weather Map
  Symbols
•Buttons (8)
•Go to next card
     ❑ Group
     ❑ Transparent
     ❑ Goes to next card
•Return to
     ❑ Group
     ❑ Transparent
     ❑ Goes to first group
       card (Card Two)
•Six: Go to explanation
  (Cloud Cover, Dew Point,
  Pressure, Temperature,
  Weather, Wind Bard)
     ❑ Transparent
     ❑ Go to appropriate
       card
•(First two buttons are
  grouped so they show
  through on next six cards)

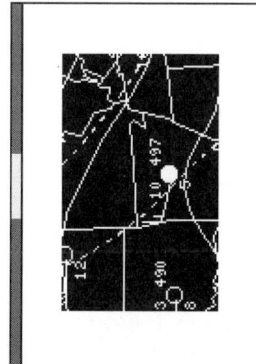

Card: ONE
•Graphic Object - Weather
  Map of USA
•Buttons
  ❑ Go next card
  •Transparent; covers card

Figure 7.2
Button Appearance dialog box

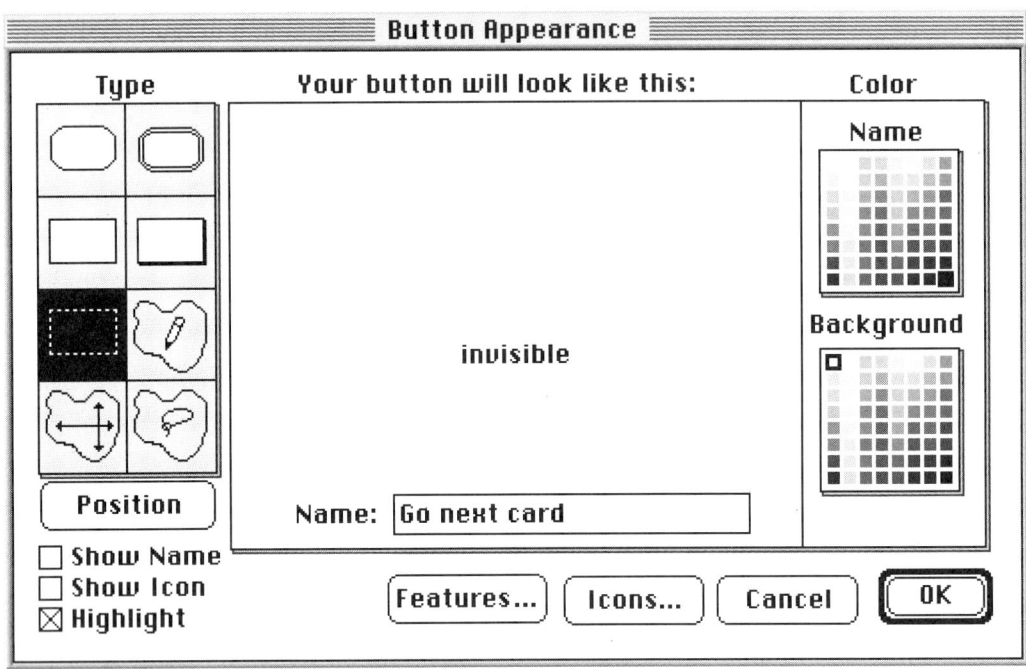

This is the transparent button style.

The marquee below is what the button will look like when it first appears on the screen. The cursor will look like ✛ and can be used to size and position the button.

❏ Enter a name for the button such as Go next card.

❏ Click the transparent button style under Type.

❏ To position the button on the screen, click Position.

Grasp the button with the ✛ cursor and drag it to the upper left corner of the card. Then drag on the lower right corner of the button until most of the card is covered by the button. When you are satisfied with the positioning of the button, click the card on an area outside the button. You will be returned to the Button Appearance dialog box.

❏ Click OK, and the Actions dialog box will appear (Figure 7.3).

❏ Under Places to Go:, select Next card, and the Transitions dialog box will appear (Figure 7.4).

❏ Select Dissolve, click OK to exit this dialog box, and then click Done.

Figure 7.3
Actions dialog box

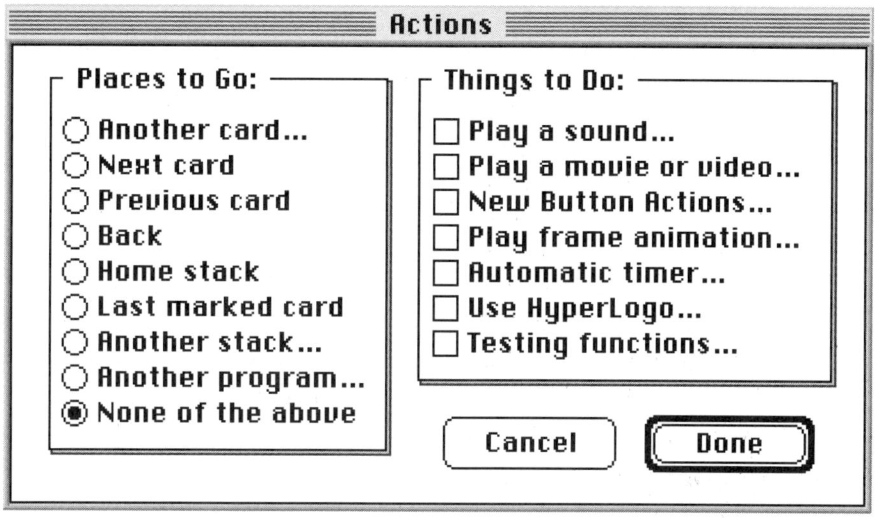

Actions

Places to Go:
- ◯ Another card...
- ◯ Next card
- ◯ Previous card
- ◯ Back
- ◯ Home stack
- ◯ Last marked card
- ◯ Another stack...
- ◯ Another program...
- ⦿ None of the above

Things to Do:
- ☐ Play a sound...
- ☐ Play a movie or video...
- ☐ New Button Actions...
- ☐ Play frame animation...
- ☐ Automatic timer...
- ☐ Use HyperLogo...
- ☐ Testing functions...

[Cancel] [**Done**]

Figure 7.4
Transitions dialog box

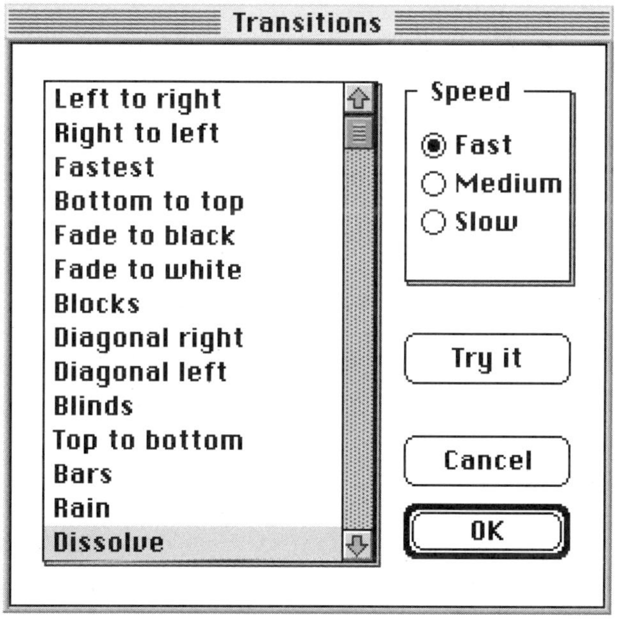

Transitions

Left to right
Right to left
Fastest
Bottom to top
Fade to black
Fade to white
Blocks
Diagonal right
Diagonal left
Blinds
Top to bottom
Bars
Rain
Dissolve

Speed
- ⦿ Fast
- ◯ Medium
- ◯ Slow

[Try it]

[Cancel]

[**OK**]

Second Card in the Stack

You've finished with the first card of your stack. Now you're ready to proceed with the second card of your stack. Choose `Edit/New Card`, and a new blank card will appear on the screen.

💾 **ADDING A GRAPHIC OBJECT TO THE CARD** Now you need to place on the card a graphic of the weather symbols you are presenting. To accomplish this,

❏ Point to `Objects/Add a Graphic Object...`. Find the graphic file `Weather` and open it.

❏ Choose one of the following: **M** double-click the Lasso tool to select the graphic or **W** use the Lasso or the Selection tool to select the graphic. Then click `OK`. Place the graphic on the far right side of the card by positioning it with the ✛ cursor.

❏ Click outside the graphic object; the `Graphic Appearance` dialog box will appear (Figure 7.5).

❏ Enter a name for the graphic object, such as `Weather symbols`.

❏ Click the `Features...` button; the `Item Features` dialog box will appear (Figure 7.6).

❏ Click `Group item` (because you want the graphic to show on all the cards that will be grouped with this card); then click `OK` to exit the `Item Features` dialog box.

❏ Click `OK` to exit the `Graphic Appearance` dialog box.

Any clip art on any grouped card will appear on every member card of that group unless you hide the picture with a nonshared item. A graphic object, on the other hand, does not have to be set to group.

Figure 7.5
Graphic Appearance dialog box

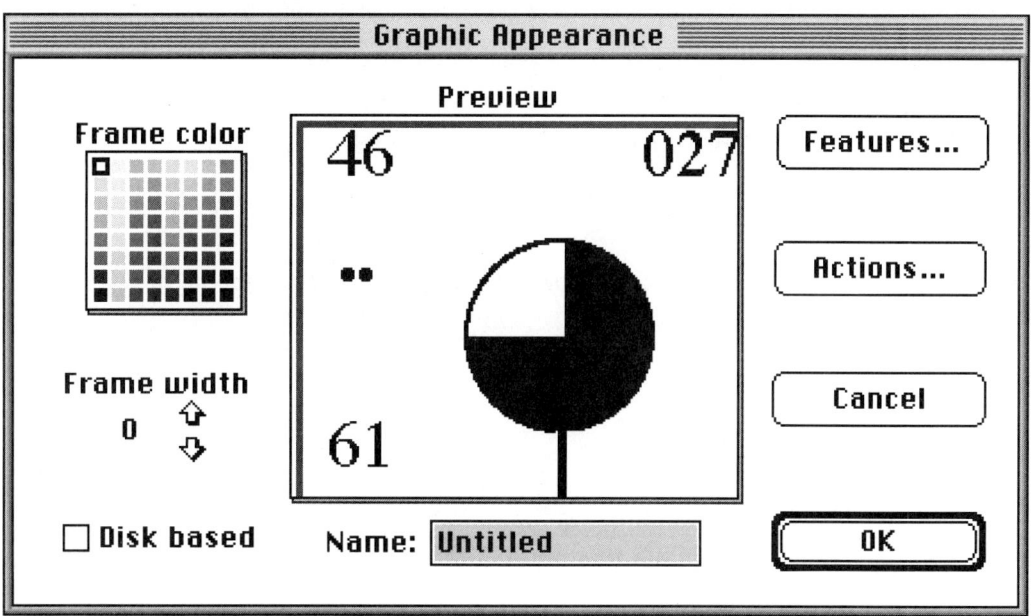

Figure 7.6
Item Features dialog box

ADDING GROUP NAVIGATION BUTTONS TO THE CARD You need a method to get to the next card, so

❏ Point to `Objects/Add a Button...`. When the `Button Appearance` dialog box (Figure 7.2) appears on the screen,

❏ Enter a name for the button, such as `Go next card`.

❏ Click the transparent button style under `Type`. You want an icon for this new button, so

❏ Click `Show Icon`.

❏ If the `Icons` dialog box (Figure 7.7) does not appear, then click the `Icons...` button.

Figure 7.7
`Icons` dialog box

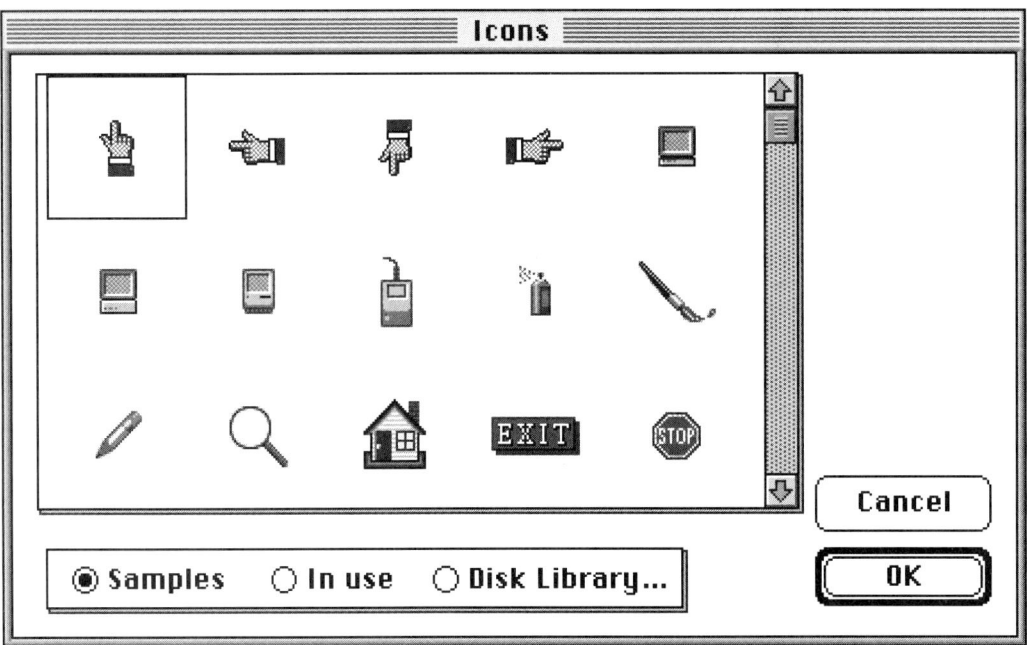

The icon we suggest you use for your button that will take the user to the next card is the

Because of its location, you will have to scroll down the list of icons (Figure 7.7).

❏ Choose the icon you want by clicking it; to see additional choices, click the scroll bar on the right side of the dialog box.

❏ Click `OK` to exit the `Icons` dialog box.

❏ To position the button on the screen, click `Position`, grasp the button with the ✛ cursor, and position the button at the lower right of the card. Then decrease the size of the button by pointing to a cor-

ner of the button and dragging toward its center. When you are satisfied with the size and position of the button, click the card on an area outside the button. You will be returned to the `Button Appearance` dialog box.

❏ Click the `Features...` button, and the `Item Features` dialog box will appear (Figure 7.8).

Figure 7.8
`Item Features` dialog box

```
┌─────────────────────────────────────────────┐
│ ═══════════    Item Features    ═══════════  │
│  ┌─────────────────────────────────────────┐ │
│  │                                         │ │
│  │  Item Type:  Button                     │ │
│  │  Space Used: N/A                        │ │
│  │  Item Owner:  N/A                       │ │
│  │  Item ID:  2                            │ │
│  │  Item Card Position: N/A                │ │
│  │                                         │ │
│  └─────────────────────────────────────────┘ │
│  ┌─────────────────────────────────────────┐ │
│  │  ☐ Locked          ☐ Hidden             │ │
│  │  ☐ Group item      ☐ No Click           │ │
│  │  ☐ Drop Off only                        │ │
│  └─────────────────────────────────────────┘ │
│  ┌──────────┐  ┌──────────┐  ┌──────────┐   │
│  │ none  ▼  │  │  Cancel  │  │    OK    │   │
│  └──────────┘  └──────────┘  └──────────┘   │
└─────────────────────────────────────────────┘
```

❏ Click `Group item` so that this button will show on all cards that will be grouped with the current card.

❏ Click `OK` to leave this dialog box and return to the `Button Appearance` dialog box.

❏ Click `OK`, and the `Actions` dialog box will appear (Figure 7.3).

❏ Under `Places to Go:`, select `Next card`, and the `Transitions` dialog box will appear (Figure 7.4).

❏ Select Right to left, click OK to exit this dialog box, and then click Done.

The second button (to return to the first card in the group, which is the second card in your stack) for this page will be similar but will differ in five ways. It will have a different

1. Name: Go back

2. Location: Lower left of the card

3. Icon:

4. Actions: Another card

5. Transition: Dissolve

You have three choices for preparing the second button:

Choice 1: You can proceed on your own with a new button, keeping the five differences in mind as you prepare the new button.

Choice 2: You can copy the first button with the **Button Edit tool** (B) or the **Pointer (Arrow) tool** from the Tool menu, paste it, and then make the five changes indicated.

Choice 3: You can use the following directions:

❏ Choose Objects/Add a Button....

❏ When the Button Appearance dialog box appears on the screen, enter a name for the button such as Go back.

❏ Click the transparent button style under Type. You want an icon for this button, so

❏ Click Show Icon.

❏ If the Icons dialog box does not appear, then click the Icons... button.

❏ Choose the icon you want by clicking it; to see additional choices, click the scroll bar on the right side of the dialog box.

❏ Click OK to exit the Icons dialog box.

❏ To position the button on the screen, click Position, grasp the button with the ✛ cursor, and position it at the lower left corner of the card. Then decrease the size of the button by pointing to a corner of the button and dragging toward its center. When you are satisfied with the size and position of the button, click the card on an area outside the button. You will be returned to the Button Appearance dialog box.

The icon we suggest you use for your button that will take the user to the next card is the

Because of its location, you will have to scroll down the list of icons (Figure 7.7).

❏ Click the `Features...` button, and the `Item Features` dialog box will appear.

❏ Click `Group item` so that this button will show on all cards grouped with the current card.

❏ Click `OK` to leave this dialog box and return to the `Button Appearance` dialog box.

❏ Click `OK,` and the `Actions` dialog box will appear.

❏ Under `Places to Go:`, select `Another card...`. When prompted to move to the card to connect to, click `OK` since the card you want to connect to is the current card. The `Transitions` dialog box will appear.

❏ Select `Dissolve,` click `OK` to exit this dialog box, and then click `Done.`

ADDING NONGROUP NAVIGATION BUTTONS TO YOUR SECOND CARD The two buttons you just placed on the second card of your stack will appear on cards two through eight because all these cards will be grouped. The first button you prepared on the second card will allow the user to navigate forward from card to card. The second button will return the user to the first card in the group, which is the second card in the stack. All the cards in the group will display the graphic that appears on card two.

We need to add six more buttons to the second card; each of these buttons will be related to one of the six items on the graphic. However, we do not want any of these buttons to appear on any other card of the group, so these buttons will not be grouped. We will outline the steps of the first button and then let you prepare the remaining five buttons. First, however, you need to add the six additional cards that will make up your stack. These six cards will be grouped with card two. While card two is showing on the screen, point to `Edit/Ready Made Cards/Group Card,` and release the mouse button. Repeat this procedure until you have six new cards, for a total of eight cards in your stack. To navigate back to card two, use `Move/Previous Card` until you come to card two; or to go forward, use `Move/Next Card` until you reach card two.

Now we are ready to add a button for each of the six weather symbols on the card.

❏ Point to `Objects/Add a Button...`.

❏ When the `Button Appearance` dialog box appears on the screen, enter the following name for the button: `Cloud Cover.`

*You can also use $\boxed{M}$ ⌘-<
and ⌘ -> or $\boxed{W}$ <ctrl>-< and
<ctrl>-> to navigate from card
to card.*

❏ Click the Drop Shadow Rectangle button style under `Type`.

❏ `Show Name` should be selected (if selected, there is an `X` to the left of the button).

❏ To position the button on the screen, click `Position`, grasp the button with the ✛ cursor, and position it at the upper left of the card (Figure 7.1). When you are satisfied with the position of the button, click the card on an area outside the button. You will be returned to the `Button Appearance` dialog box.

❏ Click `OK`, and the `Actions` dialog box will appear.

❏ Under `Places to Go:`, select `Another card...`. When prompted to move to the card to connect to, go to card three by clicking on the appropriate arrow. Then click `OK`. The `Transitions` dialog box will appear.

❏ Scroll down to `Iris open`, click `OK` to exit this dialog box, and then click `Done`.

You've completed the first button in this collection of six buttons. Try out the button by clicking it with the Browse tool; return by clicking the return button.

To assist in aligning the remaining five buttons, use the Line tool (Tools menu) to draw a guide line for the left margin of the `Cloud Cover` button. Then you can align the remaining five buttons more precisely with this first content button. Each of the buttons will vary from each other in two respects: each button will have a unique name, and each button will have a unique destination. The following are the suggested name and destination for each of the remaining five buttons:

Button Number	Suggested Name	Destination
2	Dew Point	Card 4
3	Pressure	Card 5
4	Temperature	Card 6
5	Weather	Card 7
6	Wind Bard	Card 8

There are at least two ways you could proceed with the remaining five buttons. You could begin with a new button for each one, or you could copy the `Cloud Cover` button and paste it. We will demonstrate the second technique because it preserves the settings that we selected on the first button in this collection. The general procedure for each button is the following:

❏ Select the previous button (begin with the Cloud Cover button) with the Button Edit tool Ⓑ or the Pointer tool ▲ from the Tools menu.

❏ Copy the button with Edit/Copy button.

❏ Paste the button with Edit/Paste button and move the new button below the other button.

❏ Double-click the pasted button and make the following changes:

1. Change the name.

2. Change the destination by

❏ Clicking the Actions... button and

❏ Click Another card....

❏ Then click the right arrow in the Connections dialog box until you see the card destination for which you were searching.

❏ Click OK to exit the Connections dialog box.

❏ Click OK to exit the Transitions dialog box.

❏ Finally, click Done to exit the Actions dialog box.

Continue until you have constructed all six of the buttons and have tested them to determine that they work properly. None of these six buttons should appear on cards three through eight, just on card two. Use the Eraser tool to erase the guide line you placed on card two.

Now you need to place the title Weather Map Symbols in a text object or field. To do this,

❏ Choose Objects/Add a Text Object... to start a new field or text object. The field will appear on the screen as a rectangle of "marching ants."

❏ Size and position the field just above the six buttons and to the left of the graphic object. Then click outside the field or text object. The Text Appearance dialog box will appear (Figure 7.9).

Figure 7.9
Text Appearance dialog box

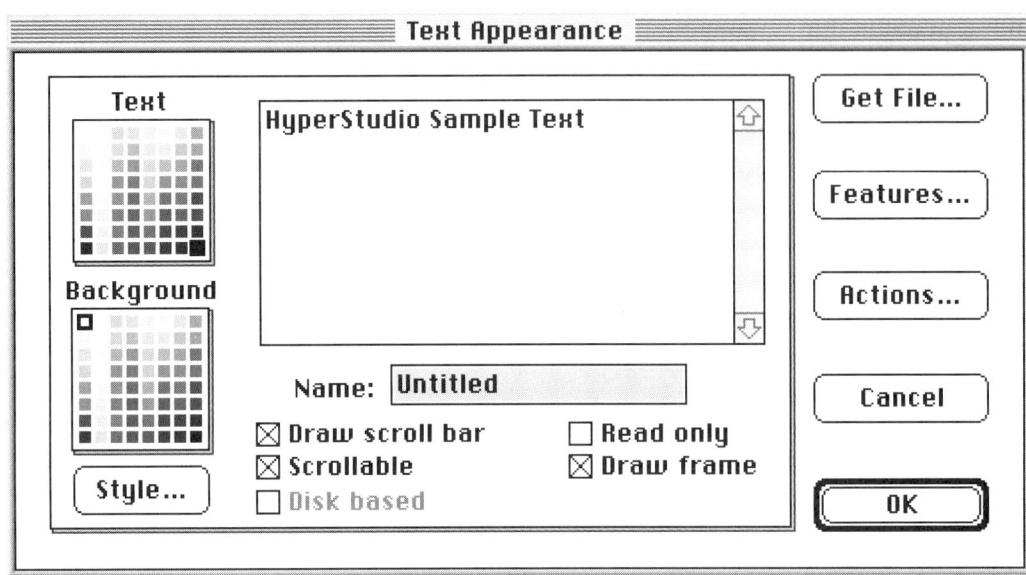

- ❏ Name the field Title.

- ❏ De-select Draw scroll bar and Scrollable by clicking them.

- ❏ Click the Style... button; set align to center and font size to 17. Then click OK to exit the Text Style dialog box.

- ❏ Set the text color by clicking the color (under Text) that you want to appear in the title.

- ❏ Click the Features... button and choose Group object because you want the title to appear on every card in the group. Click OK to exit Item Features.

- ❏ Click OK to exit the Text Appearance dialog box.

- ❏ Enter the text Weather Map Symbols into the field.

- ❏ Double-click the field with the pointer; de-select Draw frame by clicking it.

- ❏ Select Read only by clicking it. Exit the dialog box by clicking OK.

Completing Cards Three Through Eight

The last six cards have the following shared items: two buttons, a title, and one graphic object. In addition, you will need to add the following items, which will not be shared, to each of these cards: a text container (field), text, and a button that identifies a weather symbol. Table 7.1 shows the characteristics of the field or text object, the name of the text file containing the text for the field, and the information for the button that will be used as a label pointing to the symbol described by the text.

Table 7.1
Information for Cards Three Through Eight

Card #	Field Attributes Selected	Field Attributes Not Selected	Text File Name	Button Name	Button Characteristics	Symbol It Points To
3	Transparent, Locked, Read only	Draw scroll bar, Allow scrolling, Draw Frame	tf1.txt	Cloud cover	Transparent, Show Name, Name Colored red	◔
4	Transparent, Locked, Read only	Draw scroll bar, Allow scrolling, Draw Frame	tf2.txt	Dew point	Transparent, Show Name, Name Colored red	61
5	Transparent, Locked, Read only	Draw scroll bar, Allow scrolling, Draw Frame	tf3.txt	Pressure	Transparent, Show Name, Name Colored red	027
6	Transparent, Locked, Read only	Draw scroll bar, Allow scrolling, Draw Frame	tf4.txt	Temperature	Transparent, Show Name, Name Colored red	46
7	Transparent, Locked, Read only	Draw scroll bar, Allow scrolling, Draw Frame	tf5.txt	Weather	Transparent, Show Name, Name Colored red	••
8	Transparent, Locked, Read only	Draw scroll bar, Allow scrolling, Draw Frame	tf6.txt	Wind bard	Transparent, Show Name, Name Colored red	⟩

The button on each card will be in a different position because each button will point to a different weather symbol; consequently, the position of the field will be different on each card. Thus, it will be easier to place the button on the card and then to place the field relative to the position of the button.

CONSTRUCTING THE BUTTON POINTERS   You need to be on card three of your stack to begin.

- ❏ Choose `Objects/Add a Button…`.
- ❏ Name the button (Table 7.1).
- ❏ Select the button characteristics (Table 7.1).
- ❏ Position the button so that it points to the appropriate weather symbol.

For cards four through eight, copy the button you just completed on page three, paste a copy on each of pages four through eight, change the name of the button, and position it in relation to the symbol with which it is associated.

CONSTRUCTING THE FIELDS   You need to be on card three to construct the text field.

- ❏ `Point to Objects/Add a Text Object…`. The field outline will appear on the screen.
- ❏ Position the field to the left of the graphic object in an area that will not interfere with the button you just placed on the card. Then click outside the field or text object.
- ❏ The `Text Appearance` dialog box will appear (Figure 7.9).
- ❏ Click the `Get File…` button and locate and open the appropriate text file (Table 7.1). You will be returned to the `Text Appearance` dialog box.
- ❏ Click the `Style…` button, choose 12 point type, and click `OK`.
- ❏ Select the following field or text object attributes: `Read Only` and, from `Features…`: `Transparent`, `Locked`. Then click `OK`.
- ❏ De-select the following attributes: `Draw scroll bar`, `Scrollable`, `Draw frame`.
- ❏ Click `OK` to exit the dialog box.

Use the technique you used for this field to construct a field on cards four through eight. Refer to Table 7.1 for the text file associated with the appropriate card.

You have completed your stack. Be sure to save the completed stack and to make a backup copy. Now you need to try out every button in the stack. Does each button perform the task it is supposed to perform? If not, then use the Button or Pointer tool to select the button and edit it.

In the Classroom

1. Prepare a stack using pictures, shapes, or letters in which each page consists of four sections. One of the items should be flipped or rotated; the students are to identify the one that is different. This activity can help students discriminate between the letters *b* and *d* and other kinds of right-left confusion.

2. Students can prepare their science laboratory reports in a stack template. You can have graphics available that are complementary to the lab activity so that students can illustrate their reports with graphics.

3. Have students prepare historical perspectives on significant events, persons, and places they are studying.

4. Design a stack with a series of activities in which students are to draw two large intersecting circles, such as one representing shapes with four sides and the other representing red shapes. Have students draw two different shapes appropriate for each of the three regions. Then have the students use the pointer to move the shapes to the appropriate region.

5. Have students construct a stack in which they compare the cost of an item, such as automobiles, over a range of time—for example, 1920, 1930, 1940, 1950, 1960, 1970, 1980, 1990, and today.

6. Construct a stack in which you or students draw three designs on a card, one with only horizontal symmetry, one with only vertical symmetry, and one with both horizontal and vertical symmetry. Ask students to identify the type of symmetry that was used.

7. Have students write a story in which they write alternate endings. Place the endings in a stack so that students can either choose the ending they prefer or choose an ending at random.

8. Prepare a stack to illustrate Mendel's experiment in which he crossed red flowers with white flowers. A variation is to do the same thing with pairs of characteristics.

9. Prepare a timeline template with HyperStudio so students can illustrate local events or world events that occurred in the year that a parent, a grandparent, or another relative was born.

10. Construct a stack illustrating the basic composition of DNA and its role in the cell and the body.

11. After a visit to an art exhibit, have students draw or paint a picture in HyperStudio or in a paint application using the same style as their favorite piece of art from the exhibit. Place all the pictures into one stack as a display for the students and their parents.

12. Construct a stack to introduce students and parents to the course or classroom on the first day or week of school.

13. Construct a stack template to use as a portfolio for a student's work in your classroom.

Questions and Answers

Q1: **What is the difference between clip art and a graphic object?**

A: In HyperStudio, clip art becomes a part of the background. If cards are set to share, all clip art on all cards of the group will show the clip art unless you block out the view with an object. A graphic object is treated as an object, and you can have that object perform certain tasks, just as buttons can perform tasks. A graphic object can be set to share or just to show on a single card.

Q2: **Must I give a name to buttons and fields?**

A: No, you do not have to name them, but it makes it much easier to edit and organize them if you give them names.

Q3: **What is Home?**

A: Home is the name of a special stack. When you click the Home button, you will be taken to that stack.

Q4: **Sometimes there is a dark color around the border of the stack. What is that?**

A: The stack you are viewing is in presentation mode. If you want to change it, go to `Edit/Preferences...`. If you want to change back to `Presentation mode,` you can choose from the following options:

- ❏ **M** A graphic you select.
- ❏ The desktop pattern.
- ❏ A color that you select.

Q5: **Why does my Home Page look different from the Home Page on other computers?**

A: There are three Home Page styles in HyperStudio 3. Depending upon the model of the computer and whether or not the computer has a CD-ROM, the Home Page may differ. In addition, the user may have changed the Home Page.

Q6: **Can I share my stacks with others who don't have a copy of HyperStudio?**

A: To share your stacks, place a copy of your stack and a copy of the HyperStudio Player on a floppy disk.

Q7: **What kind of graphics can I use with HyperStudio?**

A: See Appendix C.

Activities

1. If you have access to a CD-ROM player, visit the following sites to get an idea of the types of things that you can construct with Hyper-Studio.

The Media Library (on CD-ROM). Click the Enter Library button.

❏ Animal Kingdom

❏ Clipart

❏ Dinosaurs

❏ HyperArt

❏ Kidamation

❏ Multipaedia

❏ Photo Gallery

❏ Screens and Backgrounds

❏ Sound and Music

Click the Exit button.

Sample Projects (on CD-ROM). You can preview the title card; if you want to look at the entire stack, click on the picture of the stack.

❏ At School

❏ Family and Community

❏ At Work

❏ Commercial

The following activities are provided to extend your working knowledge of HyperStudio.

2. **Preparing a Quiz.** The following directions show you how to use HyperStudio to collect data when you give a quiz or conduct a survey, for example. Open the file `Prctice1`. We have already prepared a quiz with three questions and associated buttons so that you can concentrate on formatting the buttons to keep track of the correct answers. In addition, we have included a button to collect the user's name. You need to format buttons a, b, c, and d on each card.

❏ Choose either the Button tool `B` or the pointer ▸ and click button `a`. The `Button Appearance` dialog box (Figure 7.2) will appear on the screen.

❏ Click the Actions button, and the `Actions` dialog box (Figure 7.3) will appear.

❏ Under `Things to Do`, click `Testing functions...`, and the `Testing` dialog box will appear (Figure 7.10).

❏ Choice a is an incorrect response, so click `be an incorrect answer`; then click `OK`.

❏ Choices b and d are also incorrect choices, so format them the same way as you formatted button a.

❏ Choice c is the correct answer, so choose `be a correct answer` for item c. One way to get to the question on the next card is to have the application move to the next card when the student gets the correct answer. Since c is the correct response for this question, choose `Next card...` under `Actions`.

Figure 7.10
`Testing` dialog box to choose the button function

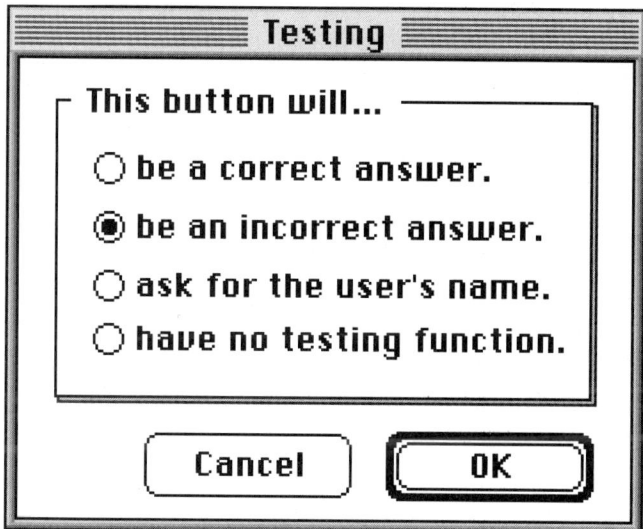

Continue to questions two and three to format the question buttons. The correct answer to the question on card two is b; question three's answer is also b.

HyperStudio generates a text file (`HS.Test.Results`) that will contain the results of a user responding to the questions in the stack.

3.   **Coloring Objects.** For practice in coloring objects in a stack, open the file `Prctice2`. Use the following procedure to color the buttons and the text in the buttons:

❏ Choose either the Button tool `B` or the pointer .

❏ Double-click a button to select it.

❑ When the Button Appearance dialog box (Figure 7.2) appears, choose a text color from Color under Name and a button (background) color under Background.

Use the following procedure to color the field and the text in the fields:

❑ Choose either the Text tool [T] or the pointer ▶ .

❑ Double-click a field to select it.

❑ When the Text Appearance dialog box (Figure 7.9) appears, choose a text color from Color under Name and a field (background) color under Background.

Use the following procedure to color the background:

❑ Double-click the Eraser tool 🖊 .

❑ Choose the color you want to "erase" in and click OK.

❑ When the Text Appearance dialog box appears, choose a text color from Color under Name and a field (background) color under Background.

❑ When the Button Appearance dialog box appears, choose a text color from Color under Name and a button (background) color under Background.

4. **Preparing a Go-to-Previous-Card Button.** Open your Weather Map stack and go to card 2. In the bottom right corner of the card there is a go-next button. You are going to make a copy of that button for your go-previous button.

❑ Select the go-next button with the Button tool or the pointer. Make a copy, paste it, and position it to the left of the go-next button.

❑ With either the Button tool or the pointer, double-click your new button.

❑ When the dialog box appears, click Icons... and select the same type of icon as the go-next button but one pointing in the opposite direction. Then click OK.

❑ When the Button Appearance dialog box appears, click Actions.

❑ Change Place to Go: to Previous card.

❑ Change Transitions to Left to right, click OK, and then click Done. Now try out your new button by clicking it with the Browse tool.

M 5. Using a QuickTime Movie. Start a new stack or use an existing stack for this activity. Add and position a new button. When the `Actions` dialog box appears,

❑ Choose `Play a movie or video…`.

❑ From the `Video/Movie Source` dialog box, click `Disk file (QuickTime movies)`.

❑ If the `QuickTime Movies` folder is on your hard drive, you will be presented with a choice of movies. Open one of the movies.

❑ Place the movie where you want it, and then click outside the boundaries of the movie.

❑ From the `QuickTime Movies` dialog box (Figure 7.11), choose `Show first frame`.

❑ Click `OK` and `Done`.

❑ Click the button to play the movie!

If there are no movies on the hard drive but you have one on a floppy disk, insert the floppy disk now and open the movie.

Figure 7.11
`QuickTime Movies` dialog box. Click `Show first frame`; then click `OK`

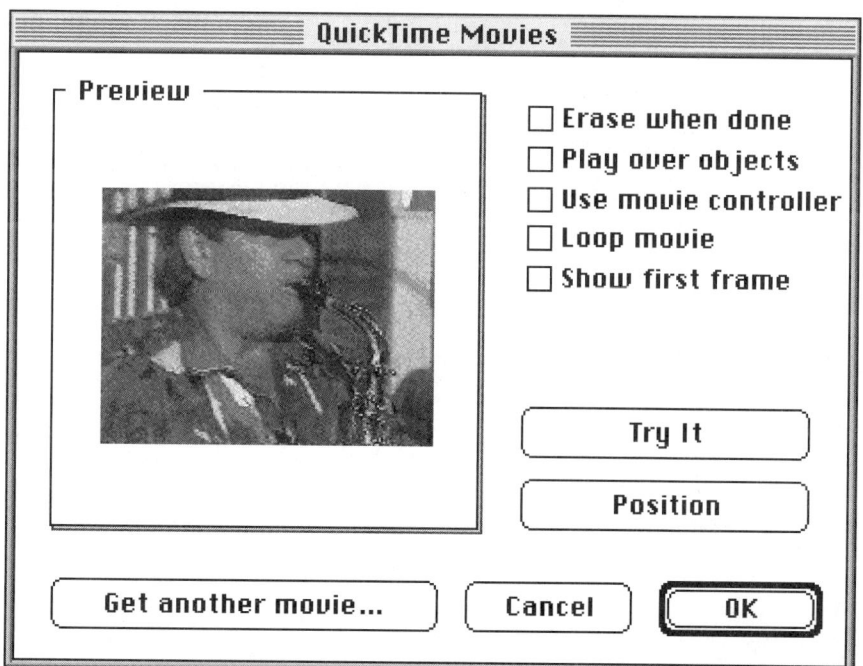

6. Playing a Sound. Start a new stack or use an existing stack. Add and position a new button.

❑ Select the Button tool or the pointer, and double-click your new button.

❑ When the dialog box appears, click `Actions...` and, under `Things to Do:`, choose `Play a sound...`.

❑ When the `Tape deck` dialog box (Figure 7.12) appears, click `Samples;` then click the sample you want to use.

❑ To exit, click OK and `Done`. With the Browse tool, click your new button to try it out.

Figure 7.12
`Tape deck` dialog box

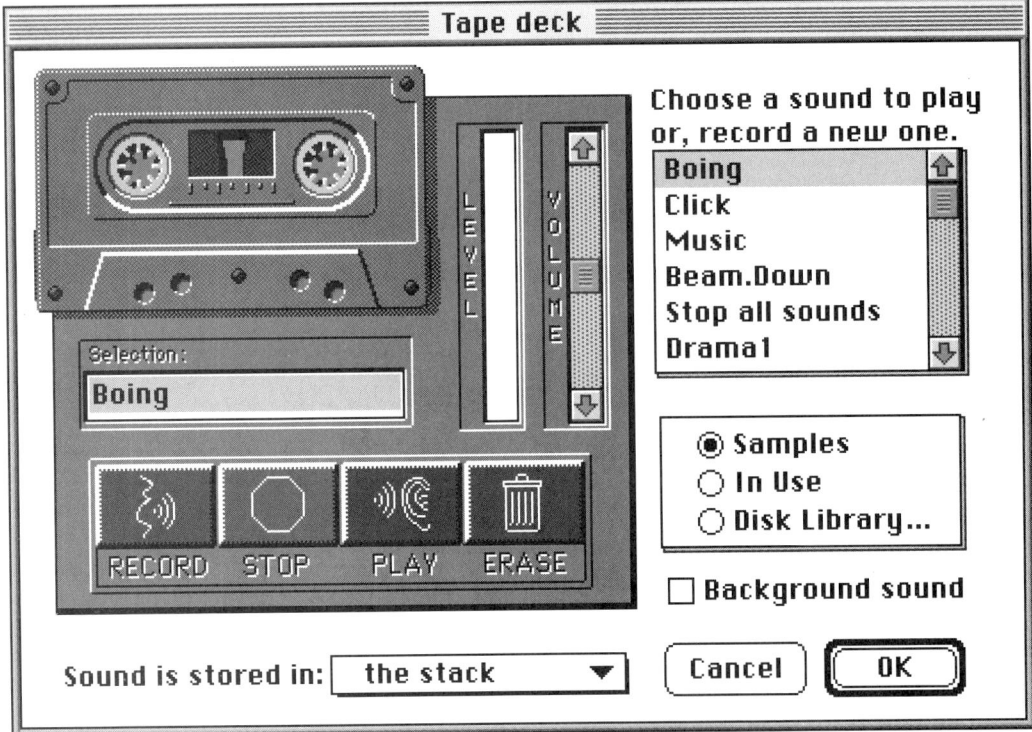

Summary

HyperStudio is a type of application referred to as hypermedia or multimedia. The basic building blocks of a stack, which is analogous to a deck of cards, are cards, buttons, and fields. Rather than organizing information sequentially, students and teachers can organize graphics, text, and sound nonsequentially by linking related ideas.

Students can also construct their own stacks with HyperStudio and can use the application in a variety of content areas. You as a teacher model the use of hypermedia in the way you present the examples in the various content areas. If you treat hypermedia as a toy, your students will probably reflect that with what they use it for, but if you use it as an instructional tool with significant examples, you increase the chances that your students will use HyperStudio in an academically productive manner.

Key Terms

button 213

Button Edit tool 222

card 213

field 213

hypermedia 212

hypertext 212

Pointer (Arrow) tool 222

stack 213

References

Babbitt, B., & Usnick, V. (1993). Hypermedia: A vehicle for connection. *Arithmetic Teacher, 40,* 430–432.

Babbitt, B. C. (1993). Hypermedia: Making the mathematics connection. *Intervention in School and Clinic, 28,* 294–301.

Bonk, C. J., *et al.* (1994). Cooperative hypermedia: The marriage of collaborative writing and mediated environments. *Computers in the Schools, 10*(1–2), 79–124.

Brigham, F. J., *et al.* (1994). *Hypermedia supports for student learning.* (ERIC Document No. ED 378965)

Carver, S., Lehrer, R., Connell, T., & Erickson, J. (1992). Learning by hypermedia: Issues of assessment and implementation. *Educational Psychologist, 27,* 385–404.

Cornelio, A. (1994). A multimedia approach to teaching library research skills. *School Library Media Activities Monthly, 10*(6), 38–40.

Edelson, D. C. (1993). Socrates, Aesop and the computer: Questioning and storytelling with multimedia. *Journal of Educational Multimedia and Hypermedia, 2,* 393–404.

Ekhaml, L. T. (1996). 100 ways of using HyperStudio in school. *School Library Media Activities Monthly, 12*(00), 36–40+.

Fernlund, P. M., & Cooper-Shoup, S. (1991). A realistic view of hypermedia in the social studies classroom. *Social Studies Review, 30*(3), 66–70.

Golson, E. (1995). Student hypertexts: The perils and promises of paths not taken. *Computers and Composition, 12,* 295–308.

Halavin, J., & Sommer, C. (1990). *Using hypertext to develop an algorithmic approach to teaching statistics.* (ERIC Document No. ED 334195)

Higgins, K., & Boone, R. (1990). Hypertext: A new vehicle for computer use in reading instruction. *Intervention in School and Clinic, 26,* 26–31.

Hinerman, F. (1994). Multimedia labs. *Science Teacher, 61*(3), 38–41.

Kaplan, N., *et al.* (1992). The Classroom Manager. Hands-on Multimedia. *Instructor, 101*(8), 105.

Lehrer, R. (1993). Authors of knowledge: Patterns of hypermedia design. In *Computers as cognitive tools,* S. Lajoie & S. Derry (Eds.), 197–227. Hillsdale, NJ: Erlbaum.

Marchionini, G. (1977). Hypermedia and learning: Freedom and chaos. *Educational Technology, 28*(11), 8–12.

Messing, J., & McLachlan, R. (1994). *History, hypermedia, and the birth of a nation.* (ERIC Document No. ED 388275)

Morris, R. L. (1995). *Dynamic multimedia instruction: An affordable solution for mixed-media integration on a single classroom television.* (ERIC Document No. ED 378964)

Patrikis, P. C., *et al.* (1990). *Multimedia and language learning. Technology in higher education: Current reflections.* (ERIC Document No. ED 358819)

Proctor, J. D., *et al.* (1995). Multimedia guiding writing modules for introductory human geography. *Journal of Geography, 94,* 571–577.

Turner, S., & Land, M. L. (1994). *HyperCard: A tool for learning.* Belmont, CA: Wadsworth.

Wiegmann, B. A. (1993). *Exploring the hyper-environment for elementary children.* (ERIC Document No. ED 370565)

Wishnietsky, D. H. (1992). *Hypermedia: The integrated learning environment. Fastback 339.* (ERIC Document No. ED 354877)

Yang, C. S., & Moore, D. M. (1995–96). Designing hypermedia systems for instruction. *Journal of Educational Technology Systems, 24,* 3–30.

Telecommunications

The World Wide Web and E-mail

OBJECTIVE

Integrate e-mail and Internet resources into classroom activities
and the curriculum.

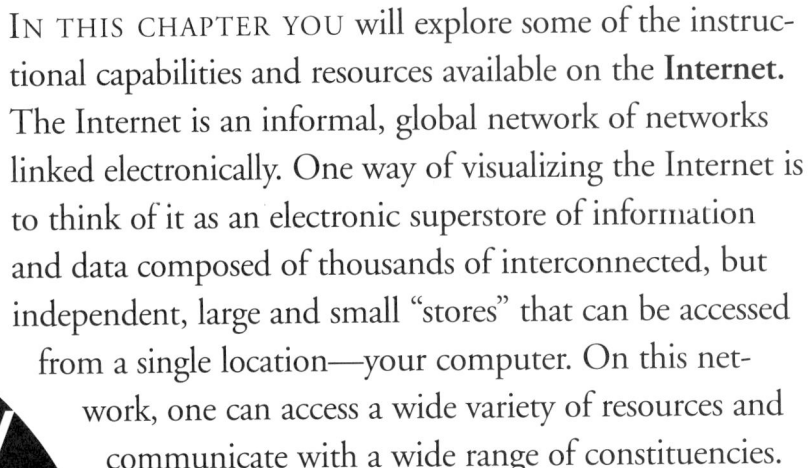

IN THIS CHAPTER YOU will explore some of the instructional capabilities and resources available on the **Internet.** The Internet is an informal, global network of networks linked electronically. One way of visualizing the Internet is to think of it as an electronic superstore of information and data composed of thousands of interconnected, but independent, large and small "stores" that can be accessed from a single location—your computer. On this network, one can access a wide variety of resources and communicate with a wide range of constituencies. No single person or entity controls the computers or the information on the Internet; in effect, the Internet is a huge electronic democracy.

Using Internet Resources in the K–12 Classroom

What does the Internet offer K–12 teachers and students? Many individuals believe that the Internet is just another fad; however, some of these same individuals also thought that desktop computers in schools in the 1970s and the 1980s were a fad and would soon disappear from schools. Others maintain that familiarity with the Internet is important for three reasons. First, use of the Internet and e-mail is an extension of one's ability to communicate, whether with another person or groups of persons anywhere on earth. Individuals in business, industry, manufacturing, the military, and higher education typically use the Internet and e-mail on a daily basis to perform duties relevant to their professions. Second, the Internet represents an enormous collection of resources and information for students and teachers. Third, because of the volume of resources on the Internet and the relative lack of quality control, there should be increased emphasis on teaching students how to find, organize, and evaluate data and information rather than just memorize information.

What kinds of things can students and teachers expect to be able to do with access to the Internet and e-mail?

- ❏ Collaborate with other students, classrooms, teachers, and experts anywhere in the world
- ❏ Study other cultures and languages
- ❏ Collect and exchange data on a wide variety of topics
- ❏ Practice communicating in a foreign language
- ❏ Solicit advice and information from experts in various fields
- ❏ Participate (electronically) in field trips
- ❏ Search for data and information in electronic databases
- ❏ Find graphics and other support materials relevant to instruction in the classroom
- ❏ Participate in online instructional activities

The World Wide Web

One of the newest parts of the Internet is called the **World Wide Web** (or WWW or W3 or the Web). The Web is a **client-server** information system that runs over the Internet; it delivers information as hypertext and hypermedia (Eager, 1994, p. 53). In the previous chapter, you worked with a hypermedia application, HyperStudio. The Web is a vast collection of hypermedia documents available on the Internet. These Web documents consist of various combinations of data that can include text, graphics, audio, and video with links or connections to other Internet resources. Web documents, then, are organized or linked together by means of hypertext. On your computer screen, these hypertext links typically take the form of underlined text, text of a different color, or icons (Figure 8.1). You can think of these links as hotspots on the screen that, when clicked, execute some kind of action such as linking to another site or going to a different part of the same document, similar to the way a button can link two cards together in HyperStudio. Consequently, by pointing and clicking, you can jump from document to document located on thousands of computers in countries all over the world—all from your computer!

Figure 8.1
The underlined phrases are links to other files or sites

Just as most of us don't repair our own automobiles or install the air conditioning unit in them, we also don't set up or maintain networks. We rely upon specialists to do that. Consequently, we assume that someone has already set up the network and properly installed the software that you will need to use a web browser. It is not within the scope of this text to attempt to guess what combinations of hardware, software, and networking exist at your site.

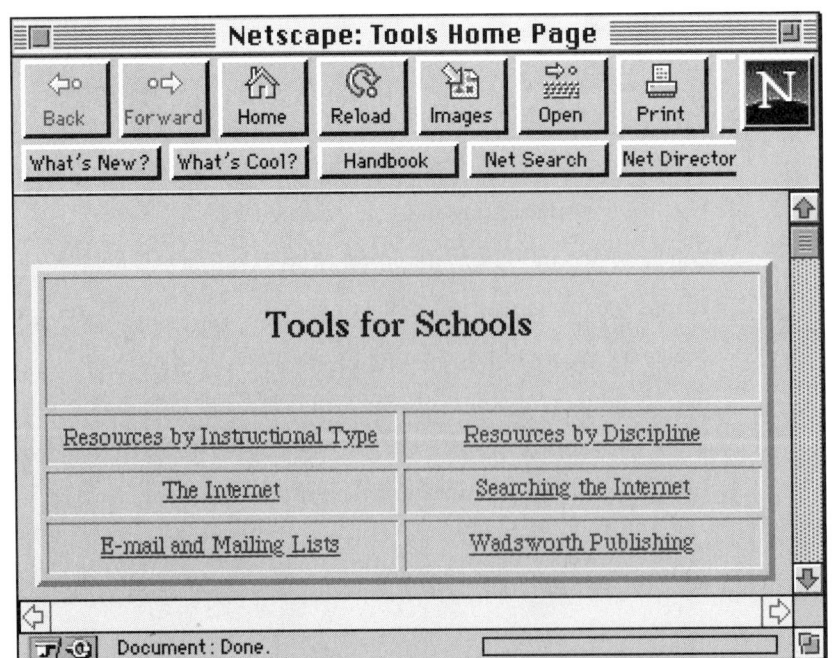

Viewing a Web Document

To view a Web document, you need a **web browser** such as Netscape or Internet Explorer. The web browser can either be on your computer or on a host computer. The activities in this chapter will assume that you are using a multimedia web browser such as Netscape or Internet Explorer on your computer.

- ❏ Start your web browser by clicking its icon.
- ❏ Choose `File/Open File...`
- ❏ Find and open the file `Tools.htm` from the `08tele` folder.

The text on the screen that is underlined or of a different color (or both) is hypertext and, when clicked, performs some kind of action. To get an idea of the types of materials, learning activities, and other educational resources located on the Internet, explore some of the sites pointed to in this document. Keep the following items in mind as you browse:

- ❏ Click once on a link to activate it. Be patient; remember that the site may be located on a computer thousands of miles away. Or the site may be busy, and you will have to try again later.

- ❏ To return to the previous document you were viewing, click the back icon 🔙 on the browser.

- ❏ If your browser is loading a page too slowly, then disable the loading of images. On Netscape, de-select `Auto Load Images` under `Options.`

- ❏ If you get a message such as `No DNS entry for this site,` you may want to try again later, check out the cable connections on your computer, or communicate this information to the person in charge of the computer lab. Or, in fact, there may be no such site anymore; Internet sites constantly appear and disappear for various reasons.

When you use your web browser to go to a site, the first document you view from the remote computer is called the **home page,** which is the interface or guide to the resources available on that computer. When you click a hot spot or a **link** on a Web page, there are addresses within those links that connect either to another server, open a file on your computer, or perform some other type of action. If you look at the bottom of your web browser when you place the mouse pointer over a link, you can see the address at the bottom of the browser.

Some people pronounce the individual letters in URL, and others call it "earl."

This address is called the Uniform Resource Locator or **URL,** and it takes the following form:

```
http://eduwww.mwsu.edu/stuff/mystuff.html
```

The WWW uses URLs to identify the location of files on other servers. The URL includes the type of resource being accessed, the address of the server, and the location of the file (Figure 8.2). Think of this address as an electronic postal address of the file you want to see, except that this address all fits on one line and there are no spaces anywhere in the address.

Figure 8.2
Parts of a Uniform Resource Locator (URL)

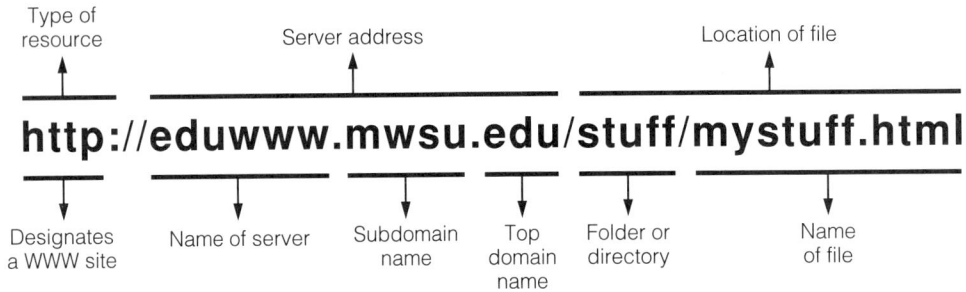

Other top domain names include com *(commercial),* gov *(government),* mil *(military),* net *(network),* org *(organization not falling into another category). Outside the United States, other countries use a two-letter domain name, such as* uk *(Great Britain) and* de *(Germany).*

1. The first part—*http*—indicates the type of site. In this case, the file is located on a WWW site and uses the Hypertext Transfer Protocol or **http** for accessing information.

2. The next part of the URL—*eduwww.mwsu.edu*—is the address of the server in which

   ❑ *eduwww* is the name of the server or computer,

   ❑ *mwsu* is the **subdomain** name of the network on which the computer resides (subdomain names frequently indicate the name of a company, university, or unit that they represent), and

   ❑ *edu* is the **top domain** name. In this case, the computer belongs to an educational institution.

Searching for Resources on the WWW

There are thousands of sites and millions of users on the Internet. Finding exactly what you are looking for can be challenging. There is no master directory; sites appear and disappear on a daily basis, so any directory will contain information

on sites that are no longer a part of the Internet. In the following section are two basic techniques for searching for resources on the Web.

USING A SEARCH ENGINE   One technique for locating information on the Internet is to use a **search engine** that has been developed especially for use on the Web. There are hundreds of engines or searchers available on the Internet. Some of these devices are actually databases rather than searchers, and they vary considerably in the areas that they search in the Internet and how focused they are.

There are basically two types of Web search engines. One type searches while you wait, and the other type searches on a scheduled basis and places the results into a database. With the latter type, your search may be conducted faster, but the information in it may not be as up-to-date as is available on a while-you-wait search. Another type of resource that is frequently referred to as a search engine or device is a database that contains a collection of information, such as telephone numbers (Wehmeyer, 1996).

In the following section, we will describe a specific search with one search engine, but the basic technique is the same for most searches with a search engine.

1. Locate one or more search engines and become familiar with how to use them.

2. Think of key phrases associated with what you want to locate and search with those phrases. Suppose that you were interested in finding graphic images on the Internet. You could search with one or more of the following phrases: clip art, icon, graphics, art.

3. When you visit an interesting site, it will probably be linked to other similar sites. Follow those links. You don't want to keep looking up the same information to return to those sites later, so you need some technique to record the location or URL of the sites. You could simply write them down on a slip of paper, but that becomes very tiresome, particularly if you find hundreds of links that you are interested in. A more effective method is to use the **bookmark** (or hotlist) feature of your browser. The bookmark allows you to save the URL so that you can quickly continue with your search. Another method of collecting URLs of your favorite sites is to copy and paste them into a word processing document, database, or other location or document as you find them.

For a brief introduction to the types of data you may encounter on the World Wide Web, see Appendix G.

To save a bookmark in Netscape, choose `Bookmarks/Add Bookmark` *when the site you want appears on the screen.*

A Sample Search In this section we will conduct a search for articles and other resources on testing or assessment. For this search, we will use the search engine Net Search at http://home.netscape.com/escapes/search/search1.html. If you are using Netscape, just click the Net Search button near the top of the browser window. When the home page for searching appears (Figure 8.3), type assessment into the space provided for your search term and then click the seek now button. In a few moments you will see the results on the screen (Figure 8.4).

Figure 8.3
Enter the word assessment and click the seek now button to begin your search

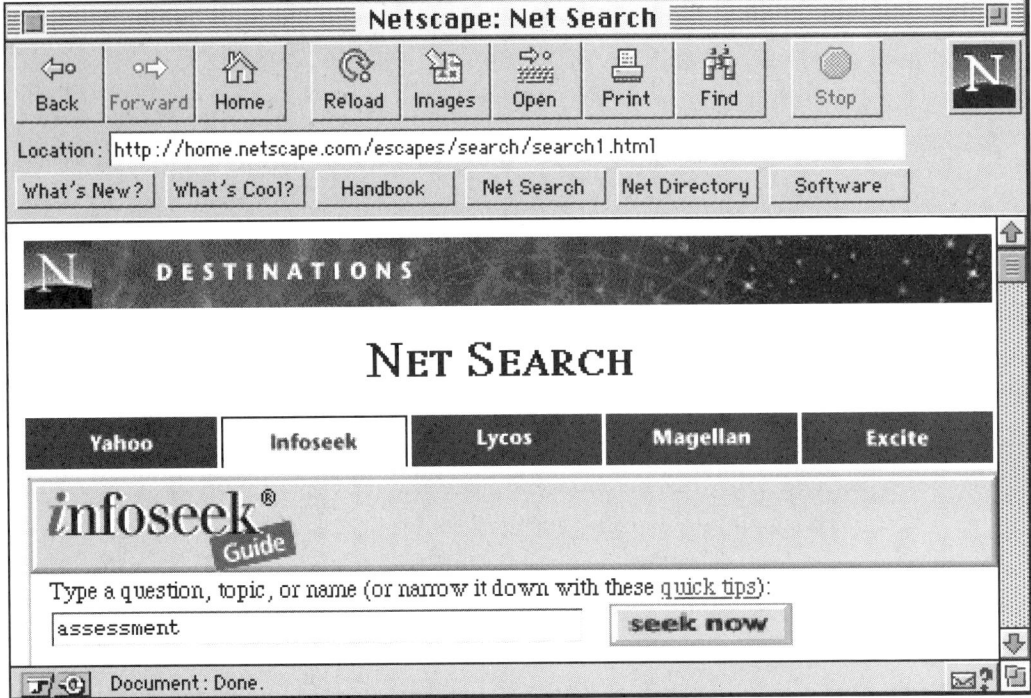

Figure 8.4
The results of your search using the term `assessment`

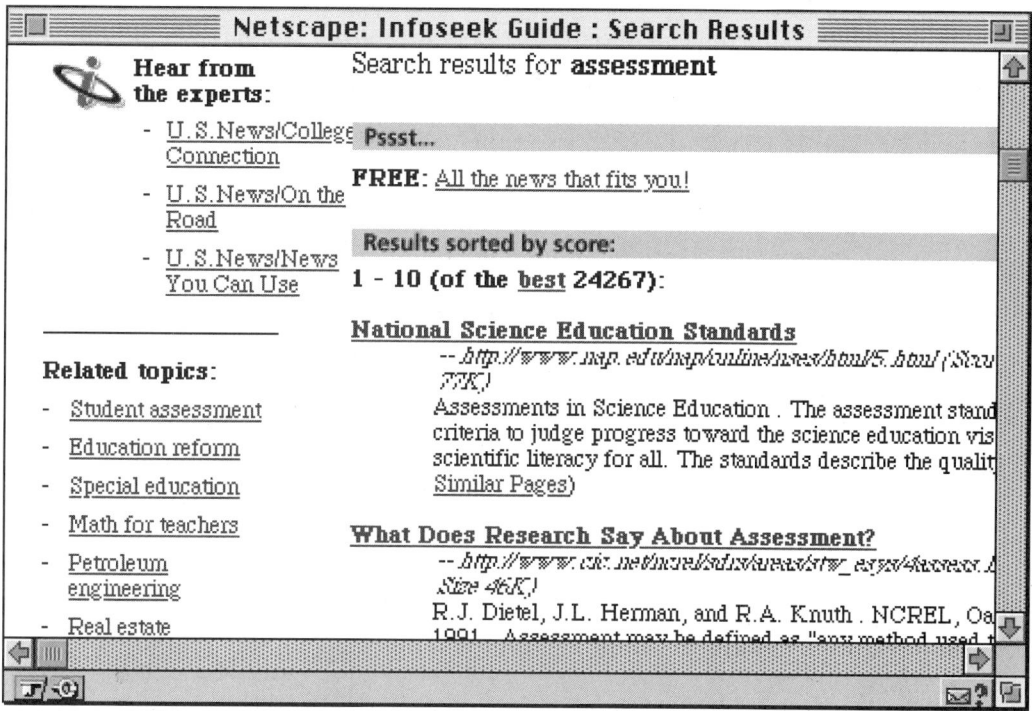

For this search, the search engine located thousands of sites; you may get more or fewer hits depending upon a variety of factors. In addition, a series of related topics appears in the browser window in our search. To go to a site, simply click the link of the site you want to visit. Typically, that site will be linked to another site or series of sites. Because of the nature of the search by a search engine, locating sites is not necessarily the same thing as finding quality sites directly related to your interests. The search engine looks for the occurrence of the phrases you entered; you must make the quality decision regarding the usefulness of the site. There will almost always be sites identified by a search that have no apparent relationship to the phrase you used in your search.

To explore with other search engines, open the file `Search.htm` (08www folder) with your web browser.

USING A SERENDIPITOUS APPROACH TO SEARCHING How else can you find sites? Other sources of Internet sites include books, news magazines, newspapers, radio, television, a friend or colleague, or just random browsing. As you follow the links associated with these sites, you may eventually find the definitive site for your topic.

Suppose someone has given you the following URL for a mathematics site:

```
http://www-groups.dcs.st-and.
ac.uk/~history/Curves/Curves.html
```

With this information, you can use your web browser to go to that site.

- ❏ Start your web browser if you haven't already done so.
- ❏ Choose `File/Open Location…`, and a dialog box will appear on the screen.
- ❏ Enter the URL (of the site you want to visit) into the dialog box and click `Open`.
- ❏ When the home page of the site appears on the screen, you can save a Bookmark to that site by choosing `Bookmark/Save Bookmark`.
- ❏ Since most sites are linked to other sites, you're on your way to finding a series of interesting sites on a topic of interest to you.

We have provided several URLs on a variety of topics. When you want to look at these sites, open the file `Tools.htm` with your web browser, click on `Resources by discipline` (Figure 8.1), and browse the topics you are interested in.

....

Preparing Your Own Web Documents

You will probably eventually want to prepare your own Web documents so that you can easily direct your students to the resources you want them to use with a particular lesson. Web documents are created with **HTML,** which stands for Hypertext Markup Language. Here is a simple example of an HTML document:

<HTML>

<HEAD>

<TITLE>Preparing HTML Documents</TITLE>

</HEAD>

<BODY>

<H1>A Simple HTML Document</H1>

This is a paragraph.<P>

This is another paragraph<P>

</BODY>

</HTML>

It is possible to construct a Web page without the HTML, HEAD, and BODY tags. Currently, most browsers will display your page correctly without these tags. However, as the WWW becomes more complicated, these tags will become increasingly important. So that you will not have to enter these tags every time you start a new Web page, we have saved a template with the name `Template` *with the tags already in the file. Or you can use the* `A new document` *item in the tag library.*

To see what this document looks like when displayed with your web browser, open (or drag-drop) the file `Barely` with your web browser. Note that the title appears at the top of the document in the title bar. An HTML document uses **tags** to tell your web browser how to display its contents. A tag is a command that deals with the page structure of a Web document as it appears on the screen. HTML tags consist of a left angle bracket < followed by the name of the tag and closed by a right angle bracket >. Tags are usually paired, for example <TITLE> and </TITLE>. The ending tag looks just like the starting tag except for a slash (/) that precedes the text within the brackets of the ending tag.

TITLES AND HEADINGS The title tag normally identifies the basic contents or purpose of the home page. The header tag <H1> is used to set off a header, much like the chapter name of a textbook appears at the beginning of the chapter. Frequently, the title and the first header of a document are the same. In a normal word processing document, a return starts a new paragraph. However, a web browser ignores the return; it starts a new paragraph when it encounters a paragraph <P> tag. Consequently, the following source code would have the identical appearance as the previous code when displayed.

<HTML><HEAD><TITLE>Preparing HTML Documents</TITLE></HEAD><BODY>

<H1>A Simple HTML Document</H1>This is a paragraph.>\<P>This is another paragraph</BODY></HTML><P>

In addition, HTML is not case sensitive; <title> is the same as <TITLE>.

PARAGRAPHS Paragraphs are created with the <P> tag. When your browser encounters a <P>, it creates a new paragraph. The browser ignores returns in your text. Let's edit the contents of the file `Barely`.

❑ Open the text file `Barely` with ClarisWorks.

❑ Delete the two paragraphs and replace them with two of your own paragraphs. Be sure there is a paragraph tag <P> located between the two paragraphs; otherwise, the web browser will display your two paragraphs as one paragraph.

❑ Save the edited document as a *text* file with the name `My.htm`.

❑ Open the edited file `My.htm` with your web browser again to observe your new paragraphs.

INLINE IMAGES To place an inline image into a Web document, you use the tag *<IMG SRC="nameOfFile.gif">*, in which you replace `nameOfFile` with the name of your graphic file. However, your graphic must be saved in GIF format before it can be displayed by a browser. In addition, you need to place the

---

If you prefer to use a text editor or if you have a special application for preparing HTML documents, you may prefer to use that application rather than ClarisWorks.

ClarisWorks has its own method for preparing HTML documents, but it is cumbersome, and we prefer to use the technique we have described here. To find out more about the ClarisWorks technique, open the stationery file named `HTML Primer`.

An exception to the pairing rule is the <P> tag; there is no such thing as </P>.

The header <Hn> tag includes an automatic paragraph marker, so you don't need to add a <P> tag.

If you want a new line but with less space than you get with the <P> tag, use the line break <BR> tag. There is no closing line break tag.

If you don't save the document as a text file, your web browser will not display it.

You will need an application such as **M** GIFConverter or **W** Graphics Workshop to convert your graphics to GIF format.

If you prefer not to type in the code for displaying an inline graphic,
❏ Open the library file Tag.
❏ Place a copy of the item Inline image into the document My.htm.
❏ Replace the text nameOfFile.gif with Mike.gif.

graphic file in the same folder as the document in which it will be displayed, or enter the pathname of the file. To practice displaying an inline graphic, we have provided a file named Mike.gif that you can use.

❏ Open the file My.htm with ClarisWorks and enter the following: *<IMG SRC="Mike.gif">* so that your document looks like

<HTML>

<HEAD>

<TITLE>Preparing HTML Documents</TITLE>

</HEAD>

<BODY>

<H1>A Simple HTML Document</H1><P>

<IMG SRC="Mike.gif">

My own paragraph.<P>

My own second paragraph.<P>

</BODY>

</HTML>

❏ Save the edited document again as a *text* file with the name My.htm. Now open (or drag and drop) the edited text file with your web browser.

❏ Open the file My.htm again with ClarisWorks and add the words *Welcome to my home page!* as shown below. Replace the text between the <TITLE> tags with your own title and the text between the header <H1> tags with your own header.

<HTML>

<HEAD>

<TITLE>My Own Title</TITLE>

</HEAD>

<BODY>

<H1>My Own Header</H1><P>

<IMG SRC="Mike.gif">Welcome to my home page!<P>

My own paragraph.<P>

My own second paragraph.<P>

</BODY>

</HTML>

❏ Save the document as a text file.

❏ Now open the text file again with your web browser. Does it appear as you had expected?

❏ Open the file again with ClarisWorks and alter the line *<IMG SRC="Mike.gif"> Welcome to my home page!>* to read *<IMG ALIGN = RIGHT SRC="Mike.gif">Welcome to my home page!>*

❏ Save the document as a text file. Now open the text file with your web browser. What was the effect of the change you made in the document this time?

HORIZONTAL LINES To add a horizontal rule or line to your Web page, use the <HR> tag. Add a horizontal line at the bottom of the my.html document with the <HR> tag.

The <HR> tag includes an automatic paragraph marker, so you don't need to add a <P> tag.

PREFORMATTED TEXT Text is normally formatted in a proportional font. However, there are times when you don't want to use a proportional font, particularly with columns of numbers. To use preformatted or monospaced text, use the <PRE></PRE> tags. Add the following code below the <HR> tag of the my.html document; do *not* use the <tab> key, but instead use spaces to line up the data into two columns:

```
<PRE>

Fiscal 1997     Fiscal 1998

1234.56         345.67

3456.78         67.43

</PRE>
```

LISTS When you need to **list** items on a home page, you can use either an unnumbered or a numbered list.

Bulleted Lists Use the <UL> and <LI> tags to present an unnumbered or **bulleted list,** such as

```
<UL>

<LI>This is the first item.

<LI>This is the second item.
```

<LI>This is the third item.

</UL>

❑ To enter a list to your My.htm document, open the file again with ClarisWorks.

❑ First, let's add a horizontal line with an <HR> tag to set off our list from the rest of the document.

❑ You can enter the appropriate code or open the library Tag and place a copy of the item List.bullet into your document below the <HR> tag you just entered. In either case, replace the three items with your own list.

Numbered Lists Use the <OL> and <LI> tags to present a numbered list, such as

<OL>

<LI>This is the first item.

<LI>This is the second item.

<LI>This is the third item.

</OL>

Enter your own numbered list by typing the list in or using the item List-numbered from the Tag file. When you open your file with a web browser, does it look like you thought it would?

LINKING You can link to other pages or documents in which the general form is <A HREF="Place URL here">Name you want to show</A>. Choose a URL you would like to use and use the sample code above to enter it into your document. You may prefer to use the item Linking in the Tag library. Regardless of the method you prefer, enter the URL you selected in place of Place URL here and a name or phrase to describe the link in place of Name you want to show. The URL should be within the double quotes.

Linking Within a List There will be occasions when you will want to use a list to present choices to a user to link to a site. In order to accomplish this, you can use the item List-nest w/link in the Tag library and replace the items in the template with your own text and URL.

We are assuming at this point that you are saving the changes as a text file and viewing your document with a web browser without being reminded each time to do so.

We want you to pick the URL so that if you are part of a class of thirty, there is less of a chance thirty people will try to access the same server at the same time!

If you type in the code yourself in ClarisWorks, be sure to not use smart quotes. See Edit/ Preferences…/Text if you are not sure if smart quotes is set.

```
            <UL>

            <LI>This.is.line.one

            <UL>

            <LI><A HREF ="Enter.URL.here">This.is.subline.one</A>

            <LI>This.is.the.next.item

            <LI>This.is.the.next.item

            </UL>

      <LI>This.is.line.two

            </UL>
```

Not all WWW browsers support every tag; if a browser doesn't support a tag, it ignores the tag.

Electronic Mail

E-mail is probably the best known and the most frequently used telecommunications tool. Even if you and your students do not have direct access to the Internet, there is a range of activities you can use in your classroom—studying other cultures and languages, collecting and exchanging data, practicing communicating in a foreign language, soliciting advice and information from experts in various fields, and participating in electronic field trips—if you have access to e-mail.

All you need to communicate with others on the Internet is to send an e-mail message to their Internet address. There are numerous e-mail applications, but they all work about the same way.

Your E-mail Address

In order to use e-mail, you will need an e-mail address. Here is my e-mail address:

    mland@nexus.mwsu.edu

An e-mail address is very similar to the URL address we discussed earlier in the chapter. Instead of a type of site (or protocol) at the beginning of the address, however, there is a user name or login name. My user name is *mland:*

- ❏ *mland,* which is a combination of the first initial of my first name and my last name. If you have an e-mail address with a university or a school system, there is probably a standard procedure for determining and issuing user names and addresses, and you probably will not be able to choose just any name.

- ❏ The user name is joined with the next part of the address with the @ symbol.

The *nexus.mwsu.edu* is the address of the server, in which

- ❏ *nexus* is the name of the server or computer on which my account resides,

- ❏ *mwsu* is the subdomain name of the network on which the computer resides (subdomain names frequently indicate the name of a company, university, or unit they represent), and

- ❏ *edu* is the top domain name. In this case, the computer belongs to an educational institution.

If I were telling you my e-mail address, I would say it this way: mland at nexus dot mwsu dot edu.

Preparing and Sending an E-mail Message with Eudora

Start Eudora; if you are prompted for your password (Figure 8.5), enter it and click OK. To begin a new message,

- ❏ Choose Message/New Message, and a new document will appear on the screen (Figure 8.6). The cursor will be on the To line, so

- ❏ Enter the e-mail address of the person to whom you want to send a message and press the <tab> key.

- ❏ The cursor will be on the Subject line. You don't have to enter the subject of your message, but it is a courtesy to enter a short description. In this case you can use something like *My first message.*

- ❏ Press <tab> until the cursor appears in the message area of the document, below the horizontal line.

- ❏ Type a brief message.

- ❏ To send your message, click the Send button at the top of the document window.

Figure 8.5
When prompted to enter your password, enter it and click OK

> *If you have your Eudora files on a floppy disk, you need to insert that disk right now. We are assuming that you have been issued an e-mail address and that you know your password.*

Please enter the mland@nexus.mwsu.edu password:

Password: [   ]

Cancel   OK

Figure 8.6
Choose Message/New Message to start a new message

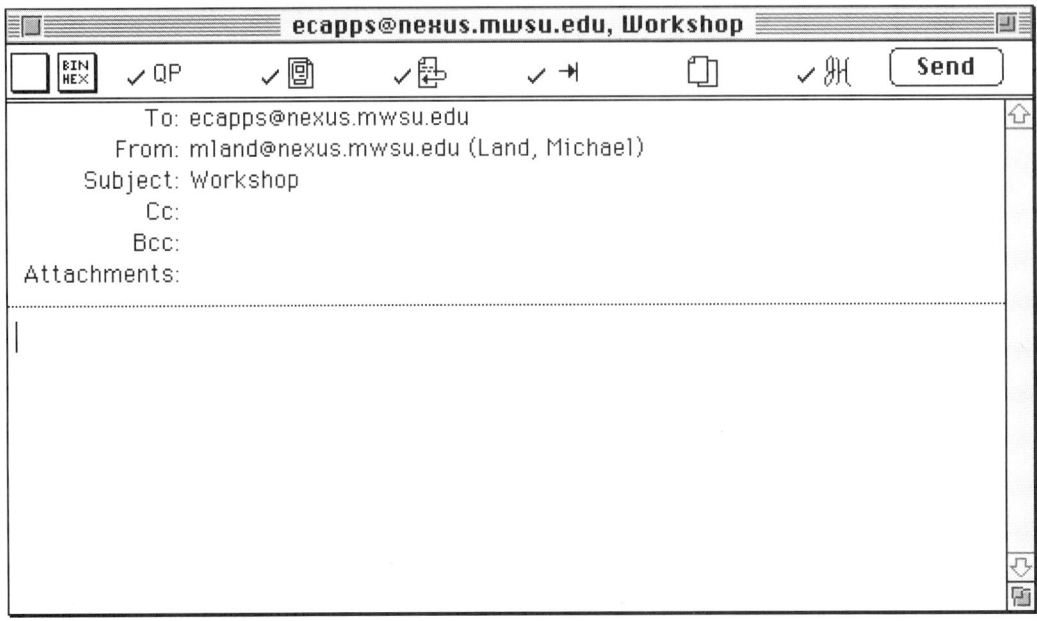

Reading, Replying to, and Forwarding Messages

Every time you start Eudora, it will check to determine if you have new mail. When you receive new mail, it will appear in the In window (Figure 8.7). If the In window does not appear but you want to view its contents, choose Mailbox/In. To read an item, click the row in which the message appears and press **M** <return> or **W** <enter>. After you have read the message, you can (1) leave the message in In, (2) delete the message with Message/ Delete, (3) reply to the message, or (4) forward the message.

Figure 8.7

The In box of Eudora showing messages received

		In			
●		TidBITS Editors	12:32 AM 8/6/96 ·	16	TidBITS#339/05-Aug-
●		TidBITS Editors	12:32 AM 8/6/96 ·	16	TidBITS#339/05-Aug-
		CyberSpLaw@aol.com	12:43 AM 8/7/96 ·	2	Re: Notification: messa
●		CyberSpLaw@aol.com	2:22 AM 8/7/96 -(	6	Cyberspace-Law#21: P
●		TidBITS Editors	10:37 PM 8/12/96	17	TidBITS#340/12-Aug-
●		TidBITS Editors	10:37 PM 8/12/96	17	TidBITS#340/12-Aug-
		Dr. Emerson Capps	2:54 PM 8/15/96 ·	3	ASCD INFO
		Dr. Emerson Capps	3:15 PM 8/15/96 ·	5	more stuff
		Alex Kennedy	3:20 PM 8/16/96 ·	2	Introduction to WEST

32/201K/0K

To reply to the message, choose

❑ Message/Reply, and the message to which you want to reply will appear on the screen with the text highlighted. Notice that the original message has a > symbol on the left margin (Figure 8.8). This is a standard procedure used to distinguish between the messages of the sender and the next recipient.

Figure 8.8

To reply to a message, choose Message/Reply, enter your reply, and click Send

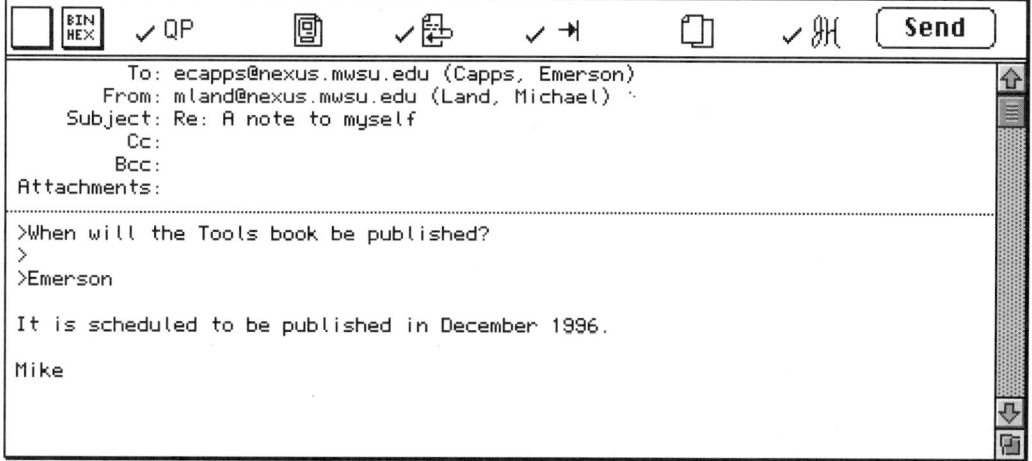

❏ You can delete as little or as much of the original message as you think necessary. Remember, though, that the person who sent the message may not recall exactly the message she or he sent, so it is a courtesy to leave that part of the message to which you are replying. Enter your reply and click `Send`.

To forward a message to another person, choose

❏ `Message/Forward,` and the message to which you want to reply will appear on the screen.

❏ Enter the e-mail address of the person to whom you want to forward the message. If you want to enter a brief message in explanation, click in the message area and type in the message.

❏ When you are ready to send the message, click `Send`.

Searching for People

The URL for the White Pages is `http://home.netscape.com/home/internet-white-pages.html.`

Where can I find someone's e-mail address? There is no one directory you can go to on the Internet to find this information. The best way is usually just to ask in person the person whose address you want! However, there are resources on the Internet that can provide assistance in locating people and organizations. If you are using Netscape, point to `Directory/Internet White Pages.`

Mailing Lists

When you use e-mail, you usually send one message to one person, although it is possible to send one message to a group of people. Suppose that you wanted to interact with a group of teachers who teach the same subjects that you do. You may want to ask questions or perhaps even answer questions from other teachers. You could use e-mail, but you may not even know who these teachers are, much less know their e-mail addresses. One way to participate with a large group is an electronic discussion referred to as an **electronic list.**

A list is sometimes called a mailing list, a distribution list, or a listserv. A listserv is actually an electronic list manager, a computer program.

SUBSCRIBING TO A LIST Suppose that a friend has given you the following information on a listserv that you are interested in joining. This list is composed of teachers who are interested in Internet access for K–12 schools:

Name of list: WVNK12-L

Administrative address: listserv@wvnvm.wvnet.edu

Posting or participating address: wvn12-l@wvnvm.wvnet.edu

❑ Open Eudora or other e-mail application and start a new message.

❑ Type in the full administrative address in the To box. In this case the address is *listserv@wvnvm.wvnet.edu* and must be typed exactly as it appears.

❑ Leave the Subject box blank. Press the <tab> key until you get to the message area.

❑ In the message area, type *subscribe* (or *sub*) followed by the name of the list followed by your name: *subscribe nameOfList Your Name*. For me, the line would look like this: *subscribe WVNK12-L Michael Land*.

❑ If Signature is on ✓ 𝔅ℋ, then turn it off by clicking the icon.

❑ Click Send. Soon you will receive mail from the list to indicate that you have been subscribed to the list or if there is an error. Keep the message you received when you have successfully joined the list. Among other things, this message tells you how to unsubscribe. Depending upon a number of factors, you may receive either a few messages or hundreds of messages over a short period of time.

POSTING TO A LIST When you want to **post,** or send a message to the individuals on the list, you start a new message and send it to the *posting* address, not the administrative address. When you want to send a message to the listserv (the application that manages the list), you send the message to the *administrative* address. Most people will send a message to the listserv only to subscribe or to unsubscribe.

FINDING A MAILING LIST There are literally thousands of lists; you can't join all of them! To find the lists you are interested in, open the file Tools.html with your web browser and click on Mailing lists in the table.

···

Netiquette

Just as there are rude people in the general population, there are also rude people on the Internet. The basic guideline is to be just as courteous online and with e-mail as you are in person.

❑ Don't say, do, or send anything electronically that you would not do in your classroom.

❑ There may be times when someone sends you or your students a rude or inflammatory message; refrain from sending that individual a

If you leave Signature *on, it will append whatever you have in your* Signature *file to the end of the message, and you may get an error from the list you are trying to subscribe to. You know* Signature *is turned off when the icon looks like* 𝔅ℋ

rather than ✓ 𝔅ℋ.

flame. **Flaming** is the term used for inflammatory messages on the Internet. If you receive a flame, either ignore it or send a calm reply.

❏ Refrain from using all CAPITALS. Using all caps is equivalent to screaming on the Internet.

❏ If you want to express emotion to convey feeling, consider using a **smiley** or **emoticon** to convey that emotion. Common emoticons include the following:

:-) a smile or grin

:-(a frown

ROTFL Rolling on the floor laughing

IMHO In my humble opinion

In the Classroom

There are numerous ways to look at the use of the Internet in the classroom. In this section, we will present two perspectives on the use of the Internet in the K–12 curriculum. The intent is to provide you with different perspectives so that you can begin planning appropriate use of telecommunications resources in your classroom.

The Internet as Global Classroom, Learning Center, and Communications Mechanism

This section presents a view of the Internet based upon what is already familiar to teachers—lesson plans, activities, materials. The groups are not mutually exclusive but are meant to be descriptive of what is available.

This approach to describing the resources available on the Internet has the advantage of using the known or familiar to approach the unknown, and increases the chances that teachers will pursue their exploration of the Internet as a source of instructional resources. To see examples of each of the following resources, open the `Tools.htm` file (in the `08www` folder) with your web browser and click on `Resources by Instructional Type`. Then click on the type of resource you want to explore:

- ❏ Lessons and Lesson Plans
- ❏ Classroom and Curriculum Activities and Resources
- ❏ Content-Area Resources
- ❏ Online Libraries, Museums, Field Trips, Tutorials, and Periodicals
- ❏ Assessment and Evaluation Resources
- ❏ Teacher Support and Information

Network-Based Educational Activity Structures

Harris (1996) has identified sixteen Internet activity structures that she classifies into three genres. Following is a brief description of each of the structures. For more information and examples of the following items, open the file `Browse.html` with your web browser and then click `Internet-based Activity Structures`.

PROBLEM-SOLVING PROJECTS These activities are community problem-solving projects (either collaborative or competitive) in which the participants can be located in various parts of the world.

Electronic Process Writing In this approach, students use e-mail to communicate with others, with a focus on writing. Students may communicate with other students or with college students, professors, or professional writers. In some cases, the writing project asks students to concentrate their feedback mainly on the *content* of each other's writing, although some projects ask writers to concentrate primarily upon the *forms* through which content is communicated.

Information Searches In these online activities, students receive clues and then use either electronic or classroom resources to answer the questions.

Parallel Problem Solving With this structure, students from two or more locations are presented with a similar problem; they solve or attempt to solve the problem and then share their problem-solving approaches electronically.

Sequential Creations In this type of activity, the participants in turn create some type of written text, such as a poem or a story, or create and add to a graphic or visual image. This product is sent electronically to other students, who add their contribution and send it on to still other students.

Simulations This type of activity is the most difficult to plan and carry through but may be the most educational. The idea is to present real-world problems to students, who then attempt to solve those problems online.

Social Action Projects The focus of this type of activity is to have students work together electronically "to create collaborative, meaningful social action projects in which children" have the main responsibility for learning about and helping to solve important global issues (Harris, 1996, p. 177).

Virtual Gatherings These activities bring students or participants together from different locations in real time to participate virtually in a computer-mediated meeting. A variation is that some participants may participate in similar activities at various project sites without direct electronic contact "in spirit" (Harris, 1996, p. 173).

INFORMATION COLLECTIONS In this group of activities, students find, collect, and compare data on a topic of interest to them or on a topic they have been assigned.

Database Creation This activity involves the collection and organization of data into database format; the database file can continue to grow and can possibly be used by the next class as an aid in studying a particular topic. The project

can be a district, city, region, state, national, or international one, depending upon the area of study and the interests and organizing capabilities of the project director.

Electronic Publishing This type of information collection and exchange occurs with the electronic publication of a document such as a magazine, newspaper, poem, or story.

Information Exchanges This type of information exchange can be on any topic that is considered to be of educational value, whether it be idioms in a particular region of the country or the types of trees in a particular region. The potential range of topics is limited only by the imagination of the teacher and the students involved.

Pooled Data Analysis Data are collected from various participating sites and then combined for analysis. The activity can be as simple as a survey on a single issue to data collection on complex topics and issues in the behavioral, earth, and life sciences.

Tele-fieldtrips In this activity, teachers and students worldwide, from their own classroom, can participate in observations of an actual field trip. A classic example of a tele-fieldtrip is MayaQuest, in which a team of cyclists and archaeologists took an expedition to Central America to study the Mayan culture. The team sent pictures (electronically) and explanations of what they experienced as they continued with their expedition.

INTERPERSONAL EXCHANGES In this category of activity, individuals communicate electronically with other individuals by using e-mail, electronic lists, newsgroups, or electronic bulletin boards.

Electronic Appearances A guest can make an electronic appearance by means of e-mail, electronic lists, newsgroups, or electronic bulletin boards. Participants, including the guest, can participate in an exchange of ideas, questions, and responses. This technique is particularly useful for appearances by current newsmakers, scientists, politicians, and specialists in a wide range of disciplines.

Electronic Mentoring This type of mentoring can be between two students or between student (or students) and a specialist from business, industry, the military, or a university. An example of this type of mentoring is Ask Dr. Math. By making the questions and responses available electronically, one can build up an archive from which others can benefit.

Global Classrooms In this type of activity, two or more classrooms study and share a common topic. Topics can range from current topics of interest in the news to literature, science, language, and cultural topics.

Impersonations In this activity, someone, perhaps a university professor or graduate student, plays the role of a famous individual and responds to questions submitted electronically. Characters can range from historical figures to characters from literature.

Keypals In this activity, students are typically paired to communicate with each other electronically with e-mail. They can select the topic of conversation themselves, or the teacher can assign topics. This type of activity can be used successfully for cultural and language activities in another county, state, or country.

Q-and-A Services In this activity structure, students submit questions electronically to an expert either by e-mail or on an electronic list.

To see examples of each of the previous resources, open the `Tools.htm` file with your web browser and click on `Resources by instructional type`.

What Are Other Schools Doing?

In one study reported by Dyrli and Kinnaman (1996b, p. 60), the most popular learning activities on the Internet (reported by schools in twenty-one states) were, in decreasing order of occurrence:

- ❏ searching for specific information online
- ❏ browsing with applications such as gopher or a WWW browser
- ❏ electronic keypal exchanges between individual students
- ❏ "electronic field trips" to museums, science centers, or with adults conducting a scientific or creative activity
- ❏ publishing class or individual products on the network
- ❏ collaborative science investigations with classes in other places
- ❏ collaborative writing projects with classes in other places
- ❏ "cultural exchanges" with classes in other places

Integrating Telecommunications into Your Classroom

Getting started is often the most difficult part of initiating a new procedure in your classroom. You and your students will need specific telecommunications skills before you can expect to be successful in integrating telecommunications into your curriculum. The students can learn and practice with these skills just prior to using them (just-in-time training) or along with their actual use in the curriculum.

Dyrli and Kinnaman (Jan 1996, p. 70) have suggested the following approach to getting started:

❑ *Review current curriculum and adapt learning experiences as online activities.* Evaluate the content (concepts, principles) and the processes (observing, inferring, predicting, measuring, communicating) of current instructional units, and determine what might be supplemented with online activities, experiences, or other resources. Examples include using online research tools, visiting online locations for specific purposes, participating in collaborative projects with other students in various places around the world, and communicating online with experts.

❑ *Join an education electronic list, discussion group, or newsgroup* to ask for resource suggestions, locate online resources, seek keypals, and initiate your own cooperative activities.

❑ *Visit education resource locations and explore the available offerings.* Find an efficient and effective way, such as the use of bookmarks, to keep URLs and descriptions of the sites of most interest to you and your students. One way is to develop a database with fields for the name of the site, the URL, and a brief description of what is available at the site.

❑ *Use Internet guides and search tools* to locate curriculum and content materials and opportunities.

❑ *Gradually move to more extensive projects and curriculum units.*

Questions and Answers

Q1: **I don't like the home page that comes up when I start Netscape on my computer. Can I change it?**

A: Yes, you can change your home page. You can use a special file that you or someone else has created, or you can link to another site. Suppose you want your home page to open with the file `Tools.htm`. For Netscape 1.n, the directions are as follows:

❑ Choose `Preferences` from the `Options` menu.

❑ Choose the `Window and Link Styles` tab.

❑ For `Home Page Location`, enter `Tools.htm`. (If you are linking to another site, enter the URL of that site instead.)

❑ Click the `OK` button.

❑ Choose `Save Options` from the `Options` menu.

For Netscape 2.n, the directions are as follows:

❑ Choose `General Preferences` from the `Options` menu.

❑ Choose the `Appearance` tab.

❑ Choose `Home Page Location` in the `Startup` section and enter `Tools.htm`. (If you are linking to another site, enter the URL of that site instead.)

❑ Click the `OK` button.

❑ Choose `Save Options` from the `Options` menu.

Q2: **What is a newsgroup?**

A: A newsgroup is comparable to a large online bulletin board organized by areas; most newsgroups are conducted by a separate USENET network (Dyrli & Kinnaman, 1996a). If you have access to a newsgroup server, you either access newsgroups with a special reader or through your web browser. You do not subscribe to a group as you do with an electronic list. Newsgroups have descriptive names; among the educational newsgroups of interest to teachers are k12.chat.teacher, k12.ed.art, k12.ed.health.pe, k12.ed.math, k12.ed.music, k12.ed.science, k12.ed.soc-studies, and k12.ed.lang.art.

Q3: **I want to send a friend a copy of a file that I prepared with ClarisWorks. Can I send it electronically?**

A: You can send a copy of the file by attaching it to a Eudora e-mail message with `Message/Attach Document...`

Q4: **Is it possible to save an e-mail message and open it up with ClarisWorks?**

A: When the message appears on the screen, use `File/Save` to save it to a disk. You can open the resulting file with ClarisWorks.

Q5: **Is it possible to send a carbon copy of an e-mail message?**

A: Yes. If you are using Eudora, enter the person's address on the `Cc` line. If you want to send a blind carbon copy to someone, enter that person's address on the `Bcc` line.

Q6: **How can I keep a copy of an e-mail message that I send to someone?**

A: There are a couple of ways to send yourself a copy of a message. You can click the 📄 icon at the top of a Eudora e-mail document until a checkmark appears to the left of the icon (when you send the message, your copy will be placed in the `Out` messages), or you can send yourself a carbon copy by typing your e-mail address on the `Cc` or `Bcc` line.

Q7: **What does *FAQ* mean?**

A: *FAQ* is the abbreviation for "frequently asked questions." Many lists and newsgroups post a file of these questions in a file called FAQ so they don't have to keep answering the same frequently asked questions!

Q8: **In Eudora, what is the difference between `New Message` and `New Message To` in the `Message` menu?**

A: If you are going to type in the address, use `New Message`. If you have entered and saved a series of addresses under `Nicknames`, you can use `New Message To` and pull down to the name of the person to whom you want to address the message, without typing. The same technique works with `Reply To` and `Forward To`.

Activities

1. Select a topic in your teaching area or major and then search with a search engine for information or resources on that topic.

2. Perform the same search on a topic in your teaching field with four different WWW search engines, and compare the results.

3. Prepare a list of potential online "experts" that you might use with your students to enrich your curriculum.

4. Identify an instructional activity or lesson that you have used or seen in a classroom that could be enhanced by some type of Internet participation. What benefit would be added to the lesson by using the Internet? Now identify a lesson that would derive little or no benefit by involving students on the Internet.

5. Prepare a home page that includes the following:
   - ❏ The name of your class or subject matter area
   - ❏ A picture of yourself or an inline graphic of some kind
   - ❏ A *list* of at least three search engines (appropriate for your teaching field) that the user can access by clicking
   - ❏ Anchors to at least three interesting sites on a topic in your teaching field

   You can start your document from scratch, use the file `Template,` or use the `A new document` item in the `Tag` library.

6. Prepare a rubric or checklist for one of the following groups of items to verify that your students (or you) can perform the indicated telecommunications skill:
   - ❏ Use an e-mail client, to include sending an e-mail message, responding to e-mail messages, attaching a file to an e-mail message, saving or storing e-mail messages, and deleting e-mail.
   - ❏ Use an electronic list, to include subscribing to, replying to a list message, replying to a single individual on a list, and unsubscribing from.
   - ❏ Search the Internet with a search engine.
   - ❏ Navigate with a graphic web browser such as Netscape.
   - ❏ Construct a simple home page.

7. Prepare bookmarks (or add them to a home page) consisting of at least ten WWW sites appropriate for your teaching field and for the grade level of your students. Document your search for these sites.

8. Select a current unit that you teach and determine what content (concepts, principles) and processes (observing, inferring, predicting, measuring, communicating) might be supplemented with online activities, experiences, or other resources.

9. If your students have separate e-mail addresses, you can use the following two activities for practice:

❏ Play an electronic version of "Gossip" by having one student send an e-mail message to another student from a list of class e-mail addresses. This student makes one change to the message and forwards it to the next student on the list. Continue until the first person receives a message from the last person on the list. Have the first person compare the original message to the message received from the last participant. If your students don't have separate addresses, a variation is to contact other schools whose students need practice sending e-mail and make it a group activity.

❏ Give each student a list of class e-mail addresses and have each student write an e-mail message to the person whose address appears immediately after his or her name on the list. If you want your students to have practice in sending carbon copies, have them send a carbon copy (Cc) to the second person and a blind carbon (Bcc) to the third person whose address comes after their address. Have students reply to each message they receive. This activity also presents a good opportunity for students to practice deleting e-mail messages. The technique ensures that each student will send and receive e-mail. You need to be sure to make adjustments if anyone is absent on the day you present this activity; otherwise, the chain will be broken by the person who is absent.

10. Prepare a list of five educational activities that *your* students could participate in with e-mail.

11. To supplement an instructional unit, develop an Internet "treasure" hunt appropriate for your students.

12. Develop an assessment device for your treasure hunt above to determine if your students have become skilled in the use of the indicated information-retrieval devices.

Summary

The influence of telecommunications on education will not be as dramatic as some suggest, but will be more dramatic than others hope. Telecommunications will have an impact on schooling because it is an outside-of-the-schools force that is pervasive in our society, whether it be in business, in the military, in higher education, or in industry. It will also have a dramatic impact upon our culture. For instance, compare the current references to the Internet in magazines, books, newspapers, television, radio, and movies to references as recent as 1994. There is a revolution occurring in the telecommunications industry; schools couldn't avoid this revolution even if they wanted to.

The traditional curriculum is typically not connected directly to the lives of most students, can become outdated quickly, and is seldom individualized. Conversely, telecommunications brings immediacy and individualization to the curriculum; brings up-to-date materials, including articles, databases, maps, reports, surveys, diagrams, film clips, photographs, and sound bites; and has the potential to transform the curriculum (Dyrli & Kinnaman, 1996a, p. 65).

It's a dynamic, exciting time to be a teacher and a student!

Key Terms

bookmark 247

bulleted list 253

client-server 244

electronic list 260

emoticon 262

flaming 262

home page 245

HTML 250

http 246

Internet 242

link 245

list 253

post 261

search engine 247

smiley 262

subdomain 246

tags 251

top domain 246

URL 246

web browser 245

World Wide Web 244

References

Armstrong, S. (1996). *Kidstuff on the Internet.* San Francisco: Sybex.

Bull, G., Bull, G., & Sigmon, T. (1996). An electronic journey. *Learning and Leading with Technology, 23*(5), 17–21.

Castro, E. (1996). *HTML for the World Wide Web.* Berkeley, CA: Peachpit Press.

Cohen, L. (1995). Safe at home: An anatomy of the World Wide Web home page (Focus on Teaching). *Business Communication Quarterly, 58*(3), 41–43.

Cotton, E. G. (1996). *The online classroom: Teaching with the Internet.* Bloomington, IN: ERIC Clearinghouse on Reading, English, and Communication.

Dubin, D. (1995). Search strategies for Internet resources. *School Library Media Quarterly, 4,* 53–54.

Dyrli, O. E. (1996). The online connection: Does your school have an acceptable use policy? *Technology & Learning, 16*(4), 18.

Dyrli, O. E., & Kinnaman, D. E. (1996a). Energizing the classroom curriculum through telecommunications. *Technology & Learning, 16*(4), 65–70.

———. (1996b). Teaching effectively with telecommunications. *Technology & Learning, 16*(5), 57–62.

Eager, B. (1994). *Using the World Wide Web.* Indianapolis: Que Corporation.

Ellsworth, J. (1994). *Education on the Internet.* Indianapolis: SAMS Publishing.

Ernst, W. (1995). *Using Netscape.* Indianapolis: Que Corporation.

Guardo, C. J., & Rivinius, S. (1995). Save before closing: Bringing technology to the liberal arts. *Liberal Education, 81*(3), 22–27.

Harris, J. (1995). *Way of the ferret: Finding and using educational resources on the Internet.* Eugene, OR: International Society for Technology in Education.

Junion-Metz, G. (1996). *K–12 resources on the Internet: An instructional guide.* Internet Workshop Series, Number 5. (ERIC Document No. ED 389316)

Lynch, P. J. (1996a). Creating graphics for the World Wide Web: File formats for web pages. *Syllabus, 9*(4), 46–48.

———. (1996b). Optimizing color graphics for the web. *Syllabus, 9*(5), 30–31.

Maxwell, C., & Grycz, C. J. (1994). *Internet yellow pages.* Indianapolis: New Riders Publishing.

Pike, M. A., *et al.* (1995). *Using the Internet.* Indianapolis: Que Corporation.

Ryder, R. J., & Hughes, T. (1997). *Internet for educators.* Upper Saddle River, NJ: Prentice-Hall.

Silva, P. U., Meagher, M. E., Valenzuela, M., & Crenshaw, S. W. (1996). E-mail: Real-life classroom experiences with foreign languages. *Learning and Leading with Technology, 23*(5), 10–12.

Smith, B. E. (1996). Mathematics resources on the World Wide Web. *Syllabus, 9*(7), 28–29.

Tennant, R. (1996a). So you want to be a web manager. *Syllabus, 9*(4), 50, 52–53.

———. (1996b). The best tools for searching the Internet. *Syllabus, 9*(5), 36–38.

Vesel, J. H. (1996). Using teleconversations to explore social issues. *Learning and Leading with Technology, 23*(5), 27–30.

Warschauer, M. (1995). *E-mail for English teaching: Bringing the Internet and computer learning networks into the language classroom.* (ERIC Document No. ED 389211)

Williams, B. (1995). *The Internet for teachers.* Foster City, CA: IDG Books Worldwide.

———. (1996). *The World Wide Web for teachers.* Foster City, CA: IDG Books Worldwide.

9

Integrating Technology into the Curriculum

O B J E C T I V E S

Plan and implement a computer-integrated curriculum.

Discuss issues related to the use of technology in the classroom.

Use teaching strategies that simplify management of technology-related instruction and enhance learning.

Evaluate lessons that use computers.

IN EARLIER CHAPTERS YOU learned to use different kinds of applications software—word processing, graphics, slide show, page layout, database, spreadsheet, hypermedia, and telecommunications. Now that you know something of how to use this software and how it might be used with your students, how do you integrate the computer into your curriculum? How do you plan and implement a curriculum that uses technology? What issues need to be considered? What classroom teaching strategies have other teachers found successful? How can you evaluate lessons that use technology?

Curriculum Planning

Technology programs usually serve one of two goals: to teach students about computers or to teach traditional content with the assistance of the computer. What is the rationale that supports each of these goals?

....

Teaching About Computers

Computer education programs that aim to teach students about computers and technology usually include objectives such as the following. The student will

- ❏ Identify the capabilities and limitations of computers.
- ❏ Describe the basic parts of a computer system.
- ❏ Demonstrate proper care of hardware and software.
- ❏ Describe the historical development of computing.
- ❏ Describe common uses of technology and their effect on society and people's lives.
- ❏ Start and operate a computer-assisted instruction (CAI) program independently.
- ❏ Be able to use the computer as a word processor.
- ❏ Write and run a simple program.
- ❏ Describe the history and use of the Internet.

The rationale for teaching students about technology is that such training provides preparation for a technological society, for a vocation, and for further academic study. Since computers play an enormous and rapidly expanding role in our society and in many of the jobs and professions our students will have in the future, it seems reasonable for them to know what a computer can do and how to use it.

Teaching with Computers

A different approach to curriculum planning is to review each objective that is already in the school's curriculum and plan how computers can be used to enhance the attainment of those objectives. The rationale is that the computer is a teaching *tool* and that students should be taught with computers and technology when such teaching provides some advantage over more conventional methods. One of those advantages is that students who use the computer in this way are using computers in the same ways that people in the world of work are using them—persons in business, industry, manufacturing, education, and the military are using computers as a tool to make them more productive in their job or profession.

There are different ways in which schools teach content with the assistance of computers. One way is by using computer-assisted instruction software to present instruction as a supplement to conventional teaching methods. The advantage of using the computer to deliver instruction is that the computer is patient, provides immediate feedback, can individualize instruction, and can provide experiences that would be impractical to provide otherwise.

Another way that computers can be used to teach traditional content is through the use of applications software. With applications software, the computer helps to make students' work easier, improve the efficiency of the teaching and learning process, and produce more professional-looking work. Word processing applications make the writing process easier, graphics illustrate an idea or express their creativity, slide show and page layout applications present students' views and work, database and spreadsheet applications search for and analyze data, hypermedia applications provide links among various types of data, and the Internet and e-mail access vast information pools and communicate with a worldwide audience. The computer, then, becomes a tool for accomplishing traditional content-area objectives across the curriculum.

Programming is another way that computers can be used to teach traditional content. In mathematics and science, students can write programs to explore relationships among variables and to solve specific problems.

Which Goal to Choose?

Given the two common goals of computer education programs, how do you decide which is more appropriate for your school or district? The two goals—teaching about computers and teaching with computers—are not mutually exclusive. A school may have several computer education programs serving different purposes. For example, a high school may have a computer science pro-

gram that prepares students for further academic study in computer science, and it may also use word processing and page layout in composition classes, databases in social sciences and science, hypermedia in other classes, spreadsheets in mathematics, and Internet resources in a variety of classes. Furthermore, a single program in computer education may serve both purposes. By using applications software in a variety of subject areas, students also learn about the computer—its capabilities and limitations, how it affects the way people work, how to use various kinds of software, and the meaning of computer terminology.

One of the major questions posed by teachers and administrators is "How do we fit computers into the curriculum without lengthening the school day?" If computer education is viewed as a new area of study that must be taught in addition to the regular curriculum, then it is difficult to find the time for a computer program without shortchanging another area of study. But if computer-related activities are designed to support the regular curriculum, they won't distract from it, they will enhance it.

Establishing a Computer-Integrated Curriculum

How does a school go about establishing a computer-integrated curriculum, one in which the computer is used as a teaching tool in traditional content areas? Planning and implementing a computer-integrated curriculum is an enormous task for a school or district to undertake. In comparison with other educational programs, computer education programs require unusually large commitments of money, personnel, facilities, and training. Not only must computers be purchased, but funds must be budgeted for maintaining the equipment; modifying the facilities; purchasing software, computer supplies, and furniture; providing teacher training; and perhaps hiring a computer resource teacher to coordinate the program. It also requires a major commitment of time from all the teachers in the school or district. Teachers of all grade levels and all subject areas should be involved in planning how the computer can best be used in their curricula, in reviewing software, in learning how to use the software, and in developing lessons and activities for their students.

Obviously, a school or district will need to implement a computer education curriculum in stages over several years, and in the process continually evaluate the plan in light of new developments in technology. In any area, curriculum planning is a process of refinement—customizing until what is taught fits the needs of teachers and students—but this is especially true in computer education because the available technology is constantly changing.

Issues in Using Computers

There are many issues that have led schools to take different paths in deciding how their computers are used. In this section, we will discuss a number of issues related to the integration of the computer into the curriculum.

Do Students Need Keyboarding Skills?

Word processing is a powerful tool for students, but if they don't know how to type, it can be a frustrating experience. Often when students first use the computer to enter information, they scan the rows of keys looking for a particular letter or symbol. Even when they become somewhat familiar with the location of commonly used keys, their "hunt and peck" method is slow. To assist students in becoming more efficient in the use of the keyboard, many schools are introducing keyboarding skills into the elementary school curriculum.

Keyboarding is learning the appropriate technique for using a computer keyboard to enter text or data. In the primary grades (K–2), the goal may simply be for the students to use the left hand for keys on the left side of the keyboard and the right hand for keys on the right. Teachers can place a piece of yarn down the middle of the keyboard as a visual reminder for the student. In the second or third grade, the home-row keys can be introduced. Small, round stickers of different colors can be placed on each home-row key and on the corresponding alphabet keys to encourage students to use the proper fingering.

Beginning about the fourth grade, some schools start more formal keyboarding instruction using software designed for that purpose (or a word processor with carefully sequenced written lessons). The overall goal is for students to be able to type as fast as they can write by hand. Emphasis is on the correct technique rather than on accuracy. Teachers have found that fourth graders are ready to learn keyboarding and can become proficient with approximately thirty hours of instruction over two or three consecutive years (Jackson & Berg, 1986). However, if students do not have an opportunity to apply the skills they have learned, their keyboarding skills may deteriorate rapidly.

Computer-using educators have divided opinions on the merits of teaching keyboarding. Some feel that keyboarding should be a prerequisite to word processing and other computer activities so that students do not develop bad keyboarding

habits. However, others feel that students should not be held back from more interesting uses of the computer until they have mastered the keyboard. The important thing to keep in mind is that keyboarding is not an end in itself but the means to more efficient use of the computer. If keyboarding is taught, it makes sense to combine it with the teaching of word processing and writing so that students can immediately apply their skills to make writing easier and more enjoyable.

Where Should the Computers Be Located?

Another issue confronting schools is the location of the computers. Should the school's computers be placed all together in a computer lab or in individual classrooms? Should they be placed on mobile carts so that they can be moved around the school as needed? Should some be placed in the learning or media center so that students have access to them throughout the day? Each arrangement offers distinct advantages and disadvantages.

COMPUTER LAB The advantage of a computer lab is that it is able to accommodate a total class at one time. Ideally, the lab should have enough computers so that there is one computer per student for the largest class size in the school. But even one computer for every two students is a workable arrangement. If the largest class size is thirty students, then fifteen computers are needed for the lab. In that case, depending upon the activity, students can work in pairs at the computers, or half of the class can work at the computers while the other half does related work that is not hands-on. For some activities, each student must have his or her own computer, but for other activities, such as searching for information in a database or conducting an Internet search, students can work in pairs and take turns as keyboarder and proofreader. Tables should be available in the computer lab so that students involved in off-computer activities can have a place to work.

CLASSROOM Locating computers in the classrooms encourages teachers to integrate the computer across the curriculum, since it is readily available at any time. Usually, the computer area is used as an activity center where students work independently or in small groups. Students can move easily from paper-and-pencil planning to keyboard activity. One of the computers can also be connected to a large screen monitor or projection system for whole-class presentations and demonstrations. If the school has more classrooms than available computers, however, this approach means that some students will not have an opportunity to use computers, whereas all students in the school are able to use the computers in a computer lab.

LAB AND CLASSROOM COMBINATION Increasing numbers of schools have both computer labs and computers in the classrooms. Then whole-group instruction can take place in the lab, while individual work is usually done in the classroom. If the school has enough computers, this is an ideal arrangement. It allows for flexibility and simplifies the teacher's job of planning and managing.

MOBILE COMPUTERS In some schools the computers are on mobile carts so that they are easily moved from the computer lab (or wherever they are kept) to the classroom and from classroom to classroom. This plan provides a maximum of flexibility, but moving computers around the building can increase the maintenance costs, and it requires careful scheduling.

MEDIA OR LEARNING CENTER A few computers should be located so that students can use them independently even when a class is scheduled in the computer lab. Students may want to work on a writing assignment, access an online database for a research report, make a cover for a science report, or compose an article for the school newspaper. The media center is an ideal place for individual computer work. Usually, the media- or learning-center specialist can provide supervision.

WHICH LOCATION IS BEST? If the goal is to integrate computers into the curriculum, it seems logical that the computers should be in the classroom, where they are readily available. But in order for students to use the computer as a tool, they must learn to use the particular software and have hands-on opportunities to practice it. Most teachers find it easier to teach the skills of using a word processor or database program to the whole class in a lab setting. If the students are comfortable using the software, though, having a computer and printer in the classroom provides more opportunities to use the computer as part of the regular curriculum.

How Can One Software Application Be Used on Several Computers?

Software can be a significant part of a school's budget, especially if separate copies are needed for each computer in the school. Although a few educational applications are in the public domain, most commercial software is copyrighted.

If software is copyrighted, the owner has the legal right to have one backup copy for archival purposes, to be used in case the original is damaged. It is not legal to make extra copies of copyrighted software to use on several computers at the same time unless the school or district has a specific agreement to that effect.

Software companies have designed various options to make multiple copies or a network copy of their software affordable for schools. Some publishers offer "lab packs" of four, six, ten, or twenty copies at a considerable discount over the single-copy price. Others offer a **site licensing agreement,** which gives the school the right to make as many copies as needed for instructional use within the school. The site licensing agreement may include a home copy option to enable the licensed school to give each student a copy of the software to use at home on a desktop or laptop computer.

Software publishers have invested millions of dollars in time and money in the development of quality software. Schools have not only a legal obligation to enforce the copyright law but also a moral one.

Do We Need an Acceptable Use Policy for the Internet?

There are sexist, racist, sexual, and other offensive materials available on the Internet, just as they are available to the public in the general marketplace. Unfortunately, the public may think of the Internet as something that has no place in the classroom because of the focus by the media on a tiny part of what is available on the Internet. Should you attempt to censor the content of the Internet? There is software that will allow you to block or filter access to certain sites. However, this approach is not without its own problems. There are tens of thousands of sites on the Internet, and there are site changes daily; it would be impossible to try to keep up with these changes.

Schools and teachers have always had the problem of monitoring student behavior; access to "inappropriate" resources on the Internet is basically the same problem, but with a twist. Perhaps a more prudent approach would be to concentrate on teaching students to take responsibility for their behavior, whether it be on the Internet, at home, at school, or elsewhere, and to communicate what is acceptable behavior regarding use of the Internet.

Prior to any incident involving use of the Internet in your school, you need to develop an acceptable use policy. Dyrli (1996) suggested giving consideration to the following items when developing the policy for a school:

1. *Review the acceptable use policy (AUP) of other schools* before constructing your own. For guidelines and examples, point your web browser at the following sites:

❏ http://www.classroom.net/classroom/aup.htm

❏ http://www.rice.edu/armadillo/acceptable.html There may be a temptation to copy the AUP of another school, but you should adopt it to the conditions and circumstances of your school.

2. *Keep your AUP brief.* One or two pages should be enough to set the guidelines.

3. *Use understandable user behavior.* Keep the language as simple and nontechnical as possible, but focus on desirable behavior.

4. *Have both students and parents sign the agreement.*

5. *Review the AUP with your students each year.*

In the Classroom

Teachers who have been using computers in both classroom and lab settings have shared with us the following teaching ideas and management suggestions:

1. Teach students how to insert a floppy disk, how to maneuver around a hard disk, how to care for floppy disks, how to use the printer properly, and how to reboot. When students successfully demonstrate these skills, they should be given a "computer operator's license" and be allowed to use software on their own.

2. "Endorsements" can be added to the computer operator's license when a student learns additional software skills.

3. Have enough blank disks so that each student has her or his own data disk. When students share a disk, one student may damage another person's file.

4. Encourage students to make backup copies of their important files. If students work in pairs, they can each make a copy of the file on their own data disks. If students are working individually, they can have a "backup partner" and save files on each other's disks.

5. Prepare a one-page reference sheet for each piece of software or software skill you introduce to students. Students can bring their reference sheets to the computer to remind them of the most commonly used procedures.

6. Keep students' data disks and reference sheets, along with blank sheets of paper for jotting down ideas and notes, in a folder with pockets. Store the folders alphabetically on a shelf in the classroom or lab so that students can find them easily when they need them.

7. Pairing students at the computer is very helpful. One student can proofread what is on the screen while the other enters information. Halfway through the task, remind them to change roles. Often students can answer each other's questions when they work in pairs.

8. When students work in pairs, be sure that each student does his or her own keyboarding. Sometimes the pair decides to let the faster typist do all the keyboarding, but then the one who proofreads does not have an opportunity to improve his or her keyboarding skills. Students learn to use software with hands-on experience, not by watching someone else.

9. Train individual students to be "classroom experts" on particular software or on particular skills. Let them help other students who have questions. Tell your students, "Ask three before me."

10. When students ask for your help, try *not* to put your hands on their keyboard or mouse. Instead, tell them which keys to press or what to do with the mouse, and let them do it themselves. Train student helpers and teacher aides to do the same thing when they are helping students.

11. If you have computers in your classroom, locate them where there will be a minimum of visual distractions for the students using them.

12. If you are working with students in a lab setting, keep a small block of wood or other object near each computer. Instead of raising their hands when they have a question, the students can put the block of wood on top of the monitor to let you know that they need help. Then their hands are free to work on another activity.

13. Remind students to save their work periodically to minimize tragedies caused by power failures or computer freezes. Post a sign near the computer area that says: "Have you saved your work lately?"

14. If your computers are not networked to a printer, then on days when lots of students will be printing, reserve some of the computers with printers for printing only. As students complete their work, they can save their work on their data disk and then take their disk to one of the computers with an available printer.

15. If you need more than one copy of something, print out one copy and then photocopy it. When students work on a project jointly, each one will want a copy.

16. Don't expect every student to need the same amount of time to complete a particular computer task. Their keyboarding skills vary, and the slower ones should not be penalized.

17. If you need to check students' work on disk, format a class data disk and have them save their work on their own data disk and on your class disk, or in a special folder on the hard drive. If your computers are networked, have students save to a folder on the server. The file name should include the student's last name and the name or number of the assignment.

18. Send a letter home to parents explaining how your students are using computers and your rationale for using software. Parents are especially interested in and supportive of the use of technology in the classroom.

Computer-Integrated Lessons and Lesson Ideas

The following samples are presented not as complete lessons but as appetizers to stimulate you to think of ways that you can supplement your current lessons and curriculum with computer activities.

1. Domestic Electronic Appliances

Content Area: Science, Social Science

Goal or Objective: To explore common electrical appliances found in the home and their impact on our lives

Applications:

❏ Word processing: students can interview parents, grandparents, or others to gather information about some of the electrical devices that have nonelectric precursors, such as lights, typewriters, cameras, and ovens. Enter these anecdotal records into a word processing document.

❏ Graphics: prepare a graphic collection of pre-electrical appliances from old catalogs, magazines, and pictures.

❏ Page layout: half the class prepares a newsletter taking the position that most electrical devices are a luxury; the other half prepares a newsletter taking the position that most electrical devices are a necessity.

❏ Database: students prepare a class database of all things electrical in their homes, including battery-operated devices. Fields could include Name of device, Source of electricity, Necessity or Luxury, Inventor, Date of invention, Comments.

❏ Telecommunications: http://www.tcns.co.uk/philips/science.html

2. Slow Down for the Curves

Content Area: Mathematics

Goal or Objective: To explore various kinds of geometric curves

Applications:

❏ Graphics: retrieve from the Internet site provided or chart with a spreadsheet.

❏ Slide show: prepare a slide show or presentation with the graphics in the student-prepared database.

❏ Page layout: class prepares a group newsletter describing something about their three or four favorite curves.

❏ Database: including as many curves as there are students in class.

❏ Spreadsheet: enter formulas for and experiment with various curves, and prepare graphs.

❏ Telecommunications:

1. http://www-groups.dcs.st-and.ac.uk/~history/Curves/Curves.html

2. http://freeabel.geom.umn.edu/

3. http://www.geom.umn.edu/apps/gallery.html

4. http://www.mathpro.com/math/glossary/glossary.html

Comments: See file `Curves` in the `05db` folder for a database slide show idea. You must use a special technique to place the graphics in the database.

3. Stormy Weather

Content Area: Science (integrated)

Goal or Objective: To explore factors affecting climate and the weather

Applications:

❏ Graphics: prepare a library of common weather symbols; have students construct weather maps illustrating current weather conditions.

❏ Database: have students keep a database of local weather data for a month.

❏ Spreadsheet: have students use their database data to construct graphs in a spreadsheet or spreadsheet frame.

❏ Hypermedia: have students construct a hypermedia stack on a selected weather topic.

❏ Telecommunications:

1. http://cissus.mobot.org/MBGnet/lesson/environment/lesson4.html

2. http://www.unidata.ucar.edu/staff/blynds/rnbw.html

3. http://covis.atmos.uiuc.edu/guide/guide.html

4. http://www.geom.umn.edu/apps/rainbow/

5. http://www.miamisci.org/hurricane/

6. http://faldo.atmos.uiuc.edu/WEATHER/weather.html

7. http://nwlink.com/~wxdude

8. http://www.weather.com/natindx.html

4. **See the USA!**

Content Area: Social Studies (integrated)

Goal or Objective: To use basic geography, technology, and writing skills

Applications:

❑ Word processing: keep travel diaries.

❑ Graphics: retrieve and produce graphics illustrative of the places "visited."

❑ Slide show: produce slide shows of favorite places "visited."

❑ Page layout: prepare newsletters communicating to others the virtues of vacationing in selected areas.

❑ Database: keep a class database of places "visited."

❑ Spreadsheet: calculate miles traveled and the cost of gasoline at the current price.

❑ Hypermedia: prepare an animation with HyperStudio showing the routes traveled.

❑ Telecommunications: find e-mail addresses of individuals who live in the areas "visited" and communicate with them.

1. http://info.er.usgs.gov/fact-sheets/finding-your-way/finding-your-way.html

2. http://www.vtourist.com/webmap/maps.htm

3. http://www.vtourist.com/vt/

Reference: Choat, D. (1991). See the U.S.A.! Teaching with technology—Curriculum connection. *Instructor, 101*(2), 75–77.

5. **Good News Bears—The Stock Market**

Content Area: Business

Goal or Objective: To gain simulated experience with the stock market

Applications:

❏ Page layout: have students prepare a newsletter article documenting their experiences "buying" and "selling" stocks.

❏ Graphics: prepare graphs with the spreadsheet illustrating changes in prices.

❏ Database: keep a database record of buying and selling transactions.

❏ Spreadsheet: copy or import data from the database to prepare charts illustrating changes in prices.

❏ Telecommunications: http://www.ncsa.uiuc.edu/edu/RSE/RSEyellow/gnb.html

Comments: Original author was Sandy Morgan.

6. Pi Math

Content Area: Mathematics

Goal or Objective: To explore the characteristics and applications of pi

Applications:

❏ Word processing: a century ago, one state legislature considered passing a law that set the value of pi to 3 to make it easier for students to use. Have students write a one-page reaction to this suggestion.

❏ Page layout: prepare a newsletter "selling" the virtues of pi as though it had just been discovered.

❏ Spreadsheet: have students discover pi either by giving them the circumference and radius of several circles or spheres, or have them measure the objects. Then students calculate the relationship between the circumference and the radius squared by dividing circumference by radius squared. Have students calculate the value of pi from 1 to 15 decimal places (the limits of ClarisWorks). Have them look for any apparent patterns.

❏ Telecommunications:

   1. http://www.ncsa.uiuc.edu/Edu/RSE/RSEorange/buttons.html

   2. http://daisy.uwaterloo.ca:80/~alopez-o/math-faq/node12.html#SECTION00510000000000000000

7. Genetics

Content Area: Biology

Goal or Objective: To explore the basic structure and function of DNA and its role in genetics

Applications:

❏ Graphics: locate DNA and genetics graphics on the Internet.

❏ Slide show: prepare and show DNA sequences.

❏ Page layout: prepare a newsletter describing the discovery of DNA.

❏ Database: have students keep a database of genetics terms.

❏ Hypermedia: construct or have students construct a tutorial on the basics of DNA and simple F1 and F2 crosses.

❏ Telecommunications:

1. http://www.biology.com/GENETICS/ GENSTUD/BG/302.1000

2. http://www.netspace.org/MendelWeb/

3. http://info.pitt.edu/~carthew/

4. http://www.ncgr.org/

Comments: At the National Center for Genome Resources site (http://www.ncgr.org/), you can download data from the genome sequence database.

8. Cinderella Stories

Content Area: Language Arts

Goal or Objective: To study common story themes such as Cinderella and compare variations of those stories

Applications:

❏ Word processing: have students write their own modern-day Cinderella (or other) story.

❏ Page layout: have students write a newsletter article as it might appear in a local paper or news magazine describing differences in the same story line.

❏ Database: prepare a database of as many variations of the Cinderella story as students can find with information on how they differ.

❏ Telecommunications: have students communicate by e-mail with other students in other countries about variations of the Cinderella or other common fairy tales: http://www.ucalgary.ca/~dkbrown/ cinderella.html.

Evaluating Lessons That Use Computers

The easiest way to use a computer in the classroom is with Computer Assisted Instruction (CAI) or the use of the computer as a tutor. This approach is popular because teachers typically continue to do with technology what they know how to do without technology, which is neither necessarily the most efficient nor the most effective approach. Increased achievement is the lure offered by the use of technology as a tutor; increased achievement, in fact, is the rationale for this approach. Since the computer is in charge and acting upon the student in these systems, if there is not increased achievement sustained over time, there may, in fact, be no justification for this approach.

To evaluate this approach to the use of technology, you should look for either:

❏ Significantly increased achievment sustained over time compared to other methods of instruction (documented by valid data collection methods rather than just by personal testimony), or

❏ Achievement at least equal to other methods of instruction accompanied by significant decreases in either cost or time.

If instructors and students use the computer as an instructional tool, the objective is to have students engaged in activities and tools (within the content areas) that are used in the work world. Increased achievement, then, would be a bonus. If we attempt to measure the effectiveness of technology with standard methods, however, we probably will not see the value of technology to education. To use the computer as a tool effectively demands that teachers and students focus more on the collection and the analysis of data in our classrooms. Current testing methods either do not measure these goals effectively or they do not measure them at all. How then can we go about measuring the use of the computer as a tool? One approach is to observe for the existence of behaviors consistent with the use of technology in this manner and consistent with the goals and objectives of the school. See Appendix H for examples of behaviors to look for when evaluating lessons where the focus is on the use of the computer as a tool.

Activities

1. You have just been placed on a committee to come up with an acceptable use policy for the Internet in your school. What factors would you consider? Would you recommend censoring or filtering out certain sites?

2. You have just been placed on a committee to recommend how technology should be used in your school. What factors should you consider? Should the input of teachers who do not have any training in the use of technology be considered just as much as that of teachers who have considerable knowledge of such use?

3. Prepare a list of ways that the technology in your school could be used for creating good public relations and positive reactions from parents and the community in general.

4. Make a list of the things a school could do to encourage teachers to integrate the use of technology into classroom activities by both teachers and students.

Summary

Computer education programs generally serve one of two purposes: to teach students about computers or to teach traditional content with the assistance of the computer. However, in many schools a single program serves both purposes. Computer activities are designed to support the regular curriculum, and, in the process, students also learn about computers.

To establish a computer-integrated curriculum, teachers review each objective that is already in the school's curriculum and plan how computers can be used to enhance the accomplishment of that objective. In addition, students may need keyboarding skills in order to use the computer more efficiently.

In evaluating lessons that use computers, it is important to consider what advantage the computer provides over the traditional ways of teaching the same lesson.

Key Terms

keyboarding 280

site licensing agreement 283

References

Balajthy, E. (1988). Keyboarding, language arts, and the elementary school child. *The Computing Teacher, 15*(5), 40–43.

Barrett, H. (1994). Technology-supported assessment portfolios. *The Computing Teacher, 21*(6), 9–12.

Becker, H. (1991). When powerful meet conventional beliefs and institutional constraints. *The Computing Teacher, 18*(8), 6–9.

Becker, J. (1993). Teaching with and about computers in secondary schools. *Communications of the ACM, 36*(5), 69–72.

Brady, H. (1991). New survey realizes what top technology teachers have learned. *Technology and Learning, 11*(4), 38–39, 42–43.

Choat, D. (1991). See the U.S.A! Teaching with technology—Curriculum connection. *Instructor, 101*(2), 75–77.

Craver, K. W. (1994). *School library media centers in the 21st century: Changes and challenges.* (ERIC Document No. ED 377871)

Duffy, T., & Bednar, A. (1991). Attempting to come to grips with alternative perspectives. *Educational Technology, 32,* 12–15.

Dwyer, D. C., *et al.* (1990). *The evolution of teachers' instructional beliefs and practices in high-access-to-technology classrooms.* (ERIC Document No. ED 325074)

Dyrli, O. E. (1996). Does your school have an acceptable use policy? *Technology & Learning, 16*(4), 20–22, 24, 26–27.

Educational technology curriculum: K–12. Living with technology: A life-long learning process. (1993). (ERIC Document No. ED 366318)

George, Y., Malcolm S., & Jeffers, L. (1993). Computer equity for the future. *Communications of the ACM, 36*(5), 78–81.

Grabe, M. (1992). Learning in technology enriched study environments. Will students study effectively? *Reading and Writing Quarterly, 8,* 321–336.

Grabe, M., & Grabe, C. (1996). *Integrating technology for meaningful learning.* Boston: Houghton Mifflin.

Janowiak, R. (1990). *Educational technology in the kindergarten through twelfth grades.* (ERIC Document No. ED 329221)

Johassen, D. H. (1995). Computer as cognitive tools: Learning with technology, not from technology. *Journal of Computing in Higher Education, 6*(2), 40–73.

Kercher, L. (1990). *Integrating technology: Strategies.* (ERIC Document No. ED 326206)

Knapp, L. R., & Glenn, A. D. (1996). *Restructuring schools with technology.* Boston: Allyn and Bacon.

Korenza, R. (1991). Learning with media. *Review of Educational Research, 61,* 179–211.

McAdoo, M. (1994). Equity: Has technology bridged the gap? *Electronic Learning, 13*(7), 24–34.

Milone, Jr., M. N., & Salpeter, J. (1996). Technology and equity issues. *Technology & Learning, 16*(4), 38–41, 44–47.

Muffoletto, R., & Knupfer, N. N. (Eds.). (1993). *Computers in education: Social, political, and historical perspectives.* (ERIC Document No. ED 366317)

Nelson, C., & Watson, J. (1991). The computer gender gap: Children's attitudes, performance, and socialization. *Journal of Educational Technology Systems, 19,* 345–353.

Orwig, A. H. (1996). Understanding public relations: A primer for schools. *Technology & Learning, 16*(4), 20–22, 24, 26–27.

Pearlman, R. (1991). Restructuring with technology: A tour of schools where it's happening. *Technology and Learning, 11*(4), 30–37.

Pina, A. A. (1992). *Design, development, and implementation of a middle school computer applications curriculum.* (ERIC Document No. ED 357731)

Salpeter, J. (1992). Are you obeying copyright law? *Technology and Learning, 12*(8), 14–23.

Sheingold, K. (1991). Restructuring for learning with technology: The potential for synergy. *Phi Delta Kappan, 23*(1), 28–36.

Smith, R., & Sclafani, S. (1989). Integrated learning systems: Guidelines for evaluation. *The Computing Teacher, 17*(3), 36–38.

Snider, J. H. (1996). Education wars: The battle over Information-Age technology. *The Futurist,* 24–28.

Sutton, R. (1991). Equity and computers in the schools: A decade of research. *Review of Educational Research, 61,* 475–503.

Thomas, L. (1996). Mathematics and quantitative tools in the classroom—Making the abstract concrete. *Syllabus, 9*(7), 10, 12.

Thomas, L., & Knezek, D. (1991). Facilitating restructured learning experiences with technology. *The Computing Teacher, 18*(6), 49–53.

Tools for the 21st century library. (1996). *Technology & Learning, 16*(5), 30.

von Wodtke, M. (1994). Thinking skills for the electronic Information Age: Applying mental capacity. *School Library Media Annual, 12,* 54–69.

Wetzel, K. (1990). Keyboarding. In *The Best of the Writing Notebook,* S. Franklin (Ed.), 46–48. Eugene, OR: The Writing Notebook.

Wiebe, J. H. (1993). *Computer tools and problem solving in mathematics.* Using Technology in the Classroom Series. (ERIC Document No. ED 365301)

Appendixes

The Macintosh Environment

To use your Macintosh efficiently, you need to be comfortable with the mouse. In addition, you need to understand how information is displayed in windows on the screen or on the Macintosh **desktop.**

Using the Mouse

The **mouse** is a pointing device you use to initiate actions on the Macintosh. When you move the mouse, a corresponding pointer called a cursor moves the same direction on the screen. To begin an action, move the mouse so the cursor is on an object or area of the screen; this action is called **pointing**. Pointing, pressing, and releasing the mouse button is called **clicking**. If you press and release the mouse button twice in rapid succession, the action is called **double clicking**.

Dragging allows you to move objects on the screen with the mouse. To move or drag an object on the screen, first point to the object with the mouse, and then press and hold the mouse button down. Move the mouse while continuing to hold down the button. Release the mouse button when the move is complete.

Selecting, or choosing, an object refers to pointing to an object and then clicking the object. When selected, the object appears highlighted.

To **pull down** a menu from the menu bar, point to the menu name with the mouse, then press and hold the mouse button. Drag the mouse downward and release the mouse button when the mouse is on the item you want.

Using Windows

You use the mouse to manipulate objects such as disks, folders, applications, and documents. These objects are usually displayed on the screen as **icons,** which are graphic representations of objects. When you double click an object, it typically opens into a **window,** which is a display area on the screen showing the contents of the object you clicked (Figure A.1). You can even double click the trash icon to see its contents.

Figure A.1
Desktop showing an active window (Tools f), an inactive window (Hard Disk), the hard disk icon, and the Trash icon

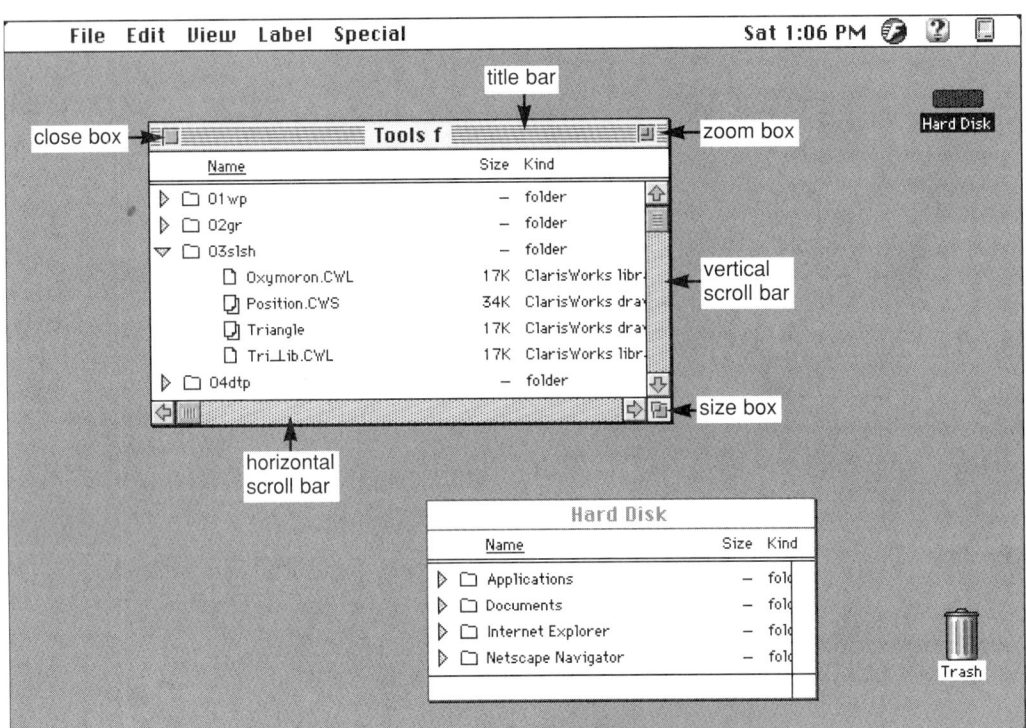

Typically, a window has a **title bar** showing the name of the object displayed in the window, a **close box** for closing the window, a **zoom box** to open the window to full size and return it to its original size, a **size box** to resize the window, and two **scroll bars** to see the contents that are beyond the edges of the window.

When more than one window is open on the screen or monitor, a striped title bar indicates which is the active window (Figure A.1). To make a different window active, click somewhere in another window.

Moving Between the Finder and an Application

You use a part of the system software called the **Finder** to work with icons and windows on your Macintosh desktop. The Finder opens automatically when you start up the Macintosh.

In System 7, an icon at the far right of the menu bar indicates whether you are in the Finder ▢ or working in an application such as ClarisWorks ▣. When you are working with an application, you can move between the application and the Finder by pulling down the menu under this icon and choosing the Finder or a different application.

Changing the Memory Allocated to an Application

When a program or application is opened, it reserves a block of memory for itself. If you are displaying the contents of a large file, you may need to increase the amount of memory reserved for the application. You can do this by increasing the memory allocation of the application in its `Info` window. If you are working in a computer laboratory, the managers of the lab may have part of the system locked so that you cannot change the memory allocation. To change the memory allocation of ClarisWorks,

- ❑ Quit ClarisWorks if it is open.
- ❑ From the `File` menu, choose `Get Info`.
- ❑ Highlight the number in the minimum size box and enter a larger number (Figure A.2). The number must be smaller than or equal to the number you place in the `Preferred size` box.
- ❑ Close the `Info` window.

When you restart ClarisWorks, you will have more memory available for working with your documents.

Figure A.2
Changing memory requirements

```
┌─────────────────────────────────────────────┐
│ ▤▣▤▤▤▤▤  ClarisWorks Info  ▤▤▤▤▤▤▤▤ │
├─────────────────────────────────────────────┤
│   ▦      ClarisWorks                         │
│          ClarisWorks 4.0v2                   │
│                                              │
│     Kind : application program               │
│     Size : 968K on disk (983,980 bytes used) │
│                                              │
│    Where : M. L. Land : ClarisWorks 4.0 Folder : │
│                                              │
│  Created : Tue, Nov 14, 1995, 10:16 AM       │
│ Modified : Tue, Nov 14, 1995, 10:41 AM       │
│  Version : ClarisWorks 4.0v2                 │
│            November, 1995                    │
│ Comments :                                   │
│  ┌───────────────────────────────────────┐  │
│  │                                       │  │
│  └───────────────────────────────────────┘  │
│         ┌┄Memory Requirements┄┄┄┄┄┐         │
│         ┊ Suggested size :  1400   K ┊       │
│         ┊ Minimum size : [1000]    K ┊       │
│ ☐ Locked┊ Preferred size : [2000]  K ┊       │
│         └┄┄┄┄┄┄┄┄┄┄┄┄┄┄┄┄┄┄┄┘         │
└─────────────────────────────────────────────┘
```

Using Folders

You can organize files on your hard drive and floppy disks in **folders.** Folders on a disk or hard drive are like folders in a filing cabinet. Folders are essential to keeping a hard disk organized; otherwise, it becomes almost impossible to find a particular file when you need it. Even when you use a floppy disk, you will probably want to use folders to organize your files.

You recognize a closed folder on the desktop by one of the following icons:

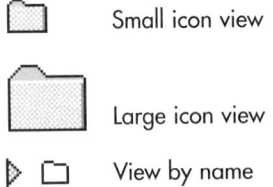

Small icon view

Large icon view

▷ ☐ View by name

To create a new, empty folder, choose `File/New Folder` while you are in the Finder. It appears with the name `untitled folder`. While it is highlighted, type a new name to change the name of the folder.

To place something into a folder, drag the item's icon to the folder. When the folder icon is highlighted, release the mouse button, and the item will appear inside the folder. If you are dragging an icon to someplace else on the same disk, it will be removed from its original location. If you are dragging an icon to a different disk, a copy of the original file will be placed on the other disk and the original will stay put.

Double clicking a folder opens its window and displays its contents.

Installing the Tools Files onto the Hard Drive

If you are working on a computer in a lab, the files from the `Tools` disks may have already been installed on the hard drive. If they have not already been installed, you can install them with the following procedure if you have access privileges to the hard drive:

❏ From the Finder, choose `File/New Folder`.

❏ Rename the folder `Tools` or `Tools Folder`.

❏ Insert the first `Tools` disk from your book and use the procedure described in the previous section to copy all the folders from the disk onto your new folder on the hard drive.

❏ Continue this procedure for each `Tools` disk.

When you have copied all the folders from each disk, remove the last floppy disk from the disk drive. Now you're ready to use the files that came with the book.

You can store folders inside of folders. Storing folders inside folders is called a **hierarchical file system.**

Formatting an Unformatted Disk

Before you can use a disk, it must be formatted. Use the following instructions to format your floppy disks.

❏ Insert a high density disk into the floppy drive.

❏ When prompted for a name, enter the name you want the disk to have.

❏ Choose the format you want, probably `Macintosh 1.4`.

❏ Click the `Initialize` button. If prompted that this procedure will erase the contents of the disk, continue.

Wait a couple of minutes and your disk will be formatted and ready to use.

If you want to erase a formatted disk, insert the disk into the disk drive and choose `Special/Erase Disk`; then click the `Erase` button.

Making Backup Copies

You should get into the habit of making a backup copy of your work. You can make a backup copy of a file either on the same disk or on a different disk. Both of the following procedures assume you are in the Finder.

BACKUP COPY ON THE SAME DISK   We will assume that your file is on a floppy disk, but the procedure is the same on a hard disk or other storage medium.

- ❏ Insert the floppy disk into the disk drive and locate the file you want to back up.
- ❏ Select the file by clicking it once.
- ❏ Choose `File/Duplicate`.

BACKUP COPY ON A DIFFERENT DISK   For this procedure, we will assume that your file is on a floppy disk, your computer has one floppy drive, and you want a backup copy on a second floppy disk.

- ❏ From the Finder, choose `File/New Folder` to place a new folder on the hard drive.
- ❏ Insert the disk containing the file you want to back up.
- ❏ Drag the file you want to back up and place it in the new folder.
- ❏ Remove the first disk and insert the disk you want to place the backup copy on.
- ❏ Drag the file onto the second disk.
- ❏ Drag the new folder (on the hard drive) to the Trash.

The Windows 95 Environment

To use your computer efficiently, you need to be comfortable with the mouse. In addition, you need to understand how information is displayed in windows on the screen or on the **desktop.**

Using the Mouse

The **mouse** is a pointing device you use to initiate actions on your computer. When you move the mouse, a corresponding pointer called a cursor moves the same direction on the screen. To begin an action, move the mouse so the cursor is on an object or area of the screen; this action is called **pointing.** Pointing, pressing, and releasing the mouse button is called **clicking.** If you press and release the mouse button twice in rapid succession, the action is called **double clicking.**

When we refer to the mouse button, we mean the left mouse button.

    Dragging allows you to move objects on the screen with the mouse. To move or drag an object on the screen, first point to the object with the mouse, and then press and hold the mouse button down. Move the mouse while continuing to hold down the button. Release the mouse button when the move is complete.

    Selecting, or choosing, an object refers to pointing to an object and then clicking the object. When selected, the object appears highlighted.

    To **pull down** a menu from the menu bar, point to the menu name with the mouse and click the mouse button. Then click the menu item you want.

Using Windows

You use the mouse to manipulate objects such as disks, folders, applications, and documents. These objects are usually displayed on the screen as **icons,** which are graphic representations of objects. When you double click an object, it typically opens into a **window,** which is a display area on the screen showing the contents of the object you clicked (Figure B.1). You can even double click the Trash icon to see its contents. Typically, a window has a **title bar** showing the name of the object displayed in the window, a **minimize icon** to reduce or minimize the window to a button on the **taskbar,** a **maximize icon** to fill the desktop with the window, and a **close icon** to close the window.

Figure B.1
Windows desktop showing an active window (Program Files), and inactive window (3½ Floppy), the computer icon (My Computer), and the Recycle Bin

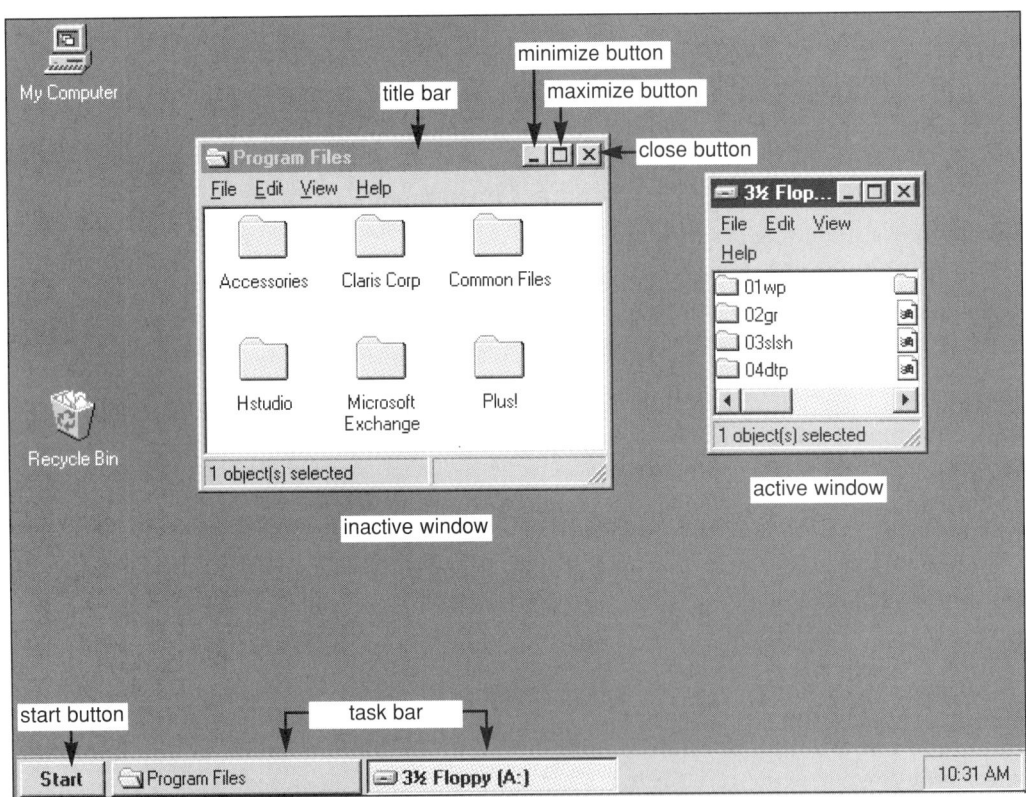

When more than one window is open on the screen or monitor, a darkened title bar indicates which is the active window (Figure B.1). To make a different window active, click somewhere in another window.

Using Folders

You can organize files on your hard drive and floppy disks in **folders.** Folders on a disk or hard drive are like folders in a filing cabinet. Folders are essential to keeping a hard disk organized; otherwise, it becomes almost impossible to find a particular file when you need it. Even when you use a floppy disk, you will probably want to use folders to organize your files.

You recognize a closed folder on the desktop by one of the following icons:

Small icon view

Large icon view

To create a new, empty folder, choose `File/New/Folder` on the desktop. It appears with the name `New Folder`. While it is highlighted, type a new name to change the name of the folder.

To place something into a folder, drag the item's icon to the folder. When the folder icon is highlighted, release the mouse button, and the item will appear inside the folder. If you are dragging an icon to someplace else on the same disk, it will be removed from its original location. If you are dragging an icon to a different disk, a copy of the original file will be placed on the other disk and the original will stay put.

Double clicking a folder icon opens its window and displays its contents.

Installing the Tools Files onto the Hard Drive

If you are working on a computer in a lab, the files from the `Tools` disks may have already been installed on the hard drive. If they have not already been installed, you can install them with the following procedure if you have access privileges to the hard drive:

❑ From the desktop, choose `File/New/Folder`.

❑ Rename the folder `Tools` or `Tools Folder`.

❑ Insert the first `Tools` disk from your book and use the procedure described in the previous section to place a copy of all of the folders from the disk into your new folder on the hard drive.

❑ Continue this procedure for the other `Tools` disk. Drag all of the folders into your new `Tools Folder`.

Do not copy the following items from the `Tools disks`: `Resource.frk`, `Fileid.dat`, `Desktop`, *and* `Finder.dat`.

When you have copied all the indicated folders from each disk, remove the last floppy disk from the disk drive. Now you're ready to use the files that came with the book.

Formatting an Unformatted Disk with Windows 95

- ❏ Insert a high density disk.
- ❏ Go to the 3¹/₂ `Floppy [A:]` drive and double click it.
- ❏ When prompted to format the disk, click `Yes`.
- ❏ When prompted, choose `Full` and then click the `Start` button.

Wait a couple of minutes for the disk to be formatted and it will be ready to use.

Making Backup Copies

You should get into the habit of making a backup copy of your work. You can make a backup copy of a file either on the same disk or on a different disk. Both of the following procedures assume you are in the Finder.

BACKUP COPY ON THE SAME DISK We will assume that your file is on a floppy disk, but the procedure is the same on a hard disk or other storage medium.

- ❏ Insert the floppy disk into the disk drive and locate the file you want to back up.
- ❏ Select the file by clicking it once.
- ❏ Choose `Edit/Copy`.
- ❏ Choose `Edit/Paste`.

BACKUP COPY ON A DIFFERENT DISK For this procedure, we will assume that your file is on a floppy disk, your computer has one floppy drive, and you want a backup copy on a second floppy disk.

- ❏ From the desktop, choose `File/New/Folder`.
- ❏ Insert the disk containing the file you want to back up.
- ❏ Drag the file you want to back up and place it in the new folder.
- ❏ Remove the first disk and insert the disk you want to place the backup copy on.
- ❏ Drag the file onto the second disk.
- ❏ Drag the new folder to the Recycle Bin.

Creating and Editing a User Dictionary in ClarisWorks

You can access a ClarisWorks dictionary from a word processing, database, drawing, or spreadsheet document or from a text frame. You can customize a user dictionary to fit the topic your students are studying.

Figure C.1
To select a dictionary or to begin a new user dictionary, choose `Edit/Writing Tools` and then either `Select` or `New` depending upon what you want to do

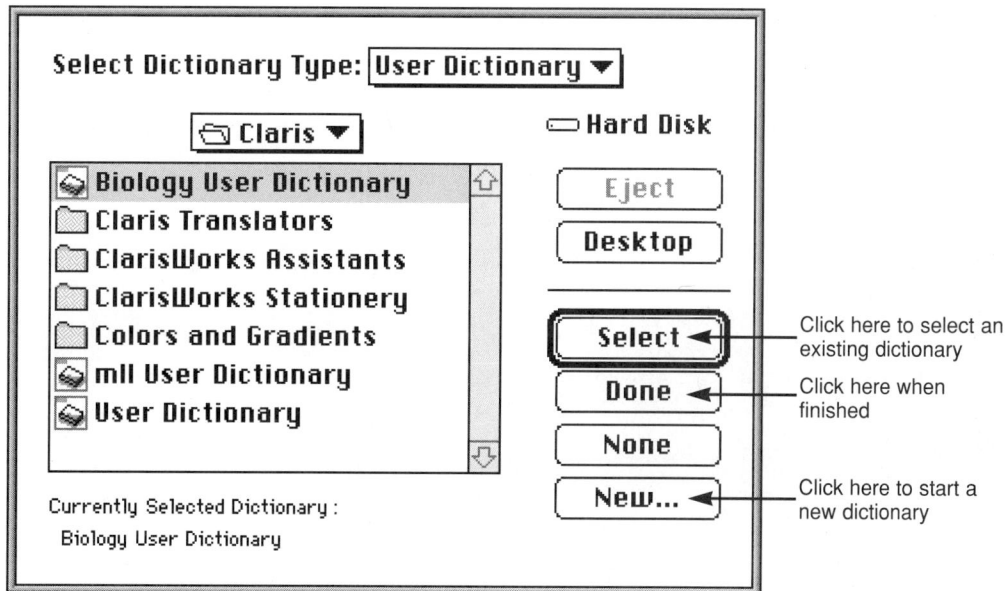

Starting a New User Dictionary

❏ Choose `Edit/Writing Tools/Select Dictionaries`.

M ❏ When the dialog box (Figure C.1) appears, click the `Select Dictionary Type` button and choose `User Dictionary`.

❏ Choose `New`, enter the name you want to use for your dictionary, point and click until you see the name of the disk or folder where you want to save the new user dictionary, and then click the `Save` button.

W ❏ From the `Select Dictionaries` dialog box, choose `User Dictionary` (*.usp) from the `Files of type` menu.

❏ Type a name into the `File` name box and click `New`.

Editing a User Dictionary

M ❏ Choose `Edit/Writing Tools/Edit User Dictionary`, and a dialog box will appear (Figure C.2).

❏ To enter a new word, type the word into the `Entry` box and click the `Add` button.

❏ To remove an existing word, click on the word and then click `Remove`.

W ❏ Choose `Edit/Writing Tools/Select Dictionaries`.

❏ Choose `User Dictionary` (*.usp) from the `Files of type` menu.

❏ Click `Edit`, type your word into the `Entry` box, then click `Add`.

❏ If you want to import words from a text file, click `Import`.

❏ If you want to export the words in a user dictionary to a text file, click `Export` and follow the directions on the screen.

Figure C.2
To edit words in a user dictionary or to enter new words, choose `Edit/Writing Tools/Edit User Dictionary`

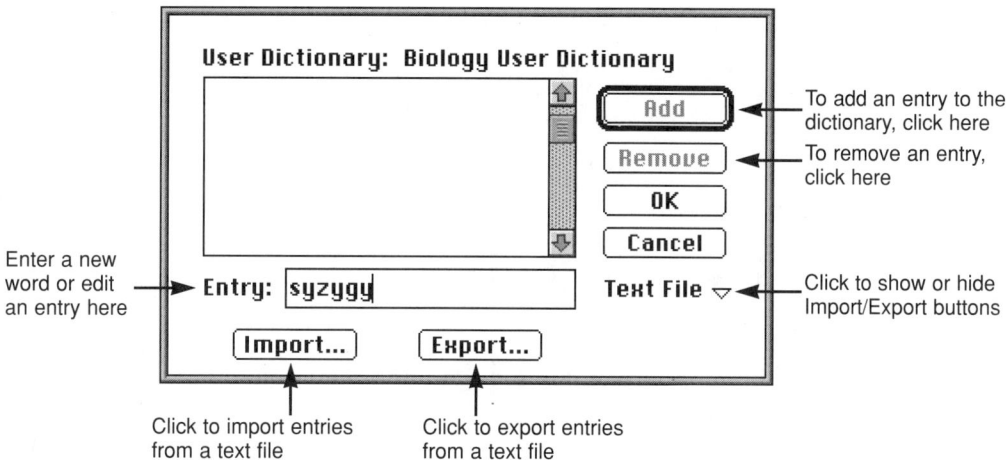

To add an entry to the dictionary, click here

To remove an entry, click here

Enter a new word or edit an entry here

Click to show or hide Import/Export buttons

Click to import entries from a text file

Click to export entries from a text file

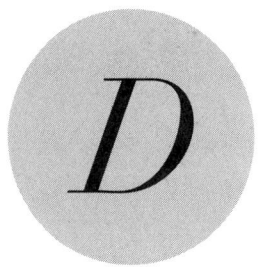

Graphic File Formats

	Claris Works4	Claris Works4	Hyper Studio3	Hyper Studio3	Netscape
	Macintosh	Windows DOS File extension	Macintosh	Windows DOS File extension	Macintosh & Windows (inline)
File Format					
Computer Graphics Metafile		CGM			
DIB-Bitmap files		DIB, BMP, RLE	BMP	BMP	
Encapsulated PostScript	EPS	EPS, AI	EPS		
Graphic Interchange Format	GIF		GIF		GIF
JPEG File Interchange Format			JPEG	JPG	JPEG
Kodak Photo CD	PHOTO CD		PHOTO CD		
MacPaint format	PNTG		PNTG		
Macintosh Picture format	PICT	PCT	PICT		
Microsoft Video		AVI			
Microsoft Windows Metafile		WMF			
Paintbrush files		PCX, PCC	PCX	PCX	
QuickTime Movie	QT		QT		
Tag Image File Format	TIFF	TIF	TIFF	TIF	
Other				BIF	

Research Highlights

What does the research say about the effectiveness of using word processing with students? The use of word processors is widespread in schools, and it is important to know what researchers are finding and reporting. Unfortunately, as in most other areas of educational research, there are few clear-cut answers or conclusive evidence about the use of word processing to teach writing. This condition should not necessarily be viewed as disturbing, however, since many of the behaviors and materials we use in the classroom have no research basis, have an unclear research basis, or may in fact have been shown to have an adverse effect. We should not hold word processing to a higher standard than we expect of other areas of research in teaching.

Teachers and researchers are concerned primarily with the effects that word processing has on students' ability to make revisions and on the quality of the writing. As with earlier studies, recent studies continue to be mixed on the effect of word processing on the ability to make revisions. Williamson (1993) reported that students reduced the use of vague references and "to be" verbs; Gregda and Hannafin (1992) reported that word processing students made more corrections and fewer errors than paper and pencil students. Poteet (1991) found that students found it easier to make changes and therefore to rewrite more to improve, a conclusion that appeared to support earlier studies finding that students spend more time revising when using word processing and that time on task is a critical element of improvement. Kantrov (1991) suggested that ease of revision may be both an advantage and a disadvantage.

The results regarding quality of writing are more mixed. Of course, quality of writing is more difficult to define and assess than revising. Gregda and Hannafin (1992) reported no significant differences in writing quality; Valeri-Gold and Deming (1991), in a review of research studies, reported "little impact on writing quality." Schramm (1991), however, in a meta-analysis of studies involving the writing samples of 836 students from kindergarten through college, reported a significant but small increase in improvement of writing for those using word processing.

With regard to other factors related to the use of word processing in teaching writing, there are reports of the following findings. The use of word processing

- ❏ promoted student thought (Brady, 1990)
- ❏ accounted for more student independence (Snyder, 1994)
- ❏ made no difference between experienced or nonexperienced writers (Schramm, 1991)
- ❏ helped motivate children to write more (D'Odorico & Zammuner, 1993)
- ❏ influenced students so that they did not perceive that assignments were difficult when asked to revise on a computer (Bright, 1990)
- ❏ was perceived by students as helpful (Williamson, 1993)
- ❏ improved student attitudes (Schramm, 1991; Valerie-Gold & Deming, 1991)
- ❏ led students to believe that it reduced the amount of time required for revising (Williamson, 1993)
- ❏ led students to write slightly longer essays (Schramm, 1991)
- ❏ was viewed as fun (Bright, 1990)
- ❏ encouraged collaboration (Brady, 1990)
- ❏ created a lively and interactive workshop environment (Brady, 1990)

Regarding teachers:

- ❏ a teacher's instructional philosophy may be the most powerful determinant of computer effectiveness (Miller & Olson, 1994)
- ❏ helped motivate teachers to write more (D'Odorico & Zammuner, 1993)
- ❏ teachers were less dominating (Snyder, 1994)
- ❏ teachers were enthusiastic about students' receptivity and response to word processing

We may be looking for the wrong outcomes, or we may be stating the results in a prejudicial manner. For instance, do the following results evoke the same image? We can report that the effects of word processing on the quality of writing are no better than when students use paper and pencil, or we can report that the use of word processing is just as effective as paper and pencil plus the stu-

dents get practice with a real-world method of writing—a computer, the device used by most professional writers!

Part of the problem with mixed results may be in the way we are conducting the research on the effects of word processing. Many studies do not control for or account for factors such as the time it took to teach the word processing skills. If the researchers considered the time on task for actual word processing work on writing, compared to the time on task with pencil and paper work on writing, would there be a difference? Cordenos (1990) reported that level of the class, size of the class, nature of the assignments, and individual versus group work all affect the efficacy of computer use.

Functions in ClarisWorks

BUSINESS AND FINANCIAL Calculates mortgage and payment values.

    FV (Future Value)

    IRR (Internal Rate of Return)

    MIRR (Modified Internal Rate of Return)

    NPER (Number of Periods)

    NPV (Net Present Value)

    PMT (Payment)

    PV (Present Value)

    RATE

DATE AND TIME Manipulates dates and times.

DATE	NOW
DATETOTEXT	SECOND
DAY	TEXTTODATE
DAYNAME	TEXTTOTIME
DAYOFYEAR	TIME
HOUR	TIMETOTEXT
MINUTE	WEEKDAY
MONTH	WEEKOFYEAR
MONTHNAME	YEAR

INFORMATION   Looks up and evaluates information in spreadsheet cells and database fields.

ALERT	INDEX
BEEP	LOOKUP
CHOOSE	MACRO
COLUMN	NA (Not Available)
ERROR	TYPE
HLOOKUP (Horizontal Look Up)	VLOOKUP (Vertical Look Up)

LOGICAL   Evaluates Boolean expressions that result in either TRUE or FALSE.

AND	ISNA (Is Not Available)
IF	ISNUMBER
ISBLANK	ISTEXT
ISERROR	NOT
ISLOGICAL	OR

NUMERIC   Performs general mathematical calculations.

ABS (Absolute)	MOD (Modulo)
BASETONUM	NUMTOBASE
EXP (Exponent)	PI
FACT (Factorial)	RAND (Random)
FRAC (Fraction)	ROUND
INT (Integer)	SIGN
LN (Natural Log)	SQRT (Square Root)
LOG	TRUNC (Truncate)
LOG10 (Log to Base 10)	

STATISTICAL   Calculates general statistics.

AVERAGE	PRODUCT
COUNT	STDEV (Standard Deviation)
COUNT2	SUM
MAX (Maximum)	VAR (Variance)
MIN (Minimum)	

TEXT Finds, compares, and manipulates text expressions.

CHAR (Character)	NUMTOTEXT
CODE (ASCII Code)	PROPER
CONCAT (Concatenate)	REPLACE
EXACT	REPT (Repeat)
FIND	RIGHT
LEFT	TEXTTONUM
LEN (Length)	TRIM
LOWER	UPPER
MID (Middle)	

TRIGONOMETRIC Creates and evaluates mathematical and scientific values.

ACOS (Arc Cosine)	DEGREES
ASIN (Arc Sine)	RADIANS
ATAN (Arc Tangent)	SIN (Sine)
ATAN2 (Arc Tangent 2)	TAN (Tangent)
COS (Cosine)	

Data and File Types on the Web

Files located on Internet servers are of two basic types: text and binary. Standard text files contain text only and are often named with the .TXT extension. All other files are binary. Binary files include such things as applications, sound files, digitized movies, and graphics. Files containing formatted text or text and graphics are also binary files.

As you explore the World Wide Web with the newest browsers, they automatically display some types of data, use helper applications to display or access other types of data and files, but may not display other types. One of the features beginning with Netscape Navigator 2 was the ability to use software plug-ins. A plug-in is a program that merges or works with another piece of software (Netscape in this case) to provide additional features as though it were a part of the original software application. There are numerous plug-ins available for Netscape. Open the file `Plugin.htm` with your web browser for information on some of the available plug-ins.

Many of the files available on the Internet will be encrypted and compressed and may require special software to decrypt and decompress them.

Text

When text is displayed by a web browser, the lines of a paragraph are wrapped to the next line by a paragraph return; this technique is called hard wrapping. If you were to highlight and copy some of the text from such a display and paste it into a word processing document, there would be a paragraph return at the end of each line where it had been wrapped when it was displayed by your browser.

Text saved as a text file may also have this characteristic since it is possible to save a text file with or without the paragraph returns at the end of each line of text. As a consequence, many of the text files available on the Internet have been saved with a paragraph return at the end of each line. It may become necessary to remove these paragraphs returns.

From `Netscape,` you can save the text appearing on the the the screen by choosing `File/Save As/Text` and the contents of the screen will be saved as a text file. Or you can choose `File/Save As/Source` and the contents will be saved with the links intact.

Text is also available on the Internet in the form of word processing files from various word processors. These binary files contain text but they also contain information regarding the formatting of text (such as font, style, and other special formatting commands) that is not saved with text files.

Graphics

Graphic binary files on the Internet typically have names that end with suffixes or extensions indicating the image format and/or information about compression and encryption. Common graphic file formats on the Internet include .GIF, .JPEG, .TIFF (or TIF), and .PICT (or .PCT). Graphic files on the Internet normally cannot be viewed online unless they are GIF or JPEG and are embedded in a Web document with HTML code. Other images need to be downloaded before they can be displayed. However, it is possible to create links to non-GIF and non-JPEG images. In this case, when a user clicks the linking icon the browser launches the appropriate helper application and the helper application displays the image.

Graphics displayed on your screen by a web browser are referred to as inline graphics. With most desktop computers and web browsers that you will be using, the inline graphics are displayed using HTML code and usually have been saved in either GIF or JPEG formats.

Open the file `graphics.htm` with a Web browser to explore some of the graphics available on the Web.

Databases

There are thousands of databases on the Internet but if the ClarisWorks database engine is the only database application you have used, you may not find these databases to be very familiar. You will find databases with and without database

engines on the Internet. For those databases that do not have an engine to search them, or provide only a simple way to search, you may find it challenging to download some of the data in a format in which it can be easily used.

Those database engines available free of charge on the Web range from the very simple, in which you click a button or two, to those in which you select from among a variety of choices. Open the file db.htm with a Web browser to explore a range of Internet databases and database or search engines.

Presentations (Slide Shows)

Slide shows on the Web typically take one of the following forms:

❏ Presentations or slide shows developed specifically for the Web with HTML code. These presentations can be accessed with a Web browser since they are in the form of Web documents.

❏ Slide shows developed with presentation software but converted into a Web document. These presentations can also be accessed with a Web browser.

❏ Slide shows developed with presentation software. These files can be downloaded and then run with the software applications that created them. In some cases, they can be run without downloading the file but still require special software.

Open the file slide.htm with a Web browser to explore some Web slide shows.

Sound

Sound resources come in a variety of file formats on the Web. Among the more common formats are .AU (Unix), .WAV (Windows), and .AIFF or .SND (Macintosh).

Movies

Movie resources come in two primary file formats on the Web: .QT (QuickTime for Macintosh and Windows) and .AVI (Windows). Movies may be available either in file format that can be downloaded or as an interactive resource.

··

Common File Extensions Found on the Web

Following is a nonexhaustive list of some of the common file extensions or suffixes found on the Web:

- ❏ **.AIFF** or **.AIF** Audio Interchange File Format for sound (Macintosh)
- ❏ **.AU** Sun audio file format
- ❏ **.AVI** Microsoft video format
- ❏ **.BIN** MacBinary file format for applications
- ❏ **.BMP** Windows bitmap file
- ❏ **.CPT** Compacted with Compact Pro
- ❏ **.GIF** CompuServe Graphics Interchange Format
- ❏ **.EXE** Executable file, usually DOS
- ❏ **.HQX** BinHex encrypted file (Macintosh)
- ❏ **.JPG** or **.JPEG** Joint Photographic Experts Group graphics format
- ❏ **.MID** MIDI music format file
- ❏ **.MPG, .MPE,** or **.MPEG** Movie Photographic Experts Group movie format
- ❏ **.QT** QuickTime movie format
- ❏ **.SEA** Selfextracting .SIT file
- ❏ **.SIT** Macintosh file compressed with Stuffit
- ❏ **.SND** Macintosh sound format
- ❏ **.TAR** Unix compressed "tar" archive
- ❏ **.TIF** or **.TIFF** Tagged Image File Format graphics format
- ❏ **.TXT** Text file format
- ❏ **.VOC** Soundblaster file
- ❏ **.WAV** WAVE audio file format
- ❏ **.Z** Unix compression scheme
- ❏ **.ZIP** DOS file format created by PHZip or Macintosh file format created by ZipIt

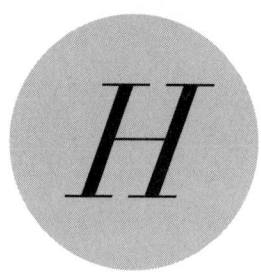

Assessing the Use of Technology as a Tool

The determination of how well a program or technique is working is one of the most critical and perhaps one of the most abused components of any program. In this appendix, we are going to present ideas for assessing and evaluating technology lessons and programs. Some of you may be disappointed that we are not going to provide an instrument that can be used directly with your program. We believe that because every program is different, each one requires a slightly different approach to evaluation. You must consider the philosophy and objectives of the school in implementing an evaluation program. If the intent or objective of using technology in your school is to provide students with opportunities to use technology to collect and analyze data and to solve problems in the content areas in a manner similar to the use of technology in the real world, then the assessment techniques for determining how well this is occurring must take this information into account. If the objective is different, then other factors must be taken into account.

Special consideration should be given to what data are going to be collected. The following items are presented to stimulate your own ideas about expectations regarding the assessment of the use of technology as a tool. This list is not meant to be exhaustive.

❏ Teachers model the use of technology expected of the students

❏ Teachers adapt the technology to the subject matter topic

❑ Teachers plan and implement instructional activities that require students to interact with technology and the subject matter content in a manner similar to individuals in that content area in the real world

❑ Teachers require students to participate in technology-related activities

❑ Teachers explain or have students discuss the relationship between the subject matter activity and the technology being used

❑ Frequency of technology use by teachers in an instructional situation

❑ Students interact with technology and the subject matter content in a manner similar to individuals in that content area in the real world

❑ Students actively participate in technology-related activities

❑ Students discuss the relationship between the subject matter activity and the technology being used

❑ Frequency of quality technology use by students in an instructional situation

❑ Examples of instructional technology used by the students

❑ Examples of instructional technology used by the teachers

❑ Classroom activities focus either on the activities themselves, the hardware and equipment, the software, or the subject matter

❑ Are the activities and assignments similar to those used in the real world of business and work? Are they best accomplished with or without technology?

❑ What is the focus of the tests and other assessment devices used by teachers?

In Figure H.1, we have presented a sample instrument that might be used to collect data on a lesson in which the teacher and students are using technology activities.

Figure H.1
Sample instrument to collect assessment data

Technology as a Tool Use
(Lesson)

The teacher had identified the appropriate technology skills the students needed to participate in the lesson:
❑ most of the skills (70–100%)
❑ some of them (40–70%)
❑ a few of them (10–40%)
❑ none of them

The students had adequate proficiency in the use of the technology skills required by the lesson:
❑ most of the students (70–100%)
❑ some of the students (40–70%)
❑ a few of the students (10–40%)

❑ most of the skills (70–100%)
❑ some of the skills (40–70%)
❑ a few of the skills (10–40%)

The focus of the lesson was on:
❑ hardware and equipment
❑ technology skills
❑ software
❑ subject matter content
❑ other activities

The students actively participated in the lesson:
❑ most of the students (70–100%)
❑ some of the studuents (40–70%)
❑ a few of the students (10–40%)
❑ none of the students

Rate the technology activities in relation to the content area:
❑ of great value
❑ of some value
❑ of questionable value
❑ of no value

❑ real world activities
❑ questionable if real world activities
❑ no one in the real world does this

The teacher's assignment or assessment of what the students learned was focused on:
❑ hardware and equipment
❑ software
❑ subject matter content
❑ the activities themselves

Mark either YES or NO for each of the following:
❑ YES ❑ NO The objectives could have been achieved more effectively without the use of technology.
❑ YES ❑ NO The technology activities interfered with the lesson.
❑ YES ❑ NO The teacher had prepared for the technology part of the lesson.
❑ YES ❑ NO The students had been prepared for the technology part of the lesson.

What were the students doing?

Briefly compare the lesson as viewed by the teacher, by the students, and by the observer.

Glossary

alley The space between text columns in a page or desktop publishing layout.

application General name for a software program such as Claris-Works. An application is used to create and edit documents.

Arc tool Graphic tool for drawing arcs of various sizes, shapes, and patterns.

backup Duplicate of an application or data disk.

Bezier curve A curve drawn through points that you specify.

Bezigon tool Graphic tool used to draw or paint a Bezier curve.

block Contiguous group of cells in a spreadsheet.

bookmark In Netscape, a technique that allows you to quickly save the address of a server so you can continue with something else. Later, you can quickly return to that server by clicking the item on the bookmark.

Brush tool Paint tool used to paint brushstrokes in a variety of shapes, sizes, colors, and patterns.

bulleted list A list of items in which each item is preceded by a character called a *bullet*, such as •, rather than being numbered.

Button Edit tool Tool in HyperStudio used to select and edit a button.

card One of the objects in a HyperStudio stack; it is the display area that appears on the screen when you have a stack open.

category Another name for *field;* a container for text or other type of data, as in a text field in a database.

cell The intersection of a row and a column in a spreadsheet.

client-server A client machine performs local tasks with local resources; a server provides shared resources and fulfills broad tasks (definition from http://go-client-server.com/ClientServerFAQ.html).

To read an interesting analogy of client-server computing, point your browser to http://www.as400.ibm.com/vans/whatis/whatis.htm.

column Vertical group of cells in a spreadsheet; in a ClarisWorks spreadsheet, the columns are indicated by a letter or letters of the alphabet.

composing stage The stage of writing in which you write a rough draft without worrying about such details as spelling, grammar, or word choice.

continue indicator Icon at the bottom of a frame indicating that the frame can be linked.

copyright The exclusive legal right to reproduce, sell, or publish artistic, literary, or musical work.

database An organized collection of data or information into fields and records.

database application Software or application that allows the user to edit, store, manipulate, and save information in an electronic database.

desktop publishing Use of a desktop or laptop computer to perform tasks such as the layout of a publication to include text columns, graphics, and the placement of text into the document.

document That which is created by an application program; the application is used to create and edit the document. For instance, ClarisWorks can be used to prepare a document. A copy of the document saved on a storage device is called a file.

drag and drop Technique for moving text or objects from one location to another with a mouse.

draw Mathematically described graphic object; often referred to as vector graphics. See *paint*.

drop shadow Technique for emphasizing or highlighting part of the border of a graphic.

electronic list A technique used to participate with a large group in an electronic discussion.

emoticon A combination of text characters used to communicate emotion. See *smiley.*

entry bar Area at the top left of the spreadsheet window in which the user enters and edits data.

Eraser Tool used to erase all or parts of a painting.

expert systems Databases containing data that represent the collected wisdom of many experts in the field, such as medical databases.

Eyedropper Graphic tool used to pick up the color and pattern of an object or painting and then to apply it to another draw object or painting.

field A container for text or other type of data, as in a text field in a database. See *category.* In HyperStudio, it is one of the objects in a stack but is called a *text object.*

file Data or information saved on a storage device such as a disk. When you store a document on a storage device, the result is referred to as a *file.* With a database, the term *file* refers also to a collection of related records.

flame, flaming Term used to refer to inflammatory messages on the Internet.

font Originally referred to an assortment of type in one size and style; now also used to refer to a family of type style such as Times or Arial.

frame A type of object; examples include text frames, paint frames, and spreadsheet frames.

Freehand tool Graphic tool used to draw curving or irregular lines.

freewriting Writing quickly, without reflection, whatever thoughts come to mind.

function Built-in formula to perform a common mathematical task, such as calculating an average or a square root.

hard copy A printed copy.

home page The first document you view from a remote computer when you access a site with a web browser.

HTML Acronym for Hypertext Markup Language, the language used to construct a document that can be viewed with a web browser.

http Acronym for Hypertext Transfer Protocol, the protocol used for accessing information on the Web.

hypermedia Term used to extend the concept of hypertext to include additional forms of media such as graphics, music, animation, and digitized audio and video. See *hypertext.*

hypertext Refers to an environment in which one can electronically browse among large chunks of text, following tangents reflecting personal interests and jumping from one chunk to another, bypassing information that is not relevant. See *hypermedia.*

inline graphics Graphic objects treated as text so that as you edit text, the position of the graphic changes as the position of the text changes. If you have the text tool selected when you paste a graphic into a text frame or word processing document, the graphic will be treated as text.

Internet An informal, global network of networks linked electronically.

invisible writing A variation of freewriting in which the computer screen is turned off.

Lasso Tool used to select all or part of a painting; particularly useful for selecting irregular shapes.

layout The placement or arrangement of text frames and other components of a newsletter or database.

Layout Popup Menu item where the user can choose to edit or view an existing layout or start a new database layout.

Line tool Graphic tool used to draw a line.

link Hotspot or hypertext on a web browser page that serves as a connection to another site or file.

link indicator Icon indicating that the contents of this frame flow into another location in a (linked) column on the same or a different page. If located at the bottom of a text frame, text is flowing out; if located at the top of a text frame, text is flowing in.

Magic Wand Paint tool used to select areas that are difficult to lasso.

mail merge A feature of many word processors in which selected data from a database is merged into a form letter.

Master Page The background of a draw document that will display on every page of the document unless covered or hidden by an object on the individual page. Can be accessed under M View or W Window.

object Term used to describe something that when selected with the pointer, has handles. Every object has a border (that you can hide if you elect) and a fill (which is the area within the border). See *draw* and *frame*.

outlining The process of grouping topics into a selected format.

Oval tool Graphic tool used to draw various kinds of ovals with various colors, patterns, and gradients.

paint Type of graphic composed of pixels or individual points on the screen; sometimes referred to as bitmapped or raster graphics.

Paint Bucket Paint tool used to fill an enclosed area with the current fill attributes.

parameter list A parameter is an expression in a function that is used to perform a calculation or action. A parameter list is a listing of all of the expressions for a particular function.

pen sample icon Indicates pen attributes currently selected.

Pencil tool Paint tool used to paint fine lines with the current fill attributes, not the pen attributes.

pixel Individual point on the computer screen that can be turned on or off; the basic element of a paint graphic.

place holder An object, such as a solid rectangle or an X, placed on a page layout to indicate where another object, such as a graphic, will, can, or should be placed.

point Measurement unit used to indicate the size of a font; 72 points = 1 inch. Also refers to the technique in which the mouse pointer is placed over an object or menu on the screen.

Pointer (Arrow) tool Tool used to select objects.

Polygon tool Graphic tool used to draw irregular polygons.

prewriting The stage of writing that includes planning what you are going to say, gathering information from other sources, and outlining and organizing your ideas.

prompted writing Writing prompted by the presence of messages in a document or file.

range In a spreadsheet, a sequence of cells on which some type of operation is to be performed, such as summing the range A1..A7.

rebus A representation of words or syllables by pictures of objects that resembles the intended words or syllables phonetically.

record All the fields or information related to the same person or thing in a database.

Rectangle tool Graphic tool used to draw rectangles of various sizes, colors, and patterns.

Regular Polygon tool Graphic tool used to draw a variety of regular polygons.

report In a database, a combination of a stored layout, search, and/or sort that can be saved with the database.

Report Popup Menu item where the user can choose to edit or view an existing report or start a new report.

reshape pointer Graphic tool used to drag an anchor point to a new location.

revision stage Stage of writing in which you reread what you have written to see how you can express your ideas more clearly and concisely. You also edit the spelling and grammar and try to find the precise word for the meaning you intend.

Rounded Rectangle tool Graphic tool used to draw rectangles with rounded corners.

row Horizontal line of cells in a spreadsheet; in ClarisWorks, cells are referred to by a numeral.

sans serif Type or font without a serif (a small finishing stroke); see *serif*.

Scrapbook Permanent storage area on the Macintosh for bits and pieces of text, graphics, and other data; accessible under the Apple icon on the menu bar.

search Systematic technique used with a database to locate records that meet specified criteria.

search engine A searching device for finding information on the Internet.

Search Popup Menu item that the user can choose to edit or view an existing search or start a new search.

Selection Rectangle tool Graphic tool used to select all or part of a paint graphic; most useful with regular shapes.

serif Type or font with a small finishing stroke; see *sans serif*.

Shortcuts Palette with various macros for common tasks performed in a particular environment.

slide show A screen-by-screen, linear presentation of a document, such as when the pages of the document are the slides, ClarisWorks is the projector, and the computer monitor is the screen.

smiley Symbols used to communicate emotion with electronic mail, such as :-).

sort To arrange in a systematic order, such as alphabetically or numerically.

Sort Popup Menu item that the user can choose to edit or view an existing sort or start a new sort.

spelling checker Software or feature of software that compares words in your document with words in its dictionary.

Spray Can Paint tool used to paint a flow of dots with the current fill attributes.

spreadsheet Application in which information is organized into intersecting rows and columns.

stack In HyperStudio, a stack is analogous to a collection of cards in which the individual cards (screens) can theoretically be viewed in any order.

stationery In ClarisWorks, refers to a file that, when opened, has the name Untitled. The purpose is to allow the user to set up a document or file with particular settings and information that will be used over and over, such as a letter template to parents.

stored report Report in a database that has been saved or stored under the icon.

stored search Search in a database that has been saved or stored under the icon.

stored sort Sort in a database that has been saved or stored under the icon.

subdomain Part of the Domain Naming System (DNS); think of the domain name portion of an e-mail address—the rightmost part of the domain name is the top domain name. Moving to the left, the next name is the subdomain name. Subdomain names in a server address frequently represent the name of a company, university, or organization.

tag A command that deals with the page structure of a Web document as it appears on the screen. Example: <P> to start a new paragraph.

template Preset form, overlay, or pattern.

text file File containing data stored in standard ASCII text format. This format removes all special coding—italics, boldface, etc. Most word processors and databases can open and display the contents of any text file.

text overflow indicator Icon at the bottom right of a text frame indicating there is more text than there is room in the text frame.

Tool panel The display or palette on the left side of a ClarisWorks word processing, draw, paint, spreadsheet, or database document window that includes the draw and/or paint tools depending upon the type of frame or document.

top domain Part of the Domain Naming System (DNS); think of the domain name portion of an e-mail address—the rightmost part of the domain name is the top domain name. Six of the most common domain names are com (commercial), edu (education), gov (government), mil (military), org (organization), and net (network). See *subdomain.*

top-of-frame indicator , Icon that identifies the top of a linked text frame to indicate if the text originated within this frame or is linked from another frame.

URL Acronym for Uniform Resource Locator; refers to the address of a web site or resource.

value In a spreadsheet, any number, formula, or function that can be used in calculations.

web browser Software used to access web sites.

white space The open area or space not occupied by text or graphics in a document; does not have to be white.

window Area on the computer screen where the contents of a document are displayed.

word wrap Feature that allows you to continue entering text or numerals and not have to press the <return> or <enter> key at the end of each line of a paragraph.

worksheet Term used to refer to that part of a spreadsheet that contains data.

World Wide Web A client-server information system that runs over the Internet; it delivers information as hypertext and hypermedia; also referred to as the Web or WWW.

Zoom Percentage box 100 Located in the lower left of a document window; indicates the viewing percentage of the document on the screen.

Index